Ska'd for Life

After leaving The Specials, Horace Panter played
with General Public and later with Specialbeat.
Today he teaches art to children with special needs
during the week, but can be found playing his bass
on weekends in various pubs around Coventry.

Horace Panter

Ska'd for Life

A PERSONAL JOURNEY WITH

The Specials

Pan Books

First published 2007 by Sidgwick & Jackson

First published in paperback 2008 by Pan Books
an imprint of Pan Macmillan , a division of Macmillan Publishers Limited
Pan Macmillan, 20 New Wharf Road, London N1 9RR
Basingstoke and Oxford
Associated companies throughout the world
www.panmacmillan.com

ISBN 978-0-330-44073-8

19 18 17 16 15 14 13

A CIP catalogue record for this book is available from
the British Library.

Typeset by SetSystems Ltd, Saffron Walden, Essex Ltd
Printed and bound by
CPI Group (UK) Ltd, Croydon, CR0 4YY

Visit **www.panmacmillan.com** to read more about all our books
and to buy them. You will also find features, author interviews and
news of any author events, and you can sign up for e-newsletters
so that you're always first to hear about our new releases.

For Helen & Denis

and Clare & Laurence

ACKNOWLEDGEMENTS

Messrs: Bradbury, Byers, Dammers, Golding, Hall and Staple, especially Lynval, who remains a supportive friend and not a bad guitar player either. Talking of guitar players, cap doffed to Neol Davies, whose brains I picked somewhat relentlessly on occasion and Big Dave Linnett, still playing!

A large thank you must go to my parents, Helen and Denis Panter, who religiously went out and bought the music press every week for nearly three years: the result being eleven scrap books of Specials and 2-Tone-related material which was invaluable for getting the chronology correct and jogging my selective memory – and making me wince a fair bit too!

Also thanks to Jeanne Kaczka, formerly of Coventry University, for information concerning the Coventry Committee Against Racism (CCAR).

Man-sized thanks to Phill Jupitus for his forewording address and to Jeff Veitch for some cool photographs.

The means of production: Ingrid Connell at the controls, applying pressure gently but firmly. Also Georgina Difford and Dusty Miller.

Huge mega-thanks to Clare, who more than anyone told me I could do this, and then helped me to do it. Thanks to Pete Chambers and Cameron Ellice for early feedback and to Richard Nason for years of support!

Good guys: Alio Maynard, Pete Gardner and Dave Reddington plus Sean Flowerdew, Kevin Harrison and Fuzz Townshend.

Picture acknowledgements

All photographs are from the author's private collection apart from on the following pages:

1: Breaker photograph courtesy of Margo Buchanan
2: Snowball massacre © Jeff Veitch
3: Warwick University gig © Jeff Veitch
6: Asleep on the bus © Colin Jones
7: Brighton Top Rank © Jeff Veitch
   Hotel room in Ireland © Jill Furmanovsky
8: © Jeff Veitch (both)
9: © Jeff Veitch
12: Specials on tv © Jeff Veitch
14: © Eugene Adabari / Rex Features
16: Sound check © Jill Furmanovksy

Contents

Foreword

To be a teenager at the birth of 2-Tone was one of the defining moments of my life. Certainly the unwieldy conventions of Seventies rock and pop music had already been given a sound kick in the bollocks with the arrival of punk, but there still seemed to be a vacuum. All of the main players were by now established and the genre-defining Sex Pistols had already broken up in the glare of the media spotlight. Callaghan was gone and we were at the dawn of Thatcherism; oh, it was quite a time to be in England.

Out in the suburbs of Essex, one of the best things about punk for me was its inclusion of the downbeat grooves and bone-shaking bass lines of Jamaican reggae. The Clash, The Ruts and The Members were all artful mimics of dub and it provided blessed relief for the pogoing masses to be able to cut loose into some serious skanking. Then it happened. I first heard the song 'Gangsters' on John Peel's show: I was utterly mesmerized. Being unfamiliar with the music of Prince Buster at the time this was totally new to me. Here was the skank and groove of reggae but delivered in a kind of psychotic double-time. I was just a naive kid from the Thames Corridor but am now proud to say that my first real taste of ska music came from Coventry.

To say that The Specials changed how I looked at music is an understatement. From the moment that I heard 'Gangsters', and the subsequent interminable wait until its actual release, I became transformed. Presumably inspired by the sounds made by these new young lions, Peely started to play lots more original early 1960s ska in his show. 'Gangsters' was finally released and made its way up the charts. And so it was that sat in front of my television I saw The Specials for the first time on *Top Of The Pops*. I don't know what I was expecting, but this band just blew me away. There was a snappy elegance to the wardrobe and a bouncing swagger to their performance that filled you with joy. Unlike most groups you saw on the show, they didn't look that happy to be there. One singer just stood immobile, staring into the camera like he wanted to smash it, while the other guy ran around the stage shouting like a madman. Here was a great British band, singing a song about the rotten state of the music business on a television show which, more than any other, defined just that. It was one of those perfect moments.

I bought their debut album the day it came out and the thing was never off of my turntable. Here was all the energy of punk but with a much keener rhythmic and melodic sensibility. Their songs held a black and white mirror up to the world around them. They told tales of debauched nights out, unemployment, racial tension, teen pregnancy, lost love, sex and forced marriage. The sawn-off shotgun rage of the punks now had a much more subtle and sharp kitchen-sink focus to its anger. The Specials rightly observed that there is as much validity to what goes on in your own life as what happens in the country at large. It was righteous indignation that you could dance to.

I never got the chance to see The Specials play live until the release of their sublime second album *More Specials*. The singalong boot-boy bounce of their early work had given way to a sleazy sophistication, the ska sounds augmented by Latin and soca rhythms. But seeing them play live at the Hammersmith Palais was a dream come true. As I was incredibly pissed on the night my recollections are hazy at best, but one great moment I clearly recall was Neville Staple climbing up the wall of speakers during the lengthy dub section of 'Stereotype', and then, as the song reached its echoing climax, leaping to the floor screaming, 'BERNIE RHODES KNOWS DON'T ARGUE . . .' And then they went into 'Gangsters' and the place went fucking mad.

Thankfully I did see them one more time performing a benefit gig for the *Morning Star* at the Rainbow in London's Finsbury Park. Myself and four mates partook of a few pints in The George Robey and then made our way over the Seven Sisters Road and into the cavernous venue. As we stood there waiting for the band to go on, one industrious individual produced a joint from his jacket and for the very first time I inhaled and experienced the now-familiar queasy euphoria. Suddenly the lights went out and we heard the unmistakable thump of 'Concrete Jungle' starting the show and in an instant the THC in our bloodstreams was swamped by a surge of adrenaline and we sprinted for the front of the hall.

What we had failed to notice as we arrived was that the crowd was a good deal younger than one might expect. By this stage the band had had a number one single and the effect seemed to be that the place was full of kids. As I powered through the crowd I was blissfully unaware of this but would love to have looked down on this strange sight

FOREWORD

from the balcony. A fifteen stone, six foot, drunk, dope-crazed ska fan cutting a swathe through a crowd of children, like an angry, tubby speedboat. I remained pinned to the front barrier all night, about twelve feet from Terry Hall. When they played 'Holiday Fortnight', we old-school fans shouted with joy at the unofficial vocal refrain, 'We are called The Specials' over Dick Cuthell and Rico Rodriguez's horn part.

That gig remains, to this day, the best live concert I ever saw and is all the more special to me because they finished the show by playing 'Ghost Town'. And that was the first time I heard it, and the last time I saw The Specials.

I am the delighted that Sir Horace Gentleman has decided to put pen to paper and tell the story of this extraordinary time in British popular culture, from his own singular perspective. It will fill a lot of the blanks in my own knowledge of the band and perhaps we might discover exactly why he ended up playing bass for the The Beat on *Top Of the Pops*. Or will we, Horace?

Phill Jupitus
April 2007

Introduction

Show time was generally around 10 o'clock, and we would shamble on. Whether we were ready or not, Neville would grab his microphone and bellow: 'GUNS' . . . a slight pause . . . 'OF NAVARONE!' Brad's snare would crack, and we'd be off – Lynval and Jerry digging into the off-beat rhythm, Rod playing clipped notes that snapped around my bass line. Terry would stand there, centre stage, a fag on as often as not, nonchalantly nodding his head to the beat while Nev careered across the stage with (hopefully) a long mike cord trailing after him, doing his trademark rabble-rousing. 'Guns of Navarone. Musical sensation designed to blow your mind!' Which kind of summed it up really.

The 'faithful', those up the front who'd seen us before, or told everyone they had, in their tonic suits or Harrington jackets, danced from the off, but the music was infectious. By the end of the evening, there was no dress code: punky-looking girls in mini-skirts and fishnet tights, kids in jeans and t-shirts, long hair, short hair, straight jeans, flared jeans, Doc Martens, baseball boots – all one sweaty, seething, rhythmic mass. Terry, at his laconic best, would look out over the crowd, leaning on his microphone stand: 'This is our last song. It's our single. It's called "Gangsters".' Neville would bellow and off we'd go again. It was the spring of 1979.

> **zeitgeist** *n*. spirit of the times; trend of thought
> and feeling in a period. [German. *Zeit*, time.
> *Geist*, spirit] (*Concise Oxford Dictionary*)

I don't like making 'socio-political statements', or pontificating about 'cultural identity in Thatcher's Britain', preferring to leave it to people who know what they're talking about, or people who get paid for saying they know what they're talking about, but . . . The Specials took the spirit of the time and turned it from negative, apathetic and nihilistic to positive. They made people dance and think at the same time. Just like the blues, where it all came from in the first place: sing about your worries and your feelings and turn them into a celebration. The Specials and the 2-Tone 'movement' became more than just pop music. We were actually out to change things: seven very different people guided by one person's vision. It was astonishing. Ironic even. In fact, irony was written right through The Specials like in a stick of rock. A band formed by a militant socialist who was sometimes later referred to as a benevolent dictator. A band that stood for unity and racial harmony but split up because they couldn't stand each other. A head-on collision between wide-eyed idealism and the coldest, most cynical of businesses. With me (sort of) in the middle.

This is not the official history of The Specials. That would be a stupendously difficult, if not impossible, task. To interview (at least) seven people, correlate all the information and then decide whose version of events was correct (was it Bracknell or Crawley? Denver, Colorado, or Norman, Oklahoma?). This would be easy compared to deciding which version was 'The Truth'.

So this is my take on events.

1

Once Upon A Time in Kettering and Coventry

Some of us are born Horace. Some achieve Horaceness. Some have Horaceness thrust upon them. The third one, that was me. On my passport it says 'Stephen Graham Panter'. The name Horace was given to me at age eleven by a history teacher, for reasons I know not. The name stuck, and after a while I got used to it, though I didn't have an enormous amount of choice. The only person who still calls me Stephen these days is my mum. I like it that way, thank you.

My passport also says Croydon as my place of birth (30 August 1953 to be precise).

I was adopted at the age of six weeks and brought up in Kettering, Northamptonshire, which was where my father, Denis, was born in 1920. He worked as a clerk on the railways until he joined the army during the Second World War. When they realized he could use a typewriter, they transferred him from the Royal Northumberland Fusiliers to the Army Service Corps. He spent most of his war in what was then called the Belgian Congo (now the Democratic Republic of Congo). He met Helen Booth in 1948, while on holiday in Jersey. They married in April 1949. My sister, Gillian, also adopted, arrived in 1957.

Kettering was then a small East Midlands market town, birthplace of William Knibb, who was one of the leading lights in the abolition of slavery campaign in Jamaica in the nineteenth century. Apart from this historical claim to fame, the Kettering area boasted a number of shoe factories. Doc Martens boots (which I was later to wear with pride) were made in nearby Irthlingborough until 2002.

Not a great deal happened in Kettering in terms of excitement, and I usually made my own adventures with the local kids in the old iron-ore quarries behind my father's vegetable allotment. I always had sticking plasters over one knee at least. My father was a better-than-average rugby player and played most weekends. Once every six weeks my mother and I would have to help make sausage, baked beans and mashed potato for 150 or so seemingly huge gentlemen at the rugby ground in Waverley Road. The club house had a one-armed bandit with an American Indian's head on it. It took sixpenny pieces, or tanners as they were called back then.

My dad bought a lilac and orange transistor radio in 1962, and from that moment I was fascinated by pop music. When I was ten years old I joined the Searchers fan club. I remember seeing them on *Thank Your Lucky Stars*, Tony Jackson standing in the middle, looking as cool as anything, warding off girls' adoring screams with a sardonic grin, a great big semi-acoustic bass guitar tucked under his chin. I knew all the words to 'Sweets for My Sweet'. The sixties were swinging, and, in my adolescent, provincial, market-town way, so was I.

What really sealed my fate were the pirate radio

stations. Radio Luxembourg was all right, if you didn't mind only hearing half of the tunes and had the patience to find the station as it veered across the dial, phasing in and out. No, the business was Radio London, Big L, 266 on the Medium Wave, playing the Small Faces, The Spencer Davis Group, Joe Tex, Wilson Pickett, The Rolling Stones, Diana Ross and The Supremes. Radio London, Tony Windsor, Chuck Blair, Paul Kay and, later, Tony Blackburn and the mighty John Peel – these were my high priests of pop, the guys who delivered, with their fingers on the pulse. I wanted to be a pirate radio DJ.

We had a copy of Cliff Richard's *Summer Holiday* LP (I played the Shadows tracks to death) and *With The Beatles* (my favourite was 'Roll Over Beethoven'), but 'Fifth Dimension (5D)' by The Byrds was the first single I ever parted cold cash for. Buying it was as much a statement of intent as a choice of music. The Byrds were psychedelic (which I understood had something to do with lots of colours and having long hair) and were part of a movement that wanted to change the world through pop music. If any world needed changing in 1966, it was mine.

I was a total pop-music nut. I bought *Record Mirror* and cut out the charts page, collected them all and held them together with a big bulldog clip. It never dawned on me that I could actually participate in creating music, and anyway I was having too much fun being a fan. Later on, I became aware of clothes and youth culture and . . . gulp . . . girls, and started to harbour secret thoughts about being a rock star.

Although never excelling at school I nonetheless managed to pass my eleven-plus exam and ended up attending Kettering Grammar School. Academic mediocrity would be my watchword for the next seven years, and I scraped into the sixth form with three O-levels. By the time I was sixteen (1969) I was regularly daydreaming through A-level English and History. A-level Art was bearable, however. I was left to my own devices as often as not and I spent my time designing psychedelic album covers for imaginary bands that I happened to play in.

I don't know how it came about, but I bought a Rosetti Bass 8 off Birrell Porter, a lad at school, for six quid. It was red and looked like a Gibson 335 semi-acoustic, with three buttons to select the pick-ups and volume and tone knobs. I couldn't play it. I didn't know how to tune it and I never asked anyone for any lessons. I just used to wear it and play in front of the full-length mirror in my bedroom to packed theatres, or sometimes to the late-night clienteles of small smoky clubs. I was usually imagining myself in one of the bands I had invented in the art room, only now I was their bass player. Around about that time I stopped going to the barber's.

We were middle-class, us Panters, but there was never any what you'd call nowadays 'disposable income'. My parents were products of a war economy and the austerity that accompanied it. My father was the director of a small furniture-removal firm – three or four vans, six or eight employees. We lived in a spacious house, kitted out with furniture that came via my father's job: tables people didn't want, settees that were going to be dumped. No rubbish, mind, but stuff that you couldn't throw away. When they moved, my dad's shed was full of jam jars brimming with screws, nuts, bolts, nails, hinges, and the neck of my Rosetti Bass 8.

Any money that I had was obtained by saving my

pocket money. An incredible feat, when, all around me, incredible records were being released almost every week and John Peel's *Top Gear* was on the radio on Sunday afternoons.

I was aware of ska and reggae, but it wasn't at the forefront of my musical tastes. I was more taken by long-haired, denim-clad lead guitarists with rows of stacked amplifiers at their backs than I was by Desmond Dekker, but there again I hadn't yet learnt to dance, and these strange tunes were synonymous with the skinheads who were always trying their best to disrupt the church youth club discos my friends and I attended. Music had no colour for me back then, it was all pop, it was in 'the charts', it had a number: 'That was Engelbert Humperdink at number four, and now, here's Fontella Bass at number eighteen.' A tune was either good or bad; the artist's race seemed irrelevant. Unfortunately, skinhead reggae classics like 'Return of the Django' or 'Double Barrel' always conjured up the image of some Neanderthal bovver boy 'smacking the nut' on some poor unfortunate. Come to think of it, it was still violent music ten to twelve years later, only by then I was playing it.

All of a sudden, in 1970 I suppose, music seemed to splinter, or I saw it differently. The Tamla Motown / Stax / Atlantic record labels represented soul music. Jimi Hendrix, Free and Cream represented rock. The psychedelic bands from California were a new counter-culture: the hippies, the underground and its press. When I started doing interviews in The Specials, I would spout on about how I was always into Stax, Booker T and The MGs and Junior Walker. OK, they were definitely an influence, but what I was really into were the blues/rock outfits! I still have the first Fleetwood Mac LP and, for reasons unknown, I bought 'Freak Out' by The Mothers of Invention – I couldn't stand it.

I was, however, coming to terms with the fact that I might like to be a rock star. The first professional pop group I ever went to see was Led Zeppelin. My friend Anthony Larcombe and I got tickets to see them at the Albert Hall in London. It scared the living daylights out of me. Blodwyn Pig, The Liverpool Scene and Led Great Gods Descending From The Heavens Zeppelin. I had never heard anything so loud in my life. The whole thing was overwhelming. Half-way through, some guy stood up and looked to me like he was having an epileptic fit, his arms flailing all over the place – the music had obviously driven him mad, but no one seemed to be bothered, no stretchers were brought, they even put a spotlight on the poor fellow. And all the while, this immense whacking noise. Dazed and confused? Yes, thank you!

Möbius was the name of the first group I was ever in. Möbius, or Möbius Trip, after the M. C. Escher drawing called 'The Möbius Strip'. The group was led by Dave Linnett, a big, long-haired kid whose parents owned a newsagent's in the middle of town. He was in the year below me at school and somehow managed to amass an enormous record collection, most of which he brought to school to let people know how hip he was. He was a genuine rebel – unlike me – and couldn't wait to leave school. He got kicked out on his last day for turning up in a denim jacket, his school blazer having been destroyed or (more likely) ceremonially burnt. I became 'cool by association' and was introduced to some of the shadier personalities of Kettering's counter-culture. Men with almost waist-length hair who had names like 'Nudge' or 'Chinny', who never seemed to work but could afford a drink. 'This is Horace, he's our bass player,' Dave would say. And there, in the smoke room of Kettering's Royal Hotel, nursing a pint of draft Guinness, coolness was bestowed upon me.

Dave had a Hofner electric guitar and a 12-string acoustic, which only had six strings on it. He had a Wem 30-watt amplifier and a 4 × 12 column speaker which had been cut in half, making two 2 × 12 cabinets. He also had a fuzz box. This meant that no matter how crappy the guitar was, it sounded enormously distorted and nasty. We played a version of Mott the Hoople's version of Little Richard's 'You Keep a Knocking' and simple, riffy tunes like Free's version of Albert King's 'The Hunter' and Cream's 'Tales of Brave Ulysses'. I handled the lead vocals as well as the bass duties. We were dreadful. Even when Dave upgraded to an Antoria SG copy and I bought a Fender Mustang-looking bass to replace the appalling Rosetti, we were still dreadful. We had a pretty busy turnover of people who wanted to be our drummer, who didn't have any drums but lots of enthusiasm. We had people who owned drum kits but couldn't play them. Once we had a guy turn up with a drum kit who could actually play. It blew us away, and we realized how awful we actually were! We settled for the guy with the drum kit who couldn't play. That way we were all in the same boat musically.

The best thing about being in a group with Dave Linnett was that I could go around saying that I was in a group . . . with Dave Linnett. He knew people who could give us a lift over to Woolaston to see groups at the Nag's

Head on a Friday. The Liverpool Scene, Supertramp, Wishbone Ash, Skid Row and, one time, The Faces, with Rod Stewart and Ronnie Wood. I wore these sweaty pub gigs like medals, and dropped them into conversations at the slightest provocation.

The kingpin Kettering muso in those days was a kid called Max Norman. He was my age, had a Gibson Les Paul Junior and wore John Lennon-type specs. He had a gorgeous girlfriend and was always surrounded by a circle of confidants, roadies and general sycophants. I was as jealous as hell. I met him about ten years later at the Hammersmith Odeon – he was setting up a PA for a gig we were doing with The Pretenders and The Who. He obviously didn't recognize me and carried on wiring up the mixing desk. I later saw him in the Mayflower Hotel in New York, when I was with General Public. I ignored him ferociously. He became a heavy metal record producer and has probably bought the Mayflower Hotel by now, if not the Hammersmith Odeon.

In their entire two years of existence, Möbius played live six times. We were dreadful every time. Sometimes more dreadful, sometimes less dreadful, but always dreadful. I was smitten. Being in a group was the best. The pinnacle of Möbius's career was when we got to play at the Rock Street youth centre in Wellingborough as first support band for Mott the Hoople. I walked on air for a month, and dined out on the fact for six. OK, we only got to play three songs before the promoter told us to get off, and I had to phone up my dad at half-eleven on a Saturday night to ask him to come and pick us and the gear up as our transport had mysteriously disappeared, but I had shared the stage with Mott and rubbed metaphorical shoulders with the High and Mighty. I sat side-stage and watched in awe as Ian Hunter sweated all over his electric piano and swore at the road crew. After that, Möbius fizzled out.

Despite failing my A-levels, September 1971 saw me start a one-year foundation course at Northampton School of Art. This was a definite higher rung up the social-climber ladder. I was officially an Art Student. My hair was now way past my collar, heading down my back as fast as I could let it grow. I could now wear my patched jeans and my fathers' old corporal's jacket every day of the week. I used to get a bus over to Northampton every day, along with a half-dozen or so fellow students from Kettering or Corby. One of the Corby contingent was a big, soft-spoken Scottish kid, Bill Drummond, who went on to become a fully fledged evil genius of pop in his own right with KLF in the nineties. Art school was definitely the way to establish your pop-star intentions, but despite all my posing I managed to get with the programme enough to land a place at Coventry's Lanchester Polytechnic, studying Fine Art. I started in October 1972. Living away from home – the real deal.

The great thing I remember about school/college/university was that every year was better than the one before it. My second year at Coventry, I finally got a handle on my degree course and met Geoff Conway, who at that time was the union secretary and owned and could play a drum kit! As I was at art college I wasn't supposed to like any kind of music that had popular appeal, so I left my Free albums in Kettering and started listening to J. J. Cale and my soul record collection. My flatmate had 'LA Woman' by The Doors, and I thought it was great – still do. Geoff and I clicked as friends as well as a rhythm section – not that we ever did any gigs, but we rehearsed a lot, and I started to realize that you had to listen as well as play. We went to see The Average White Band at Coventry Tech. – 40p. They had just recorded their second album (the white one) and were just about to go off to America to become famous and for their drummer to die of drug-related causes (he thought it was coke, but it was heroin – sick; he was a brilliant drummer). The gig was, and still is, one of the best I have ever been to in my life. Geoff and I went out and bought the album and played it to death. Whenever I hear 'Pick Up the Pieces', it all comes back.

As far as this book is concerned, another important event in my second year at art college was the new influx of first-year students. They were a far more gregarious mix than my year. We had the usual cliques and social circles, but no characters. The year below, however, more than made up for our rather boring collection of serious young artists.

The 'new boys' as we called them were loud, aggressive, funny and didn't seem to give a toss. One of them was Jerry Dammers. Jerry was born in India in 1955. His father was a clergyman and for a time in the sixties and seventies was canon of Coventry Cathedral. His parents subsequently moved to Bristol. Jerry seemed to spend most of his childhood rebelling against any kind of authority. A philosophy he still adheres to! He'd done his foundation art course at Nottingham (similar to the one I had done at Northampton) and was now starting his degree course at the Art Faculty at the Lanchester Polytechnic. I remember Jerry in tartan trousers, grown-out mod haircut, complete with sideburns, walking into the art studios on the fifth floor, singing, 'I shot the sheriff' at the top of his voice. What a strange lyric, I thought.

We held an art school 'do' in the back room of the Hand and Hart in Gosford Street. A tremendously drunken affair, which ended with Jerry playing boogie-woogie and Fats Domino tunes on the pub piano, its lid and its player both being awash with beer. An excellent night was had by all, although not too many people turned in to college the next morning.

A collection of college musos would congregate from time to time in a room in the student union building to 'jam'. My hatred of this activity dates back to my college band days. I did not seem to be as excited as the other musicians (most of whom played guitar, their ability ranging from unbearable to competent) at playing a piece of music that lasted around twenty minutes in the same key (usually E) with no change in tempo and little dynamics. Jerry would occasionally put his head round the door, especially if there was a keyboard being abused. I don't recall him joining in with our 'college jams', but he did ask Geoff and me to help him record some background music for a cartoon film he was making. We duly obliged. He wanted us to play along to a keyboard track that he had recorded, but this proved too difficult for us, so we recorded the whole thing live. It was a funky way of spending an afternoon, playing music.

Geoff and I had a house at the Gulson Road end of Bramble Street in Coventry. Across the road was a pub, the Hare and Hounds, and diagonally across Gulson Road was a chip shop. We considered ourselves extremely fortunate. I made a sign which we stuck in the window above the front door. It said: 'It's only Rock and Roll'.

Geoff had the big attic room at the top. I had the front room downstairs. Above me, in the second bedroom, was Bob Carter, who was doing a science course, and the upstairs back bedroom was the domain of Andy Wilson, who was on a 'year out' and working in the architect's department of the council. Later on, we were joined by Bob's girlfriend, Stella Clifford, who was studying Social Science (whatever that was). We had a great 'gestalt' vibe at Bramble Street. Geoff was a fantastic cook (curries a speciality), Bob was musical director, Andy was 'father figure' and Stella kept us in line!

Bob was probably the most influential musician in my life. He played piano, guitar, wrote songs and could sing. I had a bass, had considerable enthusiasm, but didn't really know how to play, how to make sense of the thing. Bob taught me the notes, octaves, fifths, thirds, all that music stuff I remember from my years in a church choir in Kettering. I started listening to bass lines and bass players. Bob had Stevie Wonder records and 'Outta Space' by Billy Preston. I learnt about grooves, and about being funky. Needless to say, before long we were the college band. We played three songs at a college revue. A blues instrumental (Bob playing guitar), a version of Carole King's 'It's Too Late' (Bob playing keyboards – he had a Hohner Clavinet, the ultimate funk toy!) and another tune that I can't remember. I couldn't sleep. It was amazing.

To enlarge our line-up we advertised in the college for two back-up singers. One was Stella (which is how she and Bob met) and the other a girl called Glennis (or was that Glynnis?). We then tried unsuccessfully to get a guitar player. We finally advertised in the *Coventry*

Evening Telegraph, and when Roy Butterworth turned up, we knew we had the guy for the gig.

Roy wasn't a student, he worked at the Dunlop, but he played the most tasteful guitar I had ever heard. He had what I would come to realize was a 'Coventry sense of humour' – dry and deadpan. He had us in stitches. We decided to call ourselves 'Alive and Smilin''. Hey, gimme a break – I was young! The band was pretty short-lived, I suppose, but it was the training I needed to learn to play with confidence. We played 'How Long' by Ace (the *Five-a-Side* album was a firm Bramble Street favourite), a storming version of Marvin Gaye's 'Ain't That Peculiar' and some tunes that Bob wrote. We were good, we had a back beat, we were funky. Bob had a great voice, and the girls filled out the choruses. People danced to us. This was the first time I'd played in front of people who were appreciative.

After college Bob and Stella moved down to London and got a flat in Wandsworth. They would be my 'London connection' for the next few years. They split up around 1980. Bob went on to be the musical director of Lynx, a London funk duo (David Grant and 'Sketch') who had hits around the time of The Specials. He later went on to co-write and produce Junior Giscome's 'Mama Used to Say' and produced the first Wham single. He died in 1988 – his pancreas failed. Stella worked in the music business (Arista/Ariola).

It was in my last year at college (1974–5) when I received an inheritance of £175. It happened that a 'music biz' friend of Bob's had a friend who had a Fender bass for sale. I was there. I rushed down to London with an empty guitar case and came back with a 1972 Sunburst Fender Precision bass – 165 quid. It looked great and sounded fantastic. I used to put it in the chair in the tiny living room in Bramble Street and just stare at it. I had the professional tool for the job. Doing an art degree just lost its appeal.

Now, I don't want to brag, but I had played at the Hammersmith Odeon long before I joined The Specials. Scottish and Newcastle Breweries sponsored a 'college band' competition, and we romped through three heats (one memorable one in Leeds, supporting Ronnie Lane's Slim Chance) to the final at London's premiere rock venue. We didn't win, but, to tell you the truth, it didn't really matter. I was a third-year art student and I HAD PLAYED THE HAMMERSMITH ODEON! Life was good.

My last year at college ended; I got a second-class Honours degree in Fine Art and I went to work on the back door of Sainsbury's, unloading lorries. Art no longer had any relevance. Rock 'n' roll was my thing now, and this job paid bills, enabled me to buy equipment and stuff. Towards the end of 1975, Bob announced that he wanted to quit the band, as he really had to get down to studying for his degree, which was fair enough, but Geoff and I were really disappointed. Bob was the 'main man' in the band. We were the rhythm section. Roy left, too, and sold his gear to buy a pedal steel guitar. He later resurfaced as a member of the Tom Robinson Band.

Geoff and I were a 'rhythm section without a band' and we eventually hooked up with Margo Buchanan, who had done vocals in Alive and Smilin' after Glennis (or Glynnis) left, and her boyfriend, guitarist Gordon Reaney. The plan was to form a band that was versatile enough to play funky/

soul stuff in discos but had a 'standard' repertoire to do working men's clubs. The band was to be called 'Breaker', which had an American CB kind of vibe. Unfortunately it was also the name of a very cheap and particularly nasty canned lager. We emptied dance floors at discotheques all over the country. We couldn't possibly compete with the new funk 12-inch releases that the DJs were playing. I remember hearing 'Get the Funk out of My Face' by the Brothers Johnson at stomach-churning volume, hairs standing up on the back of my neck, and thinking how the hell can we follow that.

Working men's clubs were another universe completely. Three half-hour spots in between several games of bingo. No fast tunes until the end, please. One time we got sent packing because people got up and danced when they weren't supposed to. Newcastle upon Tyne, Sunderland and Middlesbrough, the graveyard of light entertainment. 'And tonight, ladies and gentlemen, all the way from . . . where are you from again? . . . The Breaker Showgroup!'

In retrospect, Breaker was on a hiding to nothing from the start, but I wanted to play, and if anything good came from my stay in the band it was that I learnt to be comfortable on stage. I always said that if you could play working men's clubs for a year and a half and still want to be a musician, you were in with a chance. Either that, or you were just stupid. However, we had a van, and any money we made went to maintaining said vehicle, so we went on the dole. Yes. Stupid.

2

Hybrids, Jaywalkers
and Automatics

The group that you know of as The Specials took some two
years to form. A slow uphill struggle; the whole thing was
cajoled, wheedled, bullied, begged, borrowed and stolen
by Jerry. It is no wonder that the whole thing fell apart by
the time of *More Specials*; he had single-handedly taken
seven very different individuals and pushed them into
creating something which had its own visual and musical
style. He must have been knackered.

In 1976, I was playing in Breaker, and Jerry was on
the Midlands soul band circuit. Pharaoh's Kingdom, Earth-
bound, The Cissy Stone Band, The Ray King Soul Band,
Nite Train, Sweet Sensation. All these bands provided
the training for a host of local musicians including Jerry
Dammers, Lynval Golding, Neol Davies, Charlie 'H' Bembridge and Silverton Hutchinson. Jerry had attempted to
get some of his own songs played (he was working with
Cissy Stone at the time), but original material was not what
the circuit demanded, unless it sounded *just* like Kool and
the Gang. I remember him coming to see Breaker at our
Monday-night residency at the Smithfield Hotel in Coven-

try city centre, and it was soon after that he approached me to play on some songs he had written. I was under the impression that he wanted to get a publishing deal initially and wasn't aware of any 'masterplan' but as I was still playing in Breaker he was probably just biding his time.

Jerry's songs were odd, to say the least, a kind of funk meets reggae style. The song that stood out for me was entitled 'Jaywalker' – it never made it on to a Specials LP, although we did have a go at it on *More Specials*, but stony silence and apathy carried the day. It appears on one of those demo LPs released by Trojan, I believe. The funk part of Jerry's tunes I didn't have that much of a problem with, but the reggae, that was a different matter!

The first black person I ever met in my life was Lynval Golding (please remember this was 1976, and I had grown up in an East Midlands market town, gone to grammar school, then to college. I had never talked with anyone outside my own race, apart from a couple of Asian guys at art school.) I went through 1977 and most of '78 thinking his name was Lymveldt – I don't know why. I suppose I thought of the Veldt in Africa – I had no idea, basically. Anyhow, he played guitar pretty well and seemed to tolerate my half-hearted attempts at reggae. Lynval and his friend Desmond (Brown – original Selecter organist) used to come around my pokey two-room flat and try their best to explain to me why the bass went like that. 'Nah, man, de bass drop like dis – buh, buh, duh, duh, duh, buh, buh, duh, duh, duh,' and so on. Reggae lessons, if you like. I eventually got it. In retrospect it would have been easier to have dragged me along to a blues dance, given me a big spliff and stood me in front of one of the walls of 18-inch bass cabinets. It was Lynval who called me Horace Gentleman because of my plummy Queen's English. Lyn had come from Jamaica at age eight, in 1960, on his own, to be met by his father and stepmother. He was brought up in Gloucester, where he met Charlie 'H' Bembridge (Selecter's drummer). They both had a very rough time at school, but their musical skills pulled them through. They both moved up to Coventry in the 1970s to play on the soul band circuit.

Anyway, Jerry, Lynval and I started learning these tunes, and soon it became obvious that we would need a drummer. Jerry and Lynval decided on the wonderfully named Silverton Hutchinson, a small, wiry man from Barbados with short hair and piercing big brown eyes. He was definitely the funkiest drummer I had ever played with and was the real deal when it came to playing reggae. I was very wary of him. His moods could change almost instantly, and he seemed to thrive on tension. He seemed older than me but was probably only in his mid-twenties. He loved to talk in philosophical mode, putting the world to rights and bemoaning its current state, expounding on the correct purposes of women and how to bring up children to respect you. This, I later came to realize, was what was called 'reasoning' and was generally accompanied by liberal amounts of marijuana. The world can be put to rights a lot easier with marijuana but, in my limited experience, seemed to revert back to its original state when the effects wore off.

To say that I was pleased to be working with these gentlemen would be something of an understatement. The music that I had (selectively!) listened to was played either by black musicians or musicians who were trying their damnedest to 'sound' black, and here I was, the white bass player, with the black drummer and guitarist. It was obvious that this wasn't just going to be a recording-session line-up. I felt mad, bad and dangerous to know, and my interest in the working men's club circuit that Breaker was slogging away on for very little financial return was fading fast. Even the dizzy heights of getting through to the final of the *Melody Maker* Folk/Rock Contest of 1977 could not dampen the fact that we were going nowhere fast. One Monday, Breaker played at the Smith-field Hotel, and The Sex Pistols and The Clash played at the Lanchester Polytechnic, about 300 yards away. I got there just as they were loading out and felt considerably older than the kids who were still milling around outside. I'd got the first Elvis Costello album and a copy of 'God Save the Queen'. Music was changing. The music press was buzzing with tales of a new movement that was sweeping away the pretentiousness and pomposity of drug-addled, laid-back rock royalty. A revolution even! Experimenting was a prerequisite, emotion was preferable over technique. It didn't seem to matter whether the music was good, as long as it was new. The music that Jerry, Lynval, Silverton and I were playing was both good and new. Pretty soon we had half a dozen tunes and we were on our way to actually becoming a group. We could even be part of this new musical revolution!

I quit Breaker and took a job driving a frozen-food van. I was able to rehearse in the evenings and, more importantly, start to save some money. Any outgoings that were incurred were generally paid by Jerry, who had saved money from the soul band circuit that he was still playing.

One of the good things about music in the late seventies was that you didn't have to actually be able to sing to be a singer. This was very good for one Tim Strickland, a tall, thin, James Dean type, who had a degree in aloofness and worked at the newly opened Virgin Records shop. He was approached to join the group and agreed although he insisted he couldn't hold a tune in a bucket. He was right, but that didn't matter in 1977, did it! I vaguely remember him from college, where I think he did a Social Science degree. He was one of those kids who was into Lou Reed and The Stooges, when everyone else listened to Genesis or Wishbone Ash. He went on to run a Museum of Pop Music, or something, in Sheffield.

So we were a group of sorts and at least we had a focal point. Tim, holding the mike stand with one hand and lyric sheets in the other, snarling out Jerry's lyrics with studied indifference, while I tried not to make a fool of myself standing at the back. I had never been very good at being cool. To this day I have dreadful dress sense and rely on others to point me in the direction of appropriate fashion! I am happy in jeans and t-shirt, but I knew this was not going to help me at the cutting edge of Coventry punk, with its bondage trousers and safety pins. It was decided I should adopt the guise of a skinhead. This made me shudder. I was definitely not a hard nut. I had never been in a fight in my life, but I got some combat trousers, some Ben Sherman shirts and a kind of wind-cheater Harrington which, together with the obligatory Doc Martens boots and a 'number four' haircut, looked convincing enough at a distance.

It was easier to get me into different clothes. Tim and Jerry were cool anyway – (drainpipe trousers, biker jacket for Tim and a Crombie overcoat for Jerry), but another matter for Lynval and definitely for Silverton, who would definitely *not* dress down for anyone. To whit, the odd mix 'n' match look that we had for the next year or so.

The band (we were called The Hybrids) played its first gig some time in October 1977 at the Heath Hotel on the Foleshill Road, Coventry. We borrowed the Ray King Soul Band's PA. There was a great big grand piano on the small stage which we couldn't move, so Jerry set his ex-church organ up facing the stage with his back to the audience. I cannot remember how we went down, but at least we went down. We played (I think) 'Do the Dog', 'Little Bitch', 'Dawning of a New Era' and a version of 'Too Much Too Young', something that later became 'Nite Klub', and I'm sure, some more stuff, but I can't remember what. A band called The Shapes headlined. They were from Leamington Spa, had a record out on their own Sofa Records label and consequently were famous. We played there again a fortnight or so later, with another Coventry punk band (Urban Blight), with us going on first. It seemed to work, and we started a fortnightly 'residency' featuring other local punk bands as headliners.

Now that punk rock was the happening youth culture, loads of kids formed groups. Being musically competent didn't matter so much as whether you looked good (which generally meant defacing an old school blazer and liberal use of safety pins). Quite a few youngsters in Coventry learnt two and a half chords, wrote songs which included the word 'bored' in the title and became legends in their own sixth-form common rooms. In real terms this meant there was an awful lot of very awful punk rock being played. Coventry suffered from this as much as anywhere else, but, as happens in these sorts of situations, the good stuff generally rises to the top.

The first Coventry band to get a record deal were The Flys: Joe Hughes and Dave Freeman (who, fifteen years later, formed The Lover Speaks and wrote 'No More I Love Yous', which Annie Lennox covered). Also in the band were Neil O'Connor (Hazel's brother) and drummer Chris King. Pete King, his brother, was the band's manager. They used to be a shit-hot funk band called Midnight Circus, but I don't suppose they told too many people about that when they signed to EMI. They got their deal and were off to London, where they rented a house before you could unfasten a safety pin. Their first album, *Waikiki Beach Refugees*, is still great, but as there was 'so much product out there' in 1977, they got lost.

One of the better 'new wave' bands was Roddy Radiation and the Wild Boys. Jerry and I went to see them upstairs at the Golden Cross. They were deafeningly loud, and I didn't stay very long. I did remember Roddy, their guitar player/singer. I had seen him around town with Doc Martens boots and spiky ginger hair. I'd also seen him at The New York Dolls gig at Warwick University a couple of years earlier. I was resplendent in flares and cheese-cloth, but he had a Teddy Boy jacket and drainpipe trousers. I always thought that the 'Radiation' nametag was a punk thing, but he told me years later it was given to him because he used to go red in the face after having imbibed alcohol.

The only punk band in Coventry worth spitting at was Squad. A kid called Scully played guitar, Sam McNulty played bass, Billy Little attempted drums, and the whole thing was held together by this charismatic, sullen vocalist called Terry Hall. Both The Flys and Roddy's band were made up of seasoned musicians, guys in their early/mid-twenties. The kids in Squad were seventeen, eighteen tops, and they were the real deal. They only usually played for half an hour, because that was all the material they had. Sometimes they played for less because Terry 'got bored', or took offence to something or someone. I once saw him do the whole set with his back to the audience.

Now I was one of the 'old guys'. When I'd got home after having discussions with people on how good the Buzzcocks were, I'd put on Herbie Hancock's 'Head Hunters' or Little Feat. As far as I was concerned, if you couldn't play, you shouldn't be on stage (despite the fact that I'd been on stage at seventeen when I couldn't play!), but I still kept going to see Squad. So did Jerry. I remember him phoning me up at midnight, rather the worse for drink, from some club in Birmingham, where Squad and The Flys were playing. 'I've just seen this amazing singer – we've got to get him in our band.' We did. Next rehearsal, there he was, looking kind of nervous and hardly saying two words to anybody, but he wanted to be in the group. So Terry Hall was in. We dumped Tim, who was pretty pissed off but 'understood'. According to *Wheels out of Gear*, a few weeks after he'd been replaced Tim was at one of our gigs and threw the remains of his pint of beer over Terry during our performance. I can't say that I remember the incident, but things could get pretty wild in Coventry's punk-rock universe in those days. If the story is accurate, I'm sure it wasn't the worst thing that happened to Terry in 1977.

Of all the members of The Specials, it was Terry that I knew the least, but there again he was very shy and often very soft-spoken. This was generally misinterpreted as aloofness or arrogance, usually by people who were jealous.

Aged eighteen, Terry was younger than us and musically, from a different generation. He was growing up with The Sex Pistols and The Clash and considered the mighty Little Feat to be boring American old farts. Extolling the virtues of side four of *Exile on Main Street* by the Rolling Stones was a non-starter. Despite this, I liked him a lot and appreciated his Coventry razor-sharp wit, which could defuse some of those tense 'spent-too-much-time-in-a-van' moments.

It was around about this time that we played our first 'big' gig, in Coventry at Tiffany's Ballroom. (Tiffany's, also known as the Locarno, looms large in the Specials' mythology. It was a dance hall / Saturday-night cattle market, and it was where groups played. Apart from the Coventry Theatre, which was a seated venue, it was the biggest gig in town.) We were the support band for Ultravox.

Lynval had access to a dark blue Transit van, and we put all the gear into it and loaded into Tiffany's – just like a real rock 'n' roll band, rubbing shoulders with 'real' pop stars, with their shiny new equipment, and the professional punk ego, which I interpreted as 'Listen, right, I'm famous, but as this is punk rock, and it's the music of the street, I'll be really condescending and make like I'm really interested in you and your cruddy little band, then I'll go and drink the bottle of vodka that's in the dressing room.' (In my eyes they had a record deal and consequently had 'sold out' . . . unlike us. I was not jealous at all.) There weren't that many people to see Ultravox, and I suppose there were even fewer to see us, but again, the important thing was that we had done it: played up there on the big stage, in the big room, with the big sound.

The next rehearsal we had, there was Roddy Radiation

himself, motorbike boots and leather jacket, clutching a spray-painted silver guitar, looking like he was defending the Alamo or something. I think Jerry thought we weren't 'punk rock' enough; I never really heard any talk about 'why we needed a lead guitarist', but I suppose we did, and here he was. The band was getting louder, and we couldn't possibly fit on the stage at the Heath Hotel — there were six of us now.

The good thing about the majority of shows that we did was that we got to go on first, which meant that I could get home at a reasonable hour and be up for work the next morning. What I missed out on was the main band and what was to me the excessive amount of alcohol that went down people's throats. I had never been comfortable around drunken people (I'm still not) and tended to keep myself to myself (usually ending up 'reasoning' with Silverton) when we started playing out of town. Both Jerry and Rod were pretty thirsty guys back then, Lynval too. By this time we were pretty much kings of the heap as far as Coventry was concerned — well, we'd pinched the guitar player and the singer from the 'competition', so we would be, wouldn't we? Squad were still going strong. Gus Chambers, 'some skinhead from Radford', as Terry described him, had joined as their singer; they'd got a new guitar player too.

The Cov Punks, as they called themselves, were a fearsome bunch. I'd never seen them fight but I'd talked to people who had; the whole thing reminded me of football violence, and I was glad that I didn't hang around at our gigs after we'd played. Their favourite bands were Manchester glam-rock rabble Slaughter and The Dogs . . . and us. But whether I liked them or not, they liked the band (which was now called The Automatics by the way) and they turned up religiously whenever we played. One memorable occasion was when we supported Sham 69, back at Tiffany's in early 1978. The atmosphere was very tense, what with Sham and their travelling skinhead following, and I was convinced that a fight was going to break out. Along with us on the bill was a band called Menace, also from London. They had a single out called 'GLC' (Greater London Council). The chorus went 'GLC, GLC, GLC, you're full of shit, shit, shit, shit, shit.' We definitely weren't in Kansas now, Toto. As it happened, we went down surprisingly well and caught the eye of the local promoter's rep, a Birmingham DJ, name of Mike Horseman (more on him later). We looked a pretty odd sight up on stage. Roddy and Terry had the 'punk' look, I suppose; I was the Woolworth's skinhead, Silverton was OK because he sat low behind his drum kit. Lynval wore his flat cap and loud checked jacket, and I can't for the life of me remember what Jerry wore, but I'm sure it was considered.

By the beginning of 1978, we had what we thought was a strong line-up, and the beginnings of a local following. One of the local nightclubs, Mr George's, had started booking punk rock shows, so we marched in. It was the sort of red-velvet-wallpaper, mirror-balls, over-priced-drinks sort of place that I used to play when I was in Breaker. We got ourselves a Monday-night residency (nothing ever happens on Mondays – let the punks have the place). Pursuing our usual policy of being first on, we (or rather, Jerry) invited local bands to headline. We still rehearsed up at the Heath Hotel, and sometimes people would drop by. I remember meeting Charly Anderson, with the longest dreadlocks I'd ever seen, and a huge bass rig that made the best sound I'd ever heard. The consensus these days is that he was no great shakes as a bass player, but back then, you could have fooled me. Also along for the vibe was a mate of Silverton's, called Neville.

Neville Staple was infamous around Coventry. He had become a father in his teens, had spent time in borstal and ran a local sound system. Stories of him around Coventry are legion. A hairdresser friend of mine tells of when Nev and one of the hard-men Coventry skinheads had a fight, and how Neville emerged triumphant. He was street-wise in a way I wasn't, and I kept him at a respectable distance until I got to know him better. Neville started meeting up with us at rehearsals (I hate the phrase 'hanging out') and came to gigs. Pretty soon he was our roadie. He would do his reggae talkover stuff on the mikes when we were setting up, which impressed me no end.

The Monday-night sessions at Mr George's took off, and the place was soon heaving. I can't remember if we actually made any money, but I was one of the few members of the band who still held down a day job, so I wasn't particularly bothered. The DJ at Mr George's was an older guy. He liked us and wanted to take us into the studio. It turned out he knew a few people in the business. His name was Pete Waterman. He organized for us to spend the day in a basement studio in Berwick Street in London, in the heart of Soho. We had very little to lose and an awful lot to gain, so we got Lynval's van, borrowed a decent organ and went down to do some recording.

The experience was pretty exciting, but the finished results were less than memorable. According to Pete

Waterman's 'must read' autobiography, he paid £600 for the session. Again, it was the sort of thing that groups did, so we kind of accepted it like a rite of passage. Mr Waterman apparently attempted to get us a deal, but there were no takers, which, in retrospect, was just as well. Our 'lost demos' turned up on a Receiver Records release a few years ago. Listening to them, they are pretty lacklustre. It's not difficult to see why no one wanted to sign us. Pete Waterman is often credited with the 'discovery' of The Specials. As Jerry said to me, 'Discovering The Specials in Coventry was a little like discovering an armchair in your front room.'

Our dealings with Mr Waterman had not brought forth superstardom or sports cars, but nobody said that we owed them any money, so we pressed on. Somehow, Jerry was introduced to Chris Gilby, the manager of The Saints, an Australian punk band who were resident in the UK. They had a 'hit' single, 'I'm Stranded' – I seem to remember owning a copy. This looked like a way in. We all traipsed down to London again to a studio in a housing estate somewhere in Tower Hamlets and recorded six or so tunes – pretty badly. It was a new experience for most of us, recording. You played the song without the words (you didn't have the vocal cues), you had headphones on (the bass sounded like a rubber band), and the singers had to sing on their own. Meanwhile, the engineer went about his tasks, looking really bored and totally uninterested. It was quite a knock to our confidence. Most of the punk bands we came into contact with were dreadful musically, whereas we could actually play. So how was it we sounded crap when we got into a studio? In retrospect, we were learning how to make records.

Once again, nothing happened with the tapes, but we got the chance of playing the Marquee with – you guessed it – The Saints. The Marquee on Wardour Street, birthplace of British pop music and one of the world's most famous rock club stages, was a shit hole. The whole place stank. A combination of over-priced flat beer, its effect on male body odour, and its exit from the digestive system. The 'backstage' area was a thin room that ran the length of the stage. It was covered in graffiti (natch!) and there was nowhere to sit, let alone change. The guys from The Saints were nice enough, though – their bass player gave me a new set of strings. I remember nothing of our performance, but I remember The Saints being abominably loud and not particularly tuneful. The place was about half-full (or half-empty). We had to borrow some petrol money to get the van home to Coventry. Soon afterwards, Jerry had a phone call from Chris Gilby, saying he was not interested in us any more and we had 'missed the boat'. Jerry's reply was, 'We are the boat, mate!' I have always admired Jerry for his determination, not to mention his turn of phrase.

And the next, please. We started getting support spots in Birmingham, due mainly to Jerry's persuasive manner with one Mike Horseman (you remember!). Mr Horseman was a man of considerable reputation in certain areas of Birmingham cool society. He was a DJ known as The Shoop, an original mod. His wife was a groovy boutique owner – the Kahn of Khan and Bell (Birmingham's premiere punk emporium – Patti Bell was married to Birmingham rock icon Steve Gibbons.) He was one of the local reps for MCP (Midland Concert Promotions), who were rapidly becoming hot-shot UK tour promoters. This seemed pretty good for business, and although superstardom and sports cars were not immediately forthcoming, it did a lot to maintain our rather bumpy momentum.

What we got for starters was a residency at the Golden Eagle, in Hurst Street, Birmingham. Legendary record producer and drunk Guy Stevens said he signed Mott the Hoople because he saw them struggle up two flights of stairs with a Hammond organ. I thought about that every time we carried Jerry's ex-church organ up the three-flight spiral staircase that led to the 'concert room' of the Golden Eagle. I also thought about this when we carried it down again! The whole building was knocked down a few years ago. I cannot say I shed a tear.

Some nights (I think it was Fridays when we played there) we'd have a good turnout; other times we'd play to twenty people. We always had a good time – and we started to get regular punters. A following even.

It was around about this time that Lynval's blue Transit van was repossessed by the guys he shared it with. I had always been under the impression that it was his van alone, but one night, at a support spot at Tiffany's in Coventry, three or four black guys turned up for the van and they left with it. We got the gear back home somehow and after that enlisted the help of Gordon Reaney, the guitarist from Breaker. Breaker had run out of steam; they had never made much money and you couldn't go through life playing 'Knock Three Times' and 'Bridge Over Troubled Water' for £30 a week, so they had decided to call it a day. Which was lucky for us Automatics as Gordon provided us with a van and himself as driver.

We did some memorable support spots in Birmingham. We played with Sham 69 (again) at a Locarno-type ballroom with the house lights on, the lighting rig for the show having failed to materialize. The local 'Sham-ites' (or should that be '69-ers'?) were somewhat subdued in the 'broad daylight' atmosphere. We also played with Steel Pulse, a heavy-duty roots reggae band from Handsworth in Birmingham. They had a huge following in Birmingham – obviously – and had just released their *Handsworth Revolution* album. They still exist today, albeit in a slightly mellower form. In 1978, they were about as militant as it was legally acceptable to be.

Now, being from Coventry and playing in Birmingham was one thing (Brummies consider Coventry, if they consider it at all, like some rarely talked-about retarded relative or, at best, an eastern suburb), but being four (out of six) white guys playing reggae-punk in front of the Handsworth Revolutionaries' home crowd was another. The Pulse very kindly let us use their equipment, my bass sounding rich, deep and HEAVY through their bass player's Cerwin Vega rig, but the crowd cut us dead. No applause. No booing. No nothing. Dead. The predominantly black crowd did not seem at all happy that four white guys were up there trying to play reggae. To say it was embarrassing was the height of understatement. We shrank back to Coventry with lessons learnt and our bravado barely intact. The gig was at the Top Rank (later to become the Hummingbird), where, some months later, we would be up on stage, facing a different kind of hostility.

Our next Birmingham port of call was Barbarella's. Weedy power-pop Blondie wannabees The Photos did this appalling single called 'Barbarella's'. The chorus went something like 'I used to go to Barbarella's / Why did they have to close it down?' The club was run by the Fewtrell family, who, back then, ran Birmingham nightlife/clubland.

It had an atmosphere to it that made me feel nervous, to say the least. Nevertheless, the place was the 'Marquee' of Birmingham, and The Clash were scheduled to play a one-off gig there. Through the auspices of Mr Horseman (I suppose) we got the support spot and dutifully turned up one Sunday afternoon. The PA was set up, but no Clash. As the afternoon turned into the evening, it became apparent that Joe and the boys weren't going to show, but there was already a not inconsiderable number of studded leather jackets and spiky hairdos congregating outside. By seven o'clock there was a plan. 'The Clash ain't coming (they'll reschedule). What we'll do is let you in the club for nothing, and you can all see a band from Coventry you've never heard of.' To say I was somewhat apprehensive would be the height of understatement, but we went on and, to my surprise, we did a cracking gig, to a largely enthusiastic audience.

It was probably one of the best moves we had made in our short career. We had 'done good' with the Birmingham punks and done more than a year's worth of 'organs up three flights of stairs' at the Golden Eagle. A fortnight later, the rescheduled gig took place, and we duly did our duty. The atmosphere was electric and, to be honest, scared the shit out of me. I was not used to such levels of energy – both on the stage and coming from the audience. I'd rarely stay to watch the main bands we'd support as I had to get up for work the next day so I was totally unprepared for the full-tilt punk onslaught that was The Clash. I left just after they started, with Gordon and the equipment. No. I fled!

It was during these 'Birmingham days' that Mike Horseman introduced us to the singer of the defunct

Killjoys. They had a minor punk hit, 'Johnny Won't Get to Heaven', and their singer was trying to get a soul band together. We met him at Barbarella's and saw a kind of kindred spirit, someone else who was looking to the past for music's future. Mike thought it would be good for us to keep in touch. The singer's name was Kevin Rowland.

The Golden Eagle residency continued, but it started to get tedious playing to the same few faces for such little return. We only got a percentage of the door takings. No punters – no money. One night after we played, Jerry's organ fell to pieces as we were manhandling it down the stairs. A metaphor perhaps. It was time to move on.

Every band worth their salt has a drugs bust: The Beatles, Stones, Small Faces, anybody with any zip about them gets busted sooner or later, and we had plenty of zip. The Horsemouth got us two dates on the current Generation X tour, Derby and Huddersfield. The Derby gig was at the Old Derby Baths – wooden boards had been placed over the pool and the stage was at one end. The sound, as you can imagine, was horrendous. Generation X were rock stars. Tony James had two *red* Marshall bass stacks, not the usual black, and a Gibson Thunderbird bass (I was jealous as hell). I thought they were crap. Some kid from the crowd must have agreed with me because he got up on the stage and smacked Billy Idol in the face. I never saw it, but Lynval and Nev did and said it was hilarious.

The next night (a Saturday) we were at Huddersfield Poly. We arrived in plenty of time, got our gear out of the van and hung around, trying to ponce something to eat, or get a cup of coffee. I'd brought my girlfriend with me so I was trying my best to be polite. Generation X soundchecked, Billy Idol, sporting a black eye from the night before, then stayed on stage, played some Buddy Holly songs, had a laugh, stayed on stage a bit longer, had a few more laughs. This was the 'fuck the support band' routine that we sometimes encountered. It still makes me angry when you've got a support act and you don't give them any time to set up. I think it is incredibly arrogant, it's also ignorant: if you want the evening to be a success, you give the opening act a chance to sound good. I have never liked Generation X since. The Billy Idol MTV Rock Star thing was rubbish, and Sigue Sigue Sputnik were dross. Me, bear grudges? Nah, mate!

Anyhow, we played, and I think we even got some money, and we set off home down the M1 to Coventry. We were travelling in Gordon's van and Silverton's car. Somewhere down the M1, near Chesterfield, the van broke down. Silverton stopped and he figured that he could take one other passenger (he already had Neville, Lynval and someone else, although I can't remember who). Roddy went off in the car.

We'd phoned the AA (breakdown and recovery service) and were just sitting in the van waiting for them. Jerry was in the front with Gordon and, being a cool sort of guy, rolled a joint to pass the time. It had just been rolled when there was a knock on the passenger window. It was the police.

'What are you doing here?'

'We've broken down. We're waiting for the AA,' Gordon said, as nonchalantly as possible.

'Oh, OK then.'

The police went away, only to appear at the window some thirty seconds later. I don't think anyone had taken a breath since Gordon's quick thinking. But they were back.

'Excuse me, sir,' the officer said to Jerry.

'Yes,' said Jerry.

'Was that a hand-rolled cigarette you had in your hand a minute ago?'

'No,' said Jerry.

'I think it was, sir. Would you come with me?'

And that was that. The police towed the van and its occupants to the nearest police station at Alfreton. Jerry was taken away and charged with possession, and the rest of us were searched and, although we weren't put in a cell, we were confined to a waiting room. My girlfriend was, by turns, scared stiff, tearful and furious. To make it worse, in the morning (after us having stayed up all night), when the police let us go, the AA said they could only take five people, and, as there were seven of us in the van, you can guess who had to hitch-hike home to Coventry with his girlfriend. We got back around 1 p.m. Not very happy. She never came with me to gigs after that.

It was now the middle of 1978, and things were starting to get serious. We had started to rehearse down at the Lanchester Polytechnic, in the same room where the dreaded college jams used to take place! Jerry came in, in what appeared to be a pretty foul mood, and said something along the lines of 'You're either in this group or not in this group! We've got a gig in Newcastle next Monday.' This was a thinly veiled threat to 'quit yer day job' and 'get serious' with the band. Apart from myself, Roddy and Terry both had day jobs. Rod worked as a painter and decorator for the council. He was the only one of us who was married. And he had a mortgage. Terry worked up by the station in some business that traded in foreign postage stamps or something.

I knew that I didn't want to be a frozen-food van driver for the rest of my life. Karen, my girlfriend at the time, (and her mother) had convinced me that I should buy a house. I had saved enough money for a house in the Earlsdon area of Coventry. It was going to cost me £7,000, and I'd got the deposit, had been to see people about a mortgage and was talking to a solicitor to do the whole deal. It felt like it was the first time in my life that I'd had to make a decision. I couldn't possibly keep mortgage payments up on this house if I was in the band – which made no money from gigs, and didn't have a record deal – and I knew Jerry's soul-band money was running out. I dumped the house. (It's probably now worth at least £150,000!) My solicitor thought I was crazy; my girlfriend (and her mother) were speechless. Not only that, but I did the gig in Newcastle. So did Terry and Rod.

I still kept my job, but The Clash tour brought all that to a head.

Our relationship with Mike Horseman was not working out. He wasn't able to get us anything like the regular work we felt we were ready for, and some other stuff was going down that I only got a sketchy picture of. It seemed somebody in the Birmingham underworld had taken a dislike to him and he was getting increasingly paranoid, probably due to the threatening phone calls he had been receiving. He had taken to recording all his phone conversations – so he could use them as evidence presumably. Whatever was going down, the Coventry Automatics went down lower on his list of priorities. He did, however, introduce us to Dave Cork.

Corky, as he was known, was currently tour manager for The Clash, a position he later held for Dexy's Midnight Runners, and as a result of the Barbarella's/Clash fiasco it was deemed that he owed us a favour. We sort of jemmied our way on tour with The Clash and into their managerial sphere of influence. Or should that be clutches?

Managers had seemed a waste of space as far as we were concerned. (Not much changes does it!) We were aiming too low – if you wanted to get known, you should go to the top. The two 'top' punk managers at the time were Malcolm McClaren and Bernie Rhodes. Malcolm had The Pistols (literally!) and Bernie managed The Clash. They were the 'scene makers', the guys who told the record companies what *they* wanted – and got it. Subversive, situationalists, all that stuff. We thought it was great – just what the punk rock ethic was about.

The Clash had just recorded their second album, *Give 'Em Enough Rope*, and had released a new single, 'White Man in Hammersmith Palais'. It was their first tour in England for a year or so and was a three-week trek around the UK. Their 'official' support act was Suicide, an arty duo from New York, but they would not be able to do the first few dates. The Coventry Automatics, then, had the distinction of opening the show for The Clash until the 'official' support joined the tour, or at least that was the plan.

Of course, it was too good to be true. The day before we were due to do our first show at Aylesbury Town Hall, Jerry received a letter from solicitors representing a band called The Automatics. This 'other' Automatics had just signed a deal with Island Records and had a single, 'When the Tanks Roll Over Poland', poised to smash into the charts at any moment. We were, therefore, and consequently, notwithstanding the party of the first part, not never, and unequivocally, ever, allowed to use the name 'Automatics', ever, again!

Now, there is a lot to be said in a name. The Sex Pistols. The Clash. A name could make you or break you. Eater. The Acme Sewage Company. The band you now know as The Specials went through lots of different monikers: The Jaywalkers, The Hybrids, The (Coventry) Automatics. None of them were brilliant and, to be honest, some of them were shite. However, nothing motivates more than a deadline, and we had less then forty-eight hours to come up with something we could call ourselves when we trod the boards with The Clash in Aylesbury. I seem to remember us sitting in the back of Gordon's van trying to pluck names out of the air. Lynval said it didn't matter what we called ourselves. He looked down at what he was holding in his hands and suggested we called ourselves 'Fags and Matches'. Thanks for your input, Lyn.

Glen Matlock's post-Pistols band The Rich Kids was doing the rounds at the time, and 'The Specials' also had a sarcastic, self-depreciating tone about it. The original plan was to call ourselves The Special AKA (also known as The Automatics), but it got shortened, as things do. So there it was, and there we were, the legendary Friars Club, Aylesbury Town Hall, 28th June 1978. The Specials. We actually managed a sound check, too. While we were playing, this little guy with black combat trousers, a big nose and even bigger glasses wandered through the hall and stood at the barricade in front of the stage and peered at us. Who was this weirdo? Why, it was Bernie Rhodes.

I read somewhere that Joe Strummer himself insisted that we stay on the tour, and it become a three-band bill, but I also heard that it was because we could get Mick Jones some good sensimilla weed, so we were kept on as herbal suppliers. Whichever way it was, we were in. Sometimes Dave Cork would get us a boarding house to stay in, other times we had to rough it, and rough it we bloody well did. I rushed back to work and announced that I *had* to have the next two weeks off. There was not a great deal they could do. I was free to be a rock 'n' roll star – on tour, on the road, on the big stage, with the big PA system, backstages, dressing rooms even. Everything that I had read about, drooled about, dreamt about was finally happening.

The Clash tour was this amazing adrenaline blur. I remember Chelsea (who were also supporting for some reason) getting pelted by spit, and their guitarist jumping all over the place. We never got a great deal of 'phlegm-abuse' – the audience were probably saving it for the main attraction; either that or they didn't consider us worthy of being gobbed at. The Clash were travelling with a 'minder' – a short-haired, barrel-chested gentleman, one Steve English. A buddy of Johnny Rotten, apparently. He was a man who was to play a peripheral role in both The Specials' and The Selecter's career. He didn't particularly like us, and we kept out of his way. I think he must have warmed to us, though, as he came to our aid one time when our van was being besieged by some malevolent 'rockabilly types' outside a hotel somewhere.

When Suicide eventually did turn up, we stayed on as the opening act, the tour now becoming a three-band bill. Nev had already made his presence felt at the sound desk, and I made friends with the monitor engineer. There was a great vibe amongst the crew, and even Johnny Green and Baker (The Clash's road crew) became approachable after a while. Suicide went down really badly. Well, what d'you expect, they had no guitars or drums, just this keyboard business and a singer. I liked them, but Alan Vega looked like a healthy Johnny Thunders. It was best to keep out of his way when they came off. He was generally covered in spit and furious with it. Looking back, it's possible Bernie got them to do the tour because he knew the reaction they'd get from the crowd, who, by the time The Clash came on, were just about ready for anything. (Despite this sounding like a typical Bernie Rhodes ploy, it was apparently Mick Jones who wanted them to support.) The tour is reasonably well documented in Johnny Green's book, *A Riot of Our Own*. The dates in Scotland were great, especially Glasgow, a particularly memorable 4 July.

The gig was at the Apollo Theatre, a notorious gig in a notorious city. Our performance was pretty good. The stage was really high, so only the most accomplished gobber could reach us. Afterwards, some guys from a local band came and congratulated us in a manner that was typically Glasgow: 'Well, at least they never threw anything at you!' The guys later went on to become Altered Images, who, with the impossibly cute Claire Grogan fronting them, had Martin Rushent produced hits in the mid-eighties. One of the guys kept saying, 'I really worship The Clash,' in his broad Glaswegian accent: 'Ah rilly warship thuh Clarsh.' It became one of those idiotic 'tour sayings'.

The Clarsh, however, were in for some serious Glasgow aggro. The venue's bouncers – renowned for their 'head-butt first, ask questions later' policy – were out for revenge. Last time Joe and the boys played the Apollo, the penguin-suited ones had received a severe drubbing. It was bouncer retribution time. As soon as the band hit the opening chords to their first tune, the bouncers piled into the crowd, indiscriminately cracking heads. Appeals for calm from the stage came to nothing. By the end of the show the Clash were understandably furious, not helped by fans outside the back door demanding to know why their heroes had done nothing to help. Outside, a tired and emotional Joe Strummer smashed a bottle on the pavement and was immediately arrested by the police. Paul Simonon went to his aid, was hit with a truncheon for his pains and also taken away. Meanwhile in the theatre, a fat female Glaswegian was stood at the front of the balcony, two spotlights trained on her, doing a striptease. I have an idea this was to distract the bouncers while the band got out of the venue. It was not a pretty sight, but kind of in keeping with the evening.

We made our way back to the hotel that The Clash were staying at. There was talk of us getting some accommodation, but nothing had been sorted out by show time, other than the promise of something later on. We lounged about in reception, totally forgotten, only to be witness to the various comings and goings to the police station, and reports on Joe's and Paul's condition and whereabouts. To make a surreal evening perfect, the lift doors opened, and out stepped 'Mister Light Entertainment' himself, Lionel Blair. He sized the situation up in a second and looked over at us. 'Had a good night, boys?' he said, and walked hurriedly through reception to the waiting limousine outside.

Joe and Paul spent the night in the cells. We slept in the van.

One of the more significant events on The Clash tour for us was the show at Crawley Leisure Centre, Saturday 8 July. A cavernous sports centre (which meant a hideous sound), it was the nearest to London the band played before the closing four nights in the capital itself. There were loads of skinheads, as opposed to the punks that usually made up the majority of the audience, and pretty nasty-looking ones at that. They weren't all National Front or British Movement, but you could see that some of them were. It was unsettling, and the point was taken. Our prospective audience wasn't going to be the punks. The punk ethic seemed to be dying on its arse. The 'second division' bands (UK Subs, 999, and so on) were nowhere near as relevant as The Pistols, who had split up, or The Clash, who were about to embark on their American saga. There were the new skinhead bands too: Sham 69, of course, The Angelic Upstarts and The Cockney Rejects had got a lot of press and were spawning imitations. They were also gathering a lot of fans. It was easy to be a disaffected youth in 1978 – unemployment was high, and inner-city frustration was commonplace. This provided perfect breeding conditions for the far right. And the young far right wanted music fast and loud to fight to.

We went down reasonably well – the hall was only half full, and we played 'Liquidator' in our set – 'Hey, skinhead! You're supposed to like this!' Suicide bombed big time: a skinhead jumped up on stage and socked Alan Vega in the face. He came off stage madder than usual and hurled a chair into the plate-glass mirror in the dressing room, shattering it. His nose was bleeding and he was on the 'next fuckin' plane home'. We left him alone with his cursings and went to watch The Clash.

Jimmy Pursey from Sham 69 – *the* skinhead band – came on stage towards the end of the show and tried to defuse the situation. He almost succeeded. I was getting used to the atmosphere and levels of adrenaline at these shows by now, but this show had a malevolence about it that was almost tangible. The audience was intimidating in the extreme, all sporting similar cropped haircuts, denim jackets, jeans, braces and shiny Doc Martens boots. Sports halls around London would have that same vibe when we played there on our own a year or so later. If there was any one pivotal moment that formed The Specials and our proactive anti-racist stance it was that show in Crawley. It was a sombre and thoughtful Specials that drove into London that night. The Flys (bless 'em) had agreed to put us up.

We returned to Birmingham's Top Rank, the scene of our somewhat humbling appearance with Steel Pulse. I'm sure I saw Boy George and Martin Degville (Sigue Sigue Sputnik – you know, the band that Tony James got together towards the end of the eighties!). They were backstage, dressed up like pantomime dames – very un-punk, but the precursor of things to come.

Now, I've never been in a fight, but those who have tell me that stuff happens in slow motion. This is what happened while I was playing. I saw it: The Beer Glass With My Name On It. It came arching out of the crowd, about ten rows back, and travelled very slowly in my direction. It was not a straight glass, but one of those dimpled pint mugs. Chunky. Heavy. I couldn't stop playing and I appeared suddenly to be rooted to the spot. All I could do was hunch my head down towards my chest and hope. The glass brushed the top of my head and crashed into The Clash's drum kit behind me. I carried on playing. I don't think anyone else in the band saw it. I started dancing a bit more after that. After all, a moving target is harder to hit!

Somewhere along the way we nicked a judo mat. Gordon's Transit was a bit higher than an ordinary tranny, so after we'd put the gear in, we'd put the judo mat on top, and three or four of us could sleep on it, while everyone else kipped on the seats. I have read somewhere that we had a tent that some of us slept in, but I have no memory of it myself.

We got paid expenses – petrol money and a bit of cash for food, but we didn't have any disposable income. The Clash used to throw out badges to the crowd, so we used to help ourselves to them when we could (there were always a couple of boxes backstage) and attempt to flog them to the fans who would inevitably turn up in the afternoon and hang around. After a fortnight or so, some of these 'hangers-on' became regular faces at the gigs, and as we had a lot of time on our hands, we hung around with them. There were two little punky girls from London who wore red brothel creepers who became fixtures on the tour. I think I was in love with both of them, but I reckon a few other people were too. There was a Scouse guy and a mixed-race kid from Hull. Come in and take a bow, Pete Wylie and Roland Gift. (You *have* heard of Roland Gift (Fine Young Cannibals) and Pete Wylie's Wah! who made the tedious eighties bearable.)

I remember doing Bury St Edmunds Corn Market Hall, attempting to sing backing vocals, on the edge of the stage while a punk girl was trying her utmost to take out the laces of my Doc Martens. I suppose the 'punk' thing to do would have been to kick her in the head, or spit at her at least. I didn't have the heart to do either. I was flattered, to tell you the truth.

The Clash tour ended with four nights at the Music Machine, an old dance hall in Camden (later to become the Camden Palace). I had had my fortnight's 'holiday' and returned to work. My plan was to work during the day (I generally finished no later than 4.30 p.m.), get a train down to London, do the gig and get a train back. I could be home by midnight, possibly earlier. By this time Rod and Terry had quit their day jobs, and I was the only member of the band working. The Music Machine gigs were great. A few fans had got tickets for all four nights, and we had made a lot of friends by the end of the run. We'd even got some press, too.

One night, The Clash were going to sound check, but Paul Simonon hadn't turned up. Johnny Green marched into the small cupboard that was our dressing room and informed me that I was doing The Clash's sound check. Just doing the tour was dying-and-going-to-heaven, but doing the sound check! I sat on the side of the stage with Paul Simonon's bass (I couldn't stand with it, the guitar almost touched the floor – Simonon was a good six inches taller than me and played real low) and I played with The Clash. I'll say that again – in big letters: I PLAYED WITH THE CLASH! We played Stevie Wonder's 'Superstition' for about ten minutes, me and Topper Headon getting seriously funky (well, I thought so) and that was it. It took about a month to get the grin off my face.

It was during the Music Machine gigs that Neville

started to become more than a roadie. One of our tunes, 'Don't Try to Love Me', had a dub section towards the end. One time we were playing it, when what would become The Staples' trademark, 'Huurrrr!!', boomed, echo drenched, out of the PA. 'Don't try to love me as I would say, / cos you know I will never never go away / Yeah, baby.' It sounded fantastic. Nev was dubbing up the band from the mixing desk, and had got a mike set up too. Bernie suggested that Nev be incorporated on stage. Funny, we were just thinking that.

After the third of the four nights I fell asleep on the train just after it left London. I woke up in Wolverhampton. The next train to Coventry was at 5.15 a.m. There was no way I was going to work that day. Actually, there was no way I was going to work anyway. Not after doing the Clash tour. Jerry was talking to Bernie Rhodes about him managing us, and although he never said a definite yes, he never said a definite no, and if you see that from an unbridled optimist's point of view (ours!), we would undoubtedly be Top of the Pops pretty soon. We had to be – I mean, we'd toured with The Clash and lived, and I'd even done their sound check!

Sex Pistols guitarist Steve Jones came down for a couple of nights to play encores and stuff (as did Sham 69's Jimmy Pursey), and I distinctly remember Mick Jones and Steve Jones having this ridiculous conversation:

> *MJ* – Ere, Steve, woss your favourite chord?
> *SJ* – E. Fuckin' great chord, E!
> *MJ* – Oh! Mine's A.
> *SJ* – Yeah, good chord, A.

I kid you not. Paul Simonon approached me and thanked me for doing his sound check. He seemed a very shy lad.

He asked me how long I'd been playing bass and I said about ten years, but only the past four years seriously. 'Yeah,' he said, 'I wonder when I'll start taking it seriously' – which was, I suppose, the perfect Clash answer. We had done it. Three weeks on tour with the most high-octane punk rock show ever – and we made £12 each! It was the greatest thing that had ever happened in my life. On the last night, Roddy took Mick Jones's stage shirt, which was a 'punk-rock-thing-to-do', I suppose.

Our 'Clash experience' prepared us for the future. We saw how they all gave one hundred per cent every night and we saw what they got back from the audience and how amazing it was. I have seen some of the world's most popular groups over the past twenty-five years, and, apart from the Specials, no one – I'll say that again, just for emphasis, NO ONE – comes close to The Clash. When we started the tour, the adrenaline levels physically scared me. By the time I reached those last four nights in Camden it became as second nature as breathing. A rarefied atmosphere indeed, and one where I definitely wanted to be.

3

The French Letter:
The Special AKA goes to Paris

We returned to Coventry like gunfighters riding into Abilene (or somewhere). Well, I did anyway. I quit my job. 'Oh, what are you going to do?' 'I'm gonna be a pop star!' I signed on the dole and waited for the record companies to come flocking up to Coventry to sign us.

Our glory was pretty short-lived. Nothing happened. So, Mohammed went to the mountain, and we travelled down to London to exist in squalor at Bernie Rhodes's rehearsal studio in Camden. Dingwalls was just next door, which, if you had any money, was bearable, but as we were now all on the dole, we didn't have money very often. Most of our time was spent rehearsing, or over the road at the Caernarvon Castle pub, patiently nursing a pint of Guinness if finances stretched that far. We'd spend three or four days a week down there, then go back to Coventry to get our dole and have a bath. I think Bernie wanted us to experience some kind of squat-life. He used to come around and harangue us with punk rhetoric: 'You gotta be good enough so some kid'll buy your record as opposed to a new pair of shoes.' He used to be connected with The

Who's management and had something to do with Marc Bolan. 'So Marc comes in and says, "I've got this song called 'The Children of the Revolution'," and I said, "What do you know about the fackin' Revolution?"' He had a Renault car which had the number plate CLA5H. One time we were in his 'office', he came in, picked up the phone, dialled and said, 'Topper! It's Bernie. Stop hanging round CBS – it cheapens the whole thing,' and put the phone down. He had a point, as we later found out. He also had a good right-hand man. Mickey Foote had produced the first Clash album, had done the out-front sound on their tour and was attempting to build a demo studio at the premises, and consequently was there a lot of the time, making partitions and wiring up stuff. We spent a fair bit of time with him, trying to figure out from him what the Rhodes phenomenon was. Bernie also managed Vic Goddard (his band, The Subway Sect, were one of the original '76 punk outfits; Lynval, Jerry and I did some demos with him – introverted guy, but the songs were good) and this outfit called The Black Arabs, who appeared in The Sex Pistols' movie. We didn't mix with them that much, but when we did, it was generally to compare our situation to The Clash and moan about Bernie and what we felt he *wasn't* doing to further anyone's career.

We slept in an upstairs room, and every now and again a rat would run over someone in their sleeping bag. Squalid would be something approaching a good description. It tested our commitment to the hilt, which from Bernie Rhodes's point of view was what he wanted, but was starting to undermine all the hard work we'd already done. It was not the best of times. Bernie still seemed interested in us, but we were becoming very dubious about him. We

49

even started talking about contracts. Things came to a head after our trip to Paris.

The following piece is a letter that I wrote to Bob Carter and Stella Clifford after I got back from Paris. It appeared in print in an edition of *Chartbusters* magazine (50p) – just to fill out a couple of pages I suppose. The original is pretty libellous, not a little bit Francophobic and now seems toe-curlingly naive. It does convey my 'snotty pop-star wannabee' persona pretty well.

21/11/78

Dear Bob and Stella,

Here is the story of how we went to Paris, and what we did (or was done) when we got there . . . and how we got back.

Originally we were given a week in Paris as a 'carrot' of some sort, to sign the management contract with Bernie Rhodes. As the planned departure date came closer, it was apparent that we were not going to sign, and the 'Paris Carrot' was becoming pretty transparent.

The departure date was set for Monday 13th, the gig being five nights (14th–18th) at the 'CLUB GIBUS' in Paris. Gordon was originally going to take us, but he has been getting pretty pissed off with the Rhodes organization, and his van needed a new engine anyway. OK. So we try someone else . . . Dennis, a roadie person we know from Coventry, said he would do it, as long as he got £35 in his hand when he got back. This was agreed to, but could he take *The Subway Sect* to Manchester on the 12th (Sunday), as their van had broken down (crank-shaft). Whilst in Manchester, Dennis has an arguement with Mickey Foote (B. Rhodes' right-hand man) and says he's not going to Paris, but he would take us down to London the next day (Monday).

We go down to London the next day. Rhodes has not got any transport for us, and spends two hours telling us what 'arseholes' our friends are for not taking us to Paris (despite the fact that − if he had not intervened − they would still have been doing so). They say they will get a van, and we'll go the next day (Tuesday). We sleep on the floor at the rehearsal studio in Camden.

Tuesday. There is still no van, and we cannot convince Dennis, who we have been phoning up, to do it . . . B. Rhodes even offered him £100. I'm beginning to get pretty fed up. So are the rest of the band. That night Jerry gets drunk and demolishes the wall telephone, destroys a door and smashes bottles around us as we sleep.

Wednesday. The plan is now this: we hire a van to take us and the gear to Dover, put the gear on the ferry, and a van from the club will meet us at Calais. Groovy, great! We are going to Paris. We arrive at Dover, and put the gear on the ferry. Fab! We leave Dover, and the crossing takes place in gale-force conditions. Later that night the ferry service is suspended because conditions are so bad. I spend all the crossing up on deck, being overwhelmed by the sheer force of the sea. (A metaphysical interlude.)

We get to Calais, and the customs will not let Silverton into the country . . . no persuading, no nothing. No visa, no entry. Silverton has a Barbados passport. Mickey Foote gives him some money to get a hotel, train fare to London, and telephone numbers and hurriedly scribbled addresses whilst he is being forced into a car at the customs and put back on the ferry.

Oh well. We didn't want to play that night anyway.

Now the fun really starts. (By the way we also learn that we are doing a support gig with *Devo* on the Sunday 19th.)

The band, minus its drummer, plus Mickey Foote (MF)

are now at Calais with the equipment (backline and instruments) and the 'van to meet us' is a Volkswagen Camper van!!

After some pretty amazing (though I say it myself) packing, we manage to get the gear, Neville, Lynval and Mickey Foote into the van. (The rest of us, Jerry, Rod, Terry and myself, must hitch. We thought there was no way the French would give a lift to two black men, especially if they didn't speak the language.) So J, T, R and I hustle round the lorry terminal at Calais for a lift to Paris, no luck, and we get kicked out by a horrible, fat, big-nosed Gendarme. It is now about 11 p.m. (French time being one hour in front of UK time) and we are outside the dock area. We finally get a lift in a Rolls-Royce — A Welshman who is delivering the car to his boss, gives us a lift, Polo mints and cigarettes. What an amazing car!! Our spirits rise a bit.

We are dropped off on the motorway at some services 80 km from Paris at around 4.30 a.m. Someone says he will take two of us, so Roddy and Jerry go. At around 5 a.m. I hustle a van driver who reluctantly agrees to take Terry and I to Paris. We get into Paris at around 6. It is still dark. We have about 80 francs (£10) between us, and the address of the gig. By now we are pretty tired. It is Thursday. At around 9 a.m. we meet Jerry and Rod outside the club and go to a café where we are charged £2.00 for 4 cups of coffee. [OK, listen, this is 1978, right, and a cup of coffee cost about 15p back then.]

4 p.m. finds us asleep on a park bench nearby, with one person down at the club waiting for someone from the rest of our party who must have arrived by now, but are probably asleep. At 6 p.m. someone arrives to take us to the hotel; it is Jan, an Australian girl who knows MF, and who has put up the van party at her flat. We have been awake for around 22 hours, check in and pass out at the hotel. Silverton is

apparently on his way back to Paris by train, having obtained a visa in London that morning. We go to the club, where the gear has been set up by Neville and Lynval, and attempt to get a good sound. There are not enough mikes and we are an amplifier short. (The ampeg combo that we took over with us blows up when tested, so Rod has to use Lynval's amp which he shares with the clavinet. Lynval, however, uses Jerry's amp along with the organ.)

We are to go on at 11.30 p.m. and again at 1.30 a.m. Silverton arrives, beaming all over his face, having single-handedly come all the way from London, no mean feat if you know Silverton.

Great! The band are assembled, and we play a pretty good set, despite the fact that everyone is totally wiped, to about 20 people. We are told that we have a pretty good sound, not too loud as is usually the case, and pretty well balanced. Girls come up to the dressing room (a remarkably rare occurrence for us, I can tell you), but we are all so shattered, we go back to the hotel, via a bar where I met a 68-year-old Englishman who tells me stories about how he was mugged in Harlem (New York) in 1948, and in Montmatre (Paris) last Sunday, by a transvestite.

Friday. I wake at around 1 p.m., and begin my tourist assault on Paris. I start at the new Georges Pompidou Centre, which is like the Tate Gallery, Science Museum, Kiddie's Playground and Library rolled into one. There's a massive Joan Miró exhibition which is very impressive, and a local Paris artists' exhibition which is also pretty good. After a couple of photos, it's down the river and on to the Louvre. All the paintings which typify the best in any era of paintings are there, and the *Mona Lisa* is absolutely amazing; it has an ambience which just isn't captured by photography.

Anyway, on to Friday's gig. Perhaps a bit of info on the

club would be a good idea. It's a small cellar type club, with a layout similar to the upstairs part of Mr George's in Coventry. Opening hours are 10.30 p.m.–5.30 a.m. and the drinks, meals, etc., are cripplingly expensive. 10 francs for a beer or orange juice. However, it does have a reasonably high stage. A lot of British punk bands have played there, probably because it is one of the two clubs in Paris to feature live music. We play to a fuller house than yesterday, and go down reasonably well. The French must be educated in the subtleties of reggae and we refused to pander to their shouts of 'Wock and Woll'. Anyway, we finish and girls come up the dressing room again, and one of them comes up to me and wipes me out with the small talk to end all small talk 'I think I would like to fuck with you,' to which I reply, somewhat taken aback, 'No thanks love.' That completely wiped me out, what the hell can you say to something like that? Sometimes I wish I was not so good-looking y'know! Anyway I have to get out of this situation somehow, so I offer to buy her a drink, and engage in a policy of talking rubbish in the hope I might bore her stiff so she goes anyway. Terry, meanwhile comes up to me and relates how a member of the audience has just asked him back to his place for some heroin . . . (One lump or two Mr Hall . . . No thanks, I've just mainlined). 'One night in Paris will wipe the smile off your silly face,' as 10cc would say.

I ask my new friend if she would not mind taking me to the Eiffel Tower the next day, as I'll probably get lost if I go on my own. Agreed. I go back to the hotel and pass out.

Basically, I think the average Parisian is rude, ignorant and selfish. I don't know whether that is because I play in a pop group (I doubt it) or because I'm not French; although they treat one another badly enough. They seem to have no regard for any human life other than their own. They fight to get on and off the Metro (Underground Railway System) and drive cars like they're extras in *Death Race 2000*. The police are pretty tyrannical, especially when drugs are involved, and a lot of youngsters we met said they were all pretty paranoid about the cops, especially the riot police, whom I saw on the Saturday.

Saturday. Somehow I manage to get out of bed and meet Miss Whatever-her-name-is. I was hoping she'd get the message and wouldn't come. Never mind. The Eiffel Tower is nothing short of magnificent, unfortunately the very top was closed, but I managed to go up the first stage and take a couple of photos.

From there we went on a pretty special pilgrimage; Jim Morrison (of the Doors) is buried in Paris, so we went along to see the grave. I took a photo which I will send to Charly, quite an emotional moment. I am too knackered to do anything else, so we go to a friend's flat and fall asleep for an hour or two.

The thing that I do like about Paris is that there is no massive redevelopment. All the exteriors of the buildings are intact and it appears to be the 'ancient city' for which it is famous.

I bid my punkette au revoir and head back to the club, where we have been promised a proper sound check and perhaps a practice. Needless to say, there is no one there to let us in, so Rod and I head back to the hotel.

Now it starts to get really good.

When Rod and I get back to the hotel, MF is having a row with the guy behind reception. Apparently he had come into MF's room and demanded the money for our stay. He took 500 francs despite protestations from a half-asleep MF. Rod and I go upstairs and leave them to it. About 10 minutes later the rest of the band arrive, and ask why the front door (plate glass) is smashed to smithereens. Nothin' to do with me mate!

A while later, someone asks us to take all our gear downstairs, but we sit tight as the hotel has got our 500 francs, so we have paid for tonight's room. Time passes. I am asleep on my bed, and Jerry is having a shower.

There is a knock at the door, and in storms the proprietress, brandishing a Coca-Cola bottle, hysterical, yelling, 'Get out of my hotel.' She goes into the shower and drags Jerry out, stark naked, threatening to 'break his head'.

The stupid cow has obviously jumped to the conclusion that 'the group' have broken her front door, and has come round after blood.

We are pushed downstairs, to reception, where two large guys take Roddy's and Lynval's guitars. These she says have been 'confiscated' because we have not paid her our bill, and have broken the door. MF by this time is at the police station, along with the owner of the club, explaining the situation.

Jan arrives and, seeing us all sitting in reception, says, 'You haven't been thrown out of the hotel already, have you?' jokingly. 'Yup,' we reply, and give a brief resumé of the situation. Jan immediately goes to pieces, comes out with a long stream of 'Facks' (she being Australian you understand) and goes off to have what we can only imagine is a nervous breakdown.

The stupid cow that re-enacted the shower scene from *Psycho* with Jerry will not listen to any sort of sense (did you honestly expect her to?) so we have reached an impasse, cos we ain't going nowhere without our guitars!

MF and the club manager arrive and the situation is: *The Damned* were at the hotel last week, and, naturally, wrecked it. They also didn't pay their bill. The money they took off

MF this morning is for *The Damned*'s bill last week, and the guitars are for our bill this week and the door. NO WAY!

The Damned have got nothing to do with us, we have paid our bill, so give us back our guitars. NO WAY. You have paid for last week's group, so pay our bill now, no money, no guitars.

And so it goes on for three hours. The police are called but do nothing. (You look after your own anyway. It's just like white people treat blacks, says Silverton, this is how we are treated, now you know what it's like to be black, etc., etc.)

Lynval and Roddy, needless to say, are thinking pretty murderous thoughts, and the rest of us are devising exquisite ways of slowly ending the life of the proprietress of the hotel.

The owner (as opposed to the manager) of the club arrives. A BIG guy, with a Big cigar, and a Big scar on his face. This is getting serious! Negotiations start and eventually, an agreement is reached. MF will pay half the money (an advance of the *Subway Sect*'s gig there in a month's time), and the manager of the club will pay the other half. The owner goes off with Rod, Terry, Silverton and Neville to get the money.

MF is pretty scared. The owner, we surmise, is probably going to get some heavies to *really* show how to demolish a hotel, which is great fun for him, but still doesn't get us our guitars. Lynval, Jerry and I go for a meal and head back to the club, where the rest of the guys plus the guitars are. The owner was considering taking his gun, which he showed to the band, but didn't. The transaction took place pretty smoothly. MF is going (to try) to get *The Damned*'s bill out of their manager (some hope!).

Saturday's gig is the best yet. This band has the ability to play at its best during the most oppressive pressure, and when things are running pretty smoothly, turn out a mediocre performance, witness Friday's gig where there were no hassles during the day. We go down great, a good clear sound (apparently), and we are the first band in about three months to get an encore. For our second encore we do the last verse unaccompanied, Jerry lurching more and more towards the audience and falling off into the crowd on the last note. 'Did you hurt anyone when you fell in the crowd?' I asked him when we got up into the dressing room. 'I hope so,' was his reply.

Our spirits are high again, and boosted by the fact that the manager wants to buy us all a drink (he MUST have liked it) and the appearance in the dressing room of Ian Dury's bass player (Norman Watt-Roy) and keyboard player (Mickey Gallagher) who enthuse wildly, which brought one of the biggest grins ever to my pretty haggard face. Anyway Mr Watt-Roy and I congratulate one another on how good players we are (ho!) and re-extol the virtues of *Little Feat, Stax and Motown* session players circa '66–'70 and *Miles Davis*. The mutual appreciation society goes on downstairs, and tales of Ian Dury debauchery are rife.

By this time (3 a.m.) we have another hotel about 75 yards from the club, so we check in, and crash out. I wonder what happened to my punkette.

Sunday morning we are kicked out the hotel again because all rooms must be vacated by 11 a.m., so we all trudge downstairs and fall asleep in front of the television. Terry, however, is not here, and Jerry and Rod, who got in at 9 a.m., after having been to a café with some girls, say he went off with one of the girls. He returns, looking pretty haggard, but in fine spirits, the guy has put everything into the last three shows. While I was nearly passing out on stage on Thursday night, he was jumping around like the loony he is.

It would appear we are not playing with *Devo* that night so we get hold of a van and get gone.

The deal is, we put the gear on the boat train to London: great! Why didn't we think of that before we ask ourselves, loads cheaper, and does not involve hitch-hiking across France at 2 in the morning. Still, there is always next time (???!!!).

We deposit the gear on the train, and go for a meal and some sightseeing, as we have about 6 hours before the train departs. A meal in a restaurant restores our health to somewhere near normal, and various alcoholic beverages induce a state of almost well-being.

We board the train, Jan comes to wish us bon voyage, and we are on our way. Sleep is priority No. 1, but is difficult on a train, especially with Rod snoring (he sounds like a chain saw) and Jerry, revelling in the effects of inebriation, bellowing 'Ça va!' out of the train window. A guard soon comes along and tells him to shut up, so that sorts that out. The crossing is OK except that every comfortable seat on the goddamn ferry is occupied by some rich American posing as a hippy. Still, I have bacon and eggs in the cafeteria, and feel quite wonderful. Terry, we have sussed, must have had his drink spiked, as he has been active and wide awake now for about 36 hours. The girl he was with gave him what she said was an Aspirin, but the drugsters amongst us ain't so sure. Anyway, he is 'coming down' and looks like a corpse.

The train gets into Victoria at 6 a.m. Jerry, Silverton and Terry have enough money to get a coach to Coventry, so off they go. MF is going to hire a van for us, so we check that the gear is all there (which it is) and go back to MF's flat where we sleep for a few hours. At 10 a.m. he books the van and goes off to hire it. At about 12 a.m., the phone rings and it's Bernie Rhodes, who wants to speak to me. I get an 'ear bender' as we who have had the misfortune to have phone conversations with the aforementioned call it, saying he is not going to get a van for us, and we 'must learn to use our own initiatives, and do things for ourselves'. I naturally thank him very much and tell him what a wonderful, genuine, warm person he is, and hang up.

At least we're back in England.

You know the rest. See y'all soon,

Horace.

We ended up back in London with our equipment and no transport to get it back to Coventry. We had no money either. I then called Bob, who lent me some cash so that I could get back to Coventry, hire a van, drive back to London, pick up our gear and take it back to Coventry.

I did not want to have anything to do with Bernie Rhodes ever again, and luckily this sentiment was shared with the rest of the band. 'Paris' became part of the band mythology, along with The Clash tour. I suppose Bernie had a point; we survived a kind of rock 'n' roll boot camp, and all this stuff was grist for the lyricist's pen. The confiscation of guitars and the dealings with 'colourful' club owners would surface on 'Gangsters', our first single.

If the Clash tour was our 'Battle of Britain', Paris was our 'Dunkirk'.

4

Ska

Up until now we had played, pretty much, the same songs we had always played: 'Do the Dog', 'Dawning of a New Era' and something that later became 'Nite Klub'. We played punky stuff, stuff that was funk-based and a couple of old reggae tunes, 'Birth Control' and 'Liquidator'. We didn't have a well-defined image, either musically or visually.

Ska fitted perfectly.

The music that pre-dated reggae, ska was a combination of traditional Caribbean mento rhythms that came out of slavery all the way back to Africa and the rhythm and blues walking bass backbeat that the late 1950s Jamaicans were hearing on their radios when they tuned in to the southern American stations. The first ska records were released in Jamaica in 1960, and the sound soon travelled to England, where it took the 'blues dance' – a kind of house party affair – by storm.

The music was also adopted by the mods. These were mainly working-class youths, who in the early- to mid-1960s were, for the first time ever in British society, in possession of what is now termed 'disposable income'. This disposable income was generally disposed of in the purchase of clothes: Italian-style close-fitting suits, 'loafer' slip-on shoes, high-collar button-down shirts. A ready-made image ripe for reinventing in fact.

Musically, it meant our punky tunes could still be played fast, but with a swing that made them eminently more danceable – like our reggae stuff – and we looked like a sixties-type soul revue. The whole thing was becoming a lot more cohesive.

> **cohesive** *a.* sticking together
> (*Concise Oxford Dictionary*)

London-based reggae band Matumbi had recently released a tune called '(Whatever Happened to) Bluebeat and Ska'. Jerry and I took it as a sign! Lynval was not impressed. Ska was 'old-man music', and he pulled his face big time, but eventually came round. Silverton quit. The last four months had not impressed him or given him a taste for stardom. To him it was squalor, a lesser standard of living than he wanted, and, like Lynval, playing this type of music was definitely not his bag. Ray King offered him £40 a week to be his drummer, which was £40 a week more than we could. Now what could we do?

There were plenty of drummers around, but no one could play reggae authentically. Even though the new ska rhythm had a straight 4/4 beat, it still had to swing like reggae. Jerry attempted the drums himself at one point, but it was obvious that he was better suited as the band's keyboard player (which is a polite way of saying he was a crap drummer!). Jerry and I ventured down to London to check out a drummer he had heard of called Seb Shelton. He was playing at the Nashville rooms in Fulham with a rising London band called The Young Bucks. We offered him Silverton's job. He turned us down.* Enter Brad.

John Edward Bradbury was a Coventry kid. He had known Jerry for years and, like Jerry and I, had done the art school bit – studying at Hull (alongside Stiff Records oddity Wreckless Eric, apparently) and then qualifying as an art teacher in Birmingham. He obviously didn't go big on art teaching as his current job was sneering at people from behind the counter at Virgin Records. Brad was a 'black music' buff: Northern Soul, Tamla, Parliament/ Funkadelic, all that funky stuff, and reggae. He could play drums good too. His current gig was in a band with Neol Davies called Transposed Men. He and Neol had recorded a reggae instrumental with Brad's brother-in-law on trombone at Roger Lomas's home studio. I remember Neol and Brad bringing an acetate of it to one of our Mr George's shows, and they stood there at the back of the club watching people dance to it and grinning to one another. 'Kingston Affair' I believe it was called. It changed its name later when it became the B-side of our first single.

Jerry voiced his doubts to me as to whether Brad was the right man for the job. Lynval, however, thought differently, and we needed a drummer quick, so he was in. It became apparent early on that we had made the right choice. Brad had the reggae groove down. With the exception of Jim Brown from UB40, I don't know of any other white drummer who could get that authentic feel. He didn't just play reggae, he could change tempo seamlessly from a

* Seb Shelton went on to play with Secret Affair and later Dexy's Midnight Runners – 'The Celtic Soul Brothers' / 'Come On Eileen' line-up.

'one-drop' reggae beat to a 'four-on-the-floor' rock section, as can be heard on 'It's Up to You', which started out as a jam and ended up one of my favourite first-album tunes. Rehearsals began with a new enthusiasm as we learnt old ska numbers like 'Monkey Man' and 'You're Wondering Now' and adapted our old material with our new ska feel. The decrepit old function room out the back of the Binley Oak at the corner of Paynes Lane and Britannia Street was our HQ, and it was here, wearing scarves and fingerless gloves in the see-your-breath freezing November of 1978, that the sound of The Specials began to take shape. We would rehearse during daytime opening hours and be visited by Guinness-soaked Irishmen, who looked on, bemused but never dismissive. Perhaps they caught a similarity between the rebel songs on the pub juke box and the new rebel music made by the chop of Lynval's guitar and the high crack of Brad's snare. It would be nice to think so.

Our attempts at courting major record companies had not been at all successful, but a lot of groups were forming their own labels and distributing them via rapidly expanding independent record distributors like Pinnacle or Rough Trade. We thought we'd be better off doing our own record on our own label. One problem: no money. One of Coventry's late-night drinking emporiums was called the Domino. A two-storey building, it was part of Coventry's hideous lower precinct. The 'ground floor' (the whole thing was a second/third-floor premises, but I'm only confusing you) was a café for shoppers by day. The upstairs was open as a club at night — it had a tiny dance floor, orange and chrome interior and stayed open till 2 a.m. It was right next to Mr George's, home to our Monday-night residency and was a popular destination for those who considered closing time to have come too early. I even did a gig there once. It was there that Jerry, Rod and Lynval made the acquaintance of James O'Boyle. He lived on Westminster Road, round the corner from where I used to live on Regent Street – bed-sit land. With as broad an Irish accent as you can get, he was a little guy with a Pancho Villa spaghetti-western-type moustache. He worked with a 'minder', a black guy called Fraser, who even Neville mentioned in revered tones. Jimbo (for that was what he liked to be called) was a ... businessman, and, for a percentage, was prepared to loan us the monies to record and print up 1,500 copies of what was to be a single.

Horizon Studios was on the top floor of a converted three-storey warehouse, up near Coventry Railway Station. The top floor had been bought by Coventry landlord, property developer, car dealer and, more recently, Tenerife resident Barry Thomas. He had planned to use the top floor as the studios for Coventry's independent radio station, but Mercia Sound (cringe!) got the franchise instead, so the place was kitted out as a professional recording studio. Once again, it was three flights of stairs, with the organ, and a real tight turn up into the studio part. The décor had been done by an ex-Lanchester student, Keith 'Preston' Robinson, from ... Preston. A skinny, spotty kid with a warm disposition. He had, by then, a penchant for amphetamines. Rumour has it, he'd work for three days straight on the paintings in the studio, disappear for a few days, then come back again. These were large canvases, some of which he had done at college – whimsy science fiction type of stuff and the reception area was painted like a jungle – real good. The rest of the studio remained unpainted – Keith died of a drug-related heart attack before he could complete it. It was comforting, yet spooky, to see his work. We were to spend quite a bit of time at Horizon during the next couple of years. The studio changed hands a few times, but the paintings always remained. They knocked the whole building down some time in the early nineties to make way for the 'Central Six' retail park.

So there we were, January 1979, set up in Studio One, to record three tunes. We did versions of 'Nite Klub', 'Too Much Too Young' and this new tune that Jerry had just written – 'Gangsters'. The versions of 'Nite Klub' and 'Too Much Too Young' never quite cut it, but 'Gangsters' went down on the second take and sounded brilliant from the word go.

Our previous studio experiences made us a bit more knowledgeable about what we could, or couldn't, do. The drum kit, guitars and organ were screened off, but the bass wasn't. I used all my stage stuff (two 1×15-inch speakers) plus an extra cabinet that I'd borrowed as well, so there was this big 'wall of bass', and it got everywhere on the other instruments' tracks and gave it its sound. Terry did a 'bored' vocal and an 'angry' vocal, and they were mixed together and sounded incredible.

'Gangsters' had so much bass on it that it had to be recut as the bass blew the needle out of the record's grooves. (I am not making this up!) To compensate for the low end, Jerry overdubbed a treble-heavy piano on. The finished thing sounded amazing. Tinny, yet heavy; bored, yet angry. Perfect. We had used the riff from Prince Buster's 'Al Capone' in the tune, and, as we didn't know what to do regarding the publishing, we left the credits blank. The song was Jerry's rant about the music (and legal) business in general, and snippets from the band's history. I always found it strange that the phrase Future will' sounded like 'Fewtrell', the Birmingham nightclub owners, but perhaps that was the result of a vivid imagination!

As I said, the other tunes from the session didn't cut it, so there was the problem about what to put on the other side. A lot of reggae singles had 'versions' on the B-side, generally by different artists. Brad had an instrumental tune that he'd done with Neol Davies; it was perfect, we all dug the tune. Jerry asked Neol to put a ska rhythm guitar on it (which he dutifully did) and handed The Selecter a career.

We were now definitely cooking with gas, and the next three or four months were, in my opinion, the most creative of the band's career. We were now injecting ska rhythms into our old repertoire and drawing on the old reggae styles for new inspiration. I had taken delivery of a new hand-made bass cabinet, a single 18-inch speaker in a reflex bin. It was brilliant. Deep. Heavy. It changed the whole sound of the band. Brad and I were gelling into a formid-able rhythm section, and my confidence as a bass player was growing daily. Neville was now an on-stage member of the band, which gave a whole new dimension to our stage presence. Neville was the wild man, moving everywhere, while Terry was the perfect foil – menacing, coy and incisive all at the same time.

There was a 'mod' revival doing the rounds – The Jam had by now released their second album, and new mod bands, like Secret Affair, The Chords and The Merton Parkas, were starting to make waves in the clubs and the press, if not in the charts. This was it, this was the handle we could use. Second-hand tonic suits, readily available in any self-respecting second-hand clothing store, Ben Sherman shirts, loafer shoes or Doc Martens. Brad professed to being an old soul-boy anyway and was able to pontificate on the width of braces and which buttons to do up on your jacket, and Lyn and Jerry became sartorial referees for the uncool, which was just me, really. Lynval was all in favour of suiting up, but not keen on buying second-hand clothes. The cry of 'Me nah wear dead man clothes!' accompanied by loud kissing of teeth followed, but he soon got with the programme. He may have even bought his suits new – he definitely looked the nattiest. Roddy wasn't that keen either. He always saw himself as a James Dean with a low-slung Les Paul guitar. A kind of 'Rebel Without a Clue'. He came around, though, and got himself a leather pork pie hat. Gosford Street, which was full of second-hand clothes stores in those days, was only just around the corner from the Binley Oak.

Our 'look' was now defined, and our record (our 'sound') was happening too. We'd finally got a cut we were happy with, that *didn't* jump out of the grooves. We had a moody, very spacey dub-style B-side. What we didn't have was a record label to release it on. It became apparent that the label had to complement the band's music, its image, and it *had* to be cool. After rehearsals, Jerry and I would sit around and come up with ideas, names, sketches: Satik and Underworld were two that I remember, but 2-Tone was the name that stood out. I got the '2' with the 'Tone' bit underneath together, but it was Jerry who used the idea of black and white check (an old mod op-art motif – one of the simplest decorative patterns in the world), and the 2-Tone man. This was a caricature of Peter Tosh taken from an early photo of The Wailers. It was a brilliant image. Simple, which said everything about us in a three-inch circle of paper. Those four years at art college were not wasted! The 2-Tone man was, somewhere along the line, given the name Walt Jabsco. This was the name on the back of a bowling shirt that Jerry had picked up somewhere. It was a joke. Grown-up journalists would actually ask us, 'What's the bloke on the record called?' A silly question. 'Walt Jabsco.' A silly name, a silly answer.

We played our first gig with Brad as our drummer and with tonic suits as our stage gear at Birmingham University (Edgbaston). A strange hall, like a medieval building – complete with rafters. It had a stage that sloped down towards the front and gave me a feeling of vertigo. The Au Pairs supported, and there weren't many people there, but we played, sounded and now looked like we meant it.

A Coventry art college lecturer and buddy of Jerry's, one Alan Harrison, said he knew The Damned's manager, Rick Rogers. Jerry went to see him and managed to get him to come up to see us at a gig at Warwick University. It was an old stomping ground for us, and that particular night, Coventry's punk contingent turned out in force, and it was a terrific gig. Rick thought we were tremendous, got very drunk and stayed at my flat afterwards. He would soon have several more allies to assist in the propping up of bars over the next few years.

He had been the Stiff Records press officer when they were making waves as the finger on-the-pulse punk/new wave label – Ian Dury, Elvis Costello and Nick Lowe were all 'Stiff recording artists'. The label had an image about it: they kicked the major labels in the teeth, then laughed at them. Rick was currently boss of his own press/publicity business, called Trigger, which was based above Ted Carroll's 'Rock On' record shop in Camden, north London, just down the road from Rehearsal Rehearsals, the old Clash HQ. The Damned's fortunes were taking a turn for the better since Rick had got them a deal with Chiswick Records and they had put out the *Machine Gun Etiquette* LP, with 'Smash It Up' as the hit single. I have an idea that relations between The Damned and Rick were a little strained by then, but I think that relations between *anybody* and The Damned could be pretty difficult in those days.

It was an intense period, the spring of 1979. Our sense of purpose was almost tangible. You had to be optimistic. It is a prerequisite when starting a group. Sometimes (well, most of the time) optimism and a belief in yourself or your band is the only thing that keeps you going after you've travelled all the way to Worcester to play to six people, and the van's broken down on the way back. Jerry, Lynval, Terry, Rod, Neville, Brad and I had come this far, we'd got this close. It couldn't possibly, possibly, fail. It was all in place.

It's a pretty well-worn cliché to say that a career in a pop group is like a roller-coaster ride. Up until now, we'd taken a reasonably measured ride, from the forming of the band through nearly two years of moving in the right direction – doing The Clash tour, going to Paris and making a record. It lulled me into a false sense of security. We had set the pace we worked at. Nothing could prepare me for the next two years, and, to carry the funfair analogy further, by the end of the ride, I was eager for it to stop, so I could get off. In fact I would have liked it to stop sooner that it did.

Rick Rogers said he would like to manage us, but at this point there'd be no contracts, no percentages. We'd talk business when record companies were interested. When there was some revenue worth having a percentage of.

We now took delivery of our single. In order to make the thing a little more visually attractive, I got a printing company to make two rubber stamps. One said 'The Special AKA: Gangsters'. The other said 'VS The Selecter', Jerry's wording. The idea came from a poster advertising a sound system battle: Jah Shaka VS Alpha Sound, or something. I don't know whether many people got the connection, but I thought it was cool. The next thing was to stamp the covers. Brad had got a load of cardboard sleeves from the Virgin record shop where he still worked, which made the single a bit more durable, and gave us a load of spare paper ones to prepare for our second print run, should it ever happen. Terry, bless him, was the only one in the band who volunteered to help me with the stamping, and we spent a not unpleasant day on our hands and knees round at my Abbey Road flat until we had blisters on our palms. We did 1,500 of them.

Jerry and I then went down to the Rough Trade shop to meet the gaffer (Geoff Travis) to see if he'd take copies of the single. He'd seen us, or heard about us, from The Clash tour, and said he'd take it. It was now officially 'in the shops'. An interesting aside: we had been invited to submit a track for inclusion on a punk double-album that a label called 'The Label' was putting together. Jerry and I dropped by The Label manager's house and he gave us this spiel about how many copies they were pressing and how it was going to be real big. We asked him who else was to be on the album and he gave us a list of all these impossibly named punk bands, like Eater and The Acme Sewage Company. Jerry and I thanked him and said we'd keep in touch. I think the album actually did come out. I'm sure the guys in the Acme Sewage Company had a copy.

The Specials, on the other hand, had got their record distributed by Rough Trade. When it came out and the first 1,500 sold out, Rough Trade took over the pressing. I don't know how many copies they sold, but I've got a silver disc for 'Gangsters' and it says it's for 250,000 copies sold. I'm glad Terry and I didn't have to stamp all those.

We'd all talked about 2-Tone, how we wanted it to be a real label, not a one-off. Most of us were firm fans of the Tamla and Stax record labels, of how these labels had their own sound. You had to just hear the intro drum fill and you knew it was a Tamla-Motown record; you also knew it was going to be good. (It was, as often as not, Benny Benjamin on drums and James Jamerson on bass, a rhythm section 'par excellence'. I'm still to this day left open-mouthed by Mr Jamerson's amazing bass lines.)

The same was true with Stax. Arthur Conley, Wilson Picket, Aretha Franklin, Otis Redding – all backed by Booker T. and the MGs (Booker T. Jones, Donald 'Duck' Dunn, Steve Cropper and Al Jackson. These guys have taught more people to play (me included) than I'm sure they realized at the time).

To make a 'label-sound' like that was our dream – to hear a tune and immediately be able to say, 'That's a 2-Tone record/band,' that would be a terrific thing to do. Punk had an overall image, and although there were attempts at putting package tours together, all the big punk outfits had their own agendas by now, and it was never a 'movement' in a unified sense. So we sat up in Coventry thinking of ourselves as the UK's Tamla-Motown. Thinking about it twenty-eight years later, it was more or less what we did.

The blur, the start of the white-knuckle ride, starts round about now. I'm generally pretty good on dates and places, but the proper chronology of this time is hard to recall. The Rick Rogers press machine started to function. We started working with a booking agency from Birmingham called Oak, run by a gentleman called John Mostyn. He had been the singer in a Birmingham band, Brent Ford and The Nylons, and used to perform with a stocking over his head. Despite all this, his agency got us some good gigs. He later went on to manage The Beat.

We were now getting regular work, 'Gangsters' was in the shops and also on the radio. I had always dug John Peel. I'm not just saying that. Being a pirate radio groupie from the age of twelve, I had listened to Peel on his *Perfumed Garden* show on Radio London, following him to the BBC, where I'd sit huddled up next to an enormous wireless every Sunday afternoon to hear *Sounds of the Seventies*. Every week night, John Peel's *Top Gear* (ten till midnight) played all sorts of weird and wonderful music – even weirder with the advent of punk. Mister Peel carried the swing. He played 'Gangsters' one Wednesday night. He played it again on the Thursday. He played it every night for the next fortnight, as often as not at the beginning of the show. I loved him. He was as responsible as anyone in getting The Specials known outside of Coventry. There are an awful lot of forty-plussers out there who owe John Peel thanks; some of them got their indie-500-pressing-single played once, others now live in mansions in Surrey with Aston Martins in the garage, cellars full of Rémy Martin and goldfish bowls full of cocaine.

I felt like I'd lost a favourite uncle when I heard the news of his death.

Now we'd got regular gigs, we needed a good PA system. Roger Lomas came to our aid. He was playing in a band called The Dodgers, who had a deal with Polydor. We'd had talks with their management company earlier, but decided to pass – they were 'old guard', or even 'boring old farts', and didn't share our vision for the band and its place in the scheme of things, but there again, before the beginning of 1979, not a lot of people did. Anyhow, the Dodgers had a crackingly good Cerwin Vega PA system – small, but very powerful. For a fee, they would transport it to our gigs, set it up and operate it for us. Gordon's van had bitten the dust by now, but we could afford to hire vans from Coventry to take us and our gear to gigs. I did most of the driving. Lyn, Nev and I were the only band members with driving licences, and I think Nev's had loads of disqualifications on it, and Lynval liked to have a drink at gigs. I was happy to take the wheel. The driver's seat was the most comfortable, when you consider that there were seven band members plus two crew (Nev's buddy Trevor Evans and his sidekick, Rex Griffiths) plus all our gear to somehow get inside a Transit van. The skills learnt working for my fathers' furniture-removal firm during college holidays came in handy. With careful packing you could get everything in and, using the speaker cabinets to sit on, make it bearable for those in the back.

Before our Oak agency period, we had got our gigs ourselves as often as not. Consistency of work was something which had eluded us. This started to change. We now started on the UK club circuit, which was booming in those days: Norwich's Boogie House, Lincoln's AJ's, Sheffield's Limit Club, and the people were coming. The 'mod revival' meant that a lot of tonic suits and parkas were in attendance. The 'skinhead' resurgence meant that there were a lot of thin red braces, brightly polished Doc Martens and Crombie coats. There were interested punks and 'studenty types' (a blanket term for 'anyone else who wasn't as yet affiliated to a fashion group' – sorry, but I couldn't think of anything else to call them!). This was good.

Because these were club gigs, the audiences were over eighteen, or supposed to be. This may very well have contributed to the fact that there was very little trouble at these gigs. The only problem gig I remember from those days was at Cheltenham, and that was only because punks from Coventry clashed with skins from Cheltenham – good old Cov punks, eh! The fight happened after we'd played, and Terry stormed on stage, grabbed the mike and shouted, 'Twats! Twats! Don't be so fucking ignorant.' Everyone stopped. I was in awe. Terry had come on as a commanding front man in the year or so he'd been in the band. Later, when we were playing big places like the Hammersmith Palais, the press would say that he looked wooden and droll beside the manic Mr Staples, which was unfair. Terry may very well have been Ernie Wise to Neville's Eric Morecambe, but when it came to saying 'the right thing', he was always there. He learnt on his feet and, as sub-sequent years have proved, learnt well.

I tried Terry's trick at another gig (I can't remember where) when there was a fight. I went up to the mike and shouted, 'Oi, twats!' No one took a blind bit of notice.

We were starting to fill these clubs, and people were buying the record. There were a few dodgy gigs, like two we had in Wales: a working men's club in Martletwy, where we were asked to stop after the third song, paid and told to go away, followed by a 'rock night' at another WMC in Swansea, where we played to a dozen local heavy-metallers.

However, most of our shows were now well attended, and on some of them we 'broke the guarantee', which meant that we got a bonus at the end of the night. (If a club capacity was, say, 500 and the promoter expected 300 to turn up, our fee was based on 300 punters turning up. If more than 300 people turned up we would get an extra percentage on top of our scheduled fee, dependent on how many over 300 there were in the club. Confused? I thought you would be!) We could tell something was happening, not just by the numbers, but by the way the crowds were dressing, dancing themselves delirious and wanting to know where we were playing next. And then actually turning up along with a dozen of their mates.

We also started to make our presence felt in the capital. It was bottom of the bill at the fabled Lyceum Ballroom in The Strand. A big dance hall, with a large overhanging balcony with individual 'boxes', chintzy maroon curtains and light fittings. The whole place looked like it had seen better days. It had. It was where the live Bob Marley album was recorded; an album that amazed me with its power, passion and atmosphere. A far cry from The Damned and the UK Subs, with whom we shared the stage this particular Sunday in April 1979. It was an important gig for Rick Rogers. He was putting The Damned on as headliners, and us as his new protégés. The UK Subs were, as always, punk cannon fodder, always able to pull in a reasonable number of Neanderthal followers from exotic places like the Isle of Sheppey or Orpington. Their singer, one Charlie Harper, is something of a punk icon. Even now – twenty-eight years later – he's playing all over the world. So, for that matter, are The Damned. I think the gig was sold out, but I'm not sure. It seemed pretty well attended, from where I was standing.

I can't remember much about our performance. We got a monitor check, of sorts, and we played. Nobody threw anything, and I think a lot of the punk-hungry punters in the front row couldn't figure us out. The UK Subs went down great. They reminded me of Steppenwolf. The Damned tried too hard. Someone disconnected the PA during the show, and the band never noticed, they were playing so loud. It got reconnected, but it wasn't a good gig. I remember it ending in silence, the band storming off stage and up to their dressing room followed by a meek Rick Rogers. We left. Looking back, it was 'out with the old' (The Damned) and 'in with the new' (us lot).

The first bit of press that I've got is a review of 'Gangsters' on 24 March 1979 in *Melody Maker*, and a review of a gig at West Hampstead's Moonlight Club in the same week's edition of *Sounds*, where I was described as a 'skinny, cropped barnet, plucking away at a concrete bass'. I have an idea it was a compliment. The review, wordy though it was, was very enthusiastic. Hell, it was a review, the first review of one of our own shows. Hold tight. I remember the gig as being not very well attended, but attended by the right people, apparently. An American woman in a three-quarter-length red velvet jacket came up to us after the show and out of the blue gave Terry a kiss.

It was Chrissie Hynde. She and her guitar player James Honeyman-Scott had come to check us out. Also, I suppose, the reviewer from *Sounds*. Rick Rogers seemed to be doing his job.

The road work continued. Roger Lomas and his PA bowed out – I think they had their own tour to do, and a soft-spoken Irishman, Del Fitzpatrick, took over. He had a whacking great big PA rig, which he carried in a 7½-ton lorry and heaved in himself. He also took our equipment, or 'back line' as we now called it, so we could all travel more comfortably in a minibus. I still did the driving.

We continued playing anywhere and everywhere, and we actually started to earn a bit of money. I'd never considered money, really. I'd always had some, but I'd lived frugally (students tended to) and didn't have a car to run or a mortgage to pay. I saved money when I was working – it helped pay for the hiring of vans and the buying and maintenance of gear. Having lots of it was something that I wasn't used to, but wasn't something that I dreamt about or lusted after. I smoked cigarettes, and liked a pint of Guinness every now and then, but that was it really. I suppose I ate, too, but from looking at photographs of myself back then, I can't have eaten very much. I remember leaving from our first gig at the Nashville Rooms in London with £80 in my pocket and thinking this was definitely the big time! There was an excitement around the band. We were being tipped as 'the next big thing' and we certainly weren't going to disagree with them. Everyone was happy to muck in and make it work. We were all pulling in the same direction. We were all

◖ N.U.S. mug shot, 1973.
Would you buy a multi-cultural
ska/punk hybrid from this man?

◖ College band style.
Lanchester Polytechnic Students
Union bar, autumn 1974.

◖ Breaker: not one of
our better photos. From left:
Geoff Conway, me,
Gordon Reaney and
(seated) Margo Buchanan.

M.G.

Eric's Dates

Members Notice
051-236 8301
9, Mathew Street,
Liverpool 2.

8½. phased

			Members	Guests
Fri 29 June	JOE JACKSON + Comsat Angels		£1·35	£1·85
Sat 30 June	THE CRAMPS + Pink Military Stand Alone -	Mat 5pm	£1·10	£1·35
		Evg 8.30	£1·10	£1·60
Mon 2 July	Rhesus Records presents THE TUNES, The DONKEYS, C. P. Lee & Gordon the Moron		75p	75p
Thur 5 July	An early sixties Tamla/Soul special with Dexy's Midnight Runners + The Upsets		60p	85p
Fri 6 July	The B52's + Fashion		£1·35	£1 85
Sat 7 July	WIRE + Manicured Noise	Mat 5pm	£1·10	£1·35
		Evg 8.30	£1·10	£1·60
Thur 12 July	Special CoRRA gig featuring Activity Minimal, Modern Eon, Chink and the Drills		60p	85p
Fri 13 July	CHELSEA + Vermillion		£1·10	£1·60
Sat 14 July	THE SPECIALS + Madness	Mat 5pm	£1·10	£1·35
		Evg 8.30	£1·25	£1·75
Thur 19 July	The return of ... ALBERTO Y LOS TRIOS PARANOIAS + John Dowie		£1·10	£1·60
Fri 20 July	THE PRETENDERS + Interview		£1·10	£1·60
Sat 21 July	THE ADVERTS + guests	Mat 5pm	£1·10	£1·35
	B·52's	Evg 8.30	£1·10	£1·60
Thur 26 July	Madcap Promotions present ADAM & THE ANTS + guests		£1·10	£1·60
Fri 27 July	SIMPLE MINDS + guests		£1·10	£1·60
Sat 28 July	STIFF LITTLE FINGERS Merton Parka's			
Mon 30 July	From New Orleans ROCKING DOPSIE & THE TWISTERS + The Opposition		£1·10	£1·60

Hours of Opening: 8.30 - 2 am (Matinee Saturdays 5 pm - 7.30 pm) We are open between mid-day and 2 pm daily except Sunday for badges, posters and membership enquiries.
SHOW TIMES: On Fridays and Saturdays the main group will be on stage at 10pm followed by the support at approx 11.30 pm when door admission prices will be reduced.
Call us on our 24 hour answering service 051-236 8301 for further information.
MEMBERSHIP OF ERIC'S is £1·10 yearly. A member is entitled to sign in two guests, and to benefit from reduced admission prices. Membership application forms are available from the Club.

○ The Coventry Snowball Massacre, 23 January 1979.

○ The Specials at Warwick University, 19 February 1979.
This was the gig where Rick Rogers first saw us and decided to become
our manager. There is something going on stage left.

○ Somewhat breathtaking: Eric's flyer from 1979.

Jerry and Nev shop for clothes in Leicester, spring 1979.
The guy in the hat was called Oscar.

4 July 1979. A motorway services station on the way back from Scotland. From left:
Me, Rex Griffiths, Nev, Trevor (E.T.) Evans, Lynval, Terry, Jerry, Rod, Brad.

The 'Lark in the Park' – an open-air show in Birmingham, 25 August 1979.

Later that same evening . . .

THE 2-TONE TOUR. ⬥ Bedders and Commie (Mark Bedford from Madness and Compton Amanour from the Selecter) and Chrissy Boy and Woody (Chris Foreman and Daniel Woodgate from Madness), Bournemouth, 21 September 1979.
⬥ Asleep on the bus. Rico and Dick Cuthell are at the front.

○ Judging by the pained expression, I'd say it was 'Little Bitch' time with its wrist-destroying octave runs. Brighton Top Rank, 19 October 1979.

◑ The 2-Tone tour. Dave Jordan (aka DJ, aka the Red Dread), Forth Road Bridge Services, 14 November 1979.

◑ And on to Ireland. Jerry asleep, with Roddy in the background, 15 November 1979.

○ Full-tilt
rock-'n'-roll posing
in South London.
Lewisham,
1 December 1979.

○ Roddy Radiation,
the King of Rock,
Lewisham.

working together. It was the happiest time of the band's life.

One of the good things about The Specials was that there were so many people in it. If someone got on your nerves, you could just spend time with someone else. Three- or four-piece bands don't have this luxury; we had safety in numbers. It also meant there were a lot of people to get to know. I suppose Jerry was the person I knew best, as I knew him from college days. I was starting to get to know Lynval better too. Terry was pretty aloof but, because there were a lot of us, he could afford to be. Or maybe it was just me. No. Paranoia set in later.

At the moment I was enjoying the ride, despite the fact that I'd get real nervous before show time. I'd huddle up in a corner and shiver. I couldn't talk to anyone, and people got the message. The moment I hit the stage I was fine. I was more than fine, in fact. It's only in recent years that I've stopped being such a bag of nerves before a gig. After gigs, that was another matter. I was in heaven. I have often thought that if I could somehow bottle the feeling I had when I came off stage after a gig and sell it to people, I could be rich, rich, RICH. People would pay thousands of pounds to feel like I felt, even on The Clash tour and especially now, late spring 1979.

Dave McCullough from *Sounds* was the journalist who reviewed our Moonlight Club gig. Rick brought him up to Coventry for our first national music press interview. It took place in a flat in Spon End. I think it was Neville's flat. We did photographs near the flat, in the precinct, and at Coventry station as the journalist and the manager (and the photographer) headed back to London. The

article appeared on 7 April, page 16. To say Mr Mc-
Cullough liked the band would be an understatement.
Using the Coventry concrete jungle approach, we came
over as the new urban revolutionaries – free your ass,
and your mind will follow. Yee ha! This was good. This
was very good.

Another trek to play at the London music business
watering holes was planned. The Hope and Anchor (where
we saw some graffiti on the toilet door: 'Madness, Bluebeat
and Ska'). The Nashville, where months earlier Jerry and I
had unsuccessfully attempted to poach Seb Shelton away
from The Young Bucks. Dingwalls, where it was ten quid
to get in and some young skinhead charged backstage
with his mates after we'd finished and declared, 'We're
The Specials' Army!' My heart sank. Wrong. Wrong.
Wrong. We'd started to put in 'Nobody is special, everyone
is special' at the end of 'Liquidator', and the last thing we
wanted was Sham 69's goon squad, but we were playing
skinhead reggae and we'd have to cope with it sooner or
later. Reversing the van out of Dingwalls, later that night,
I almost ran over some long-haired guy who was urinating
against the club wall. I'm glad I didn't. It was Lemmy from
Motörhead!

We returned to The Moonlight Club, who were doing a
week-long run of shows that were being recorded. Decca
Studios were just next door, and they ran cables from the
club. The plan was to release a live Moonlight Club
compilation album. We wanted to do the gig, but were not
too sure about the album. We had no publishing contract
on our songs and needed all our material for our own LP,
which we were sure we were going to make. The gig was
fantastic. Packed. We played great, too, and there was a

brilliant bit of impromptu banter between Lyn and Nev before 'Too Hot':

> *Lynval* – The Rude Boys get hot now!
> *Neville* – Rude Boy hot *all the time*!

Jerry had mentioned the 'Rude Boy' tag in the *Sounds* article. It was a great idea – we weren't affiliated to the 'mod revival' and we weren't a 'skinhead band'; we had our own identity and (naively) hoped that our fans would. A 'rude boy' was a Jamaican expression for a street hooligan, a young, cocksure youth with more attitude than he knew what to do with – a sort of Caribbean mod, but without the disposable income. Rude Boys caught on. Rude Girls, too.

As far as the Moonlight Club compilation album went, we thought that our version of 'Long Shot Kick de Bucket', a Pioneers tune that we'd recently put in the set, was the tune we'd like to use. It was representative of the band's style, a snappy little crowd-pleaser, in fact, but it meant we still had all our original songs for our own album. The Moonlight Club album never happened, but the tapes of our performance were duly mixed and released as a bootleg later in the year. Apparently it was selling on a par with our first album in Europe during the early months of 1980, so someone must have made a heap of cash on it. This information was not divulged on the sleeve notes that appeared when *Live at the Moonlight Club* was 'officially' released by Chrysalis in 1992. I've often wondered how they came to get hold of the tapes, and whether anybody was prosecuted for releasing an illegal bootleg. Probably just regular music business business.

We also played the Fulham Greyhound, where Mick Jagger (plus bodyguard) was in attendance. We played the intro to 'Little Bitch', and apparently he muttered something about us nicking it from The Stones and left. A couple of friends of mine who'd been at the show came up to me afterwards and said, 'There was this guy standing near us – looked just like Mick Jagger.'

We were back at the Lyceum on Sunday 27 May to play a show with Delta Five and The Mekons, headlined by The Gang of Four. This was the end of a tour they'd been doing, and we were brought in to swell the numbers, I suppose. When we arrived, the stage manager wanted us to use the Gang of Four's equipment, but we declined. Reggae drums don't sound like Go4 drums; reggae bass don't sound like Go4 bass. The stage manager was pissed off. It meant the back line had to be remiked. Tough, mate. Consequently we never got a sound check, but played for two or three minutes anyway until someone told us to stop because the doors were opening. This bit of needle put us in the right frame of mind. We went on second and played a stormer. According to the press, we stole the show, despite *Sounds* correspondent Garry Bushell mistaking Lynval for Neville. The gig was great, we knew we'd trashed the rest of the bill, and as much as I hate all that competitive stuff . . .

To make a good day perfect, the two punky girls from The Clash tour were there, looking as gorgeous as ever, and, as we were loading our gear away at the end, a Mr Costello came up to us and said he'd really liked our single. Very cool. I have a picture-sleeve copy of 'Alison' on Stiff, and a copy of his album *My Aim is True*; to get a wink from someone like that was praise indeed. In fact, it was just the beginning. *Round Table*, a Radio 1 show where pop stars and DJs (that's radio presenters, not dance music specialists!) pontificated on that week's new releases, played 'Gangsters', and Elvis Costello was on the panel. He said it was 'one of the best records he'd heard in the last ten years'. We would see more of Mr Costello.

We were busy doing our thing, Rick was busy doing his. I remember him coming up to us at the end of our gig at the Greyhound in Fulham, with wide-eyed amazement, reeling off the names of at least half a dozen record company executives who were at that moment propping up the bar. Warner Brothers, CBS, Island, Chrysalis, Polydor, A&M, Arista, Virgin, all, apparently, with tongues hanging out and chequebooks at the ready. Furtively looking over his shoulder, he beamed at us and rubbed his hands with glee. It was his moment as much as ours.

Wednesday afternoon at Rick's office: I could tell something was up, but I didn't know what it was. 'Horace, could you nip over the road and get me a copy of *Melody Maker*?' The *Melody Maker* cost 18p on 19 May 1979, but the photo on the front cover was of me, Rod and Nev on stage at The Gang of Four show, and the beam on my face was worth millions. The front cover of *Melody Maker*. I think I'd like my BMW in white, if you please!

A week later, we had our *New Musical Express* interview published. Adrian Thrills is one of the nicer journalists I've met − unassuming, polite and very easy to get along with. He seemed to have been waiting most of his life for a band like The Specials. He was a soul-boy who'd got excited by punk − like us really.

The Specials signed with Chrysalis Records on 8 June 1979. Roy Eldridge, their head of A&R, said, 'The

Specials are the most exciting band I've ever seen.'
Our records would still be released on 2-Tone, albeit
marketed by Chrysalis. We had a clause in the contract
which said we could release up to ten other singles by
other bands on 2-Tone, and we had a budget of £1,000 per
project. Back then, Chrysalis was still an independent
record label. They'd previously signed Generation X and
the rather splendid Leyton Buzzards, but it was heavy-
weights like Jethro Tull that made them their money. They
were the only company to agree to all our requests regarding the 2-Tone label, and Rick considered them the best
of the bunch.

That evening we returned to the Nashville. Madness,
who were now not just a name on a pub bog door, nervously opened the show. The place was packed to the
rafters; there was a queue right round the block. Some
of the Chrysalis bigwigs came over to see us, but stayed
within the safe confines of the dressing room. Johnny
Rotten came along, took a look at the queue and went
home. There was such a crush at the door that one of the
curved glass windows broke. I have little recollection of
the actual performance, but by now, the adrenaline rush
was commonplace. I have a picture in my mind of us in
our rented van driving away from the gig back to Coventry. I would be very surprised if I had any sleep that
night.

We had done it. We were now professional musicians.
We could sign off the dole. We could write 'musician' on
our passport application forms.

Two years of transit vans, gear up two flights of stairs,
petrol receipts, signing on, sharing £250 between nine
of us (after we'd paid for the van and the petrol and the

agent). Two years of begging, hustling, borrowing and sheer bloody-minded determination had paid off. It was not just the end of one chapter, but the beginning of another. We hadn't finished. We'd just started.

5

The Dawning of a New Era

There was little time to take a breath. The iron was hot, and so were we. A two-month club tour was set up: June, through July, to finish early August, when we'd record an album, to be released in the autumn. If I thought the past six months had been hectic, I hadn't seen nothin' yet!

Rough Trade and Chrysalis had come to some agreement over 'Gangsters'. Chrysalis would take it over once Rough Trade had sold out, but in the meantime, Chrysalis would promote it in the UK and start marketing it in Europe. Having a record company like Chrysalis behind us meant that the publicity and promotion now went big time. Photo sessions and interviews quickly became commonplace and were both deemed necessary to get exposure. The 'music mags' were infinitely preferable to the 'dailies', who generally treated us like dullards. Our photo appeared in the *Sun* newspaper on Friday 23 June along with the following comments:

If it's rude, it must be Special
The Specials are a new group being widely tipped for the top. They have been adopted as the musical representatives of the Rude Boys,

that special brand of aggressive youngsters, who
are a cross between Mods and Skinheads.

Once it's in the press, that's it. You can't recall eight
million copies of the *Sun* and rewrite the pop page. We
were now aggressive youngsters, then.

We got the cover of *Smash Hits*, the 'teeny' magazine,
where they put our photo in the wrong way round (I
became Lynval Golding), reproduced the lyrics to 'Gangsters', commented on our footwear and sunglasses and
lumped us in with the mod revival.

In between belting up and down motorways, losing
sleep and a good pint of sweat every night, we did a John
Peel session, Jerry keeping the engineers there till way
past bedtime to get the mix right. We also signed a
publishing deal. Rick's Stiff Records days meant he was
reasonably close with Jake Riviera, Stiff supremo Dave
Robinson's business partner and Elvis Costello's manager.
We elected to go with Jake's publishing company, Plangent
Visions, which was managed by a gentleman called Peter
Barnes. We all trooped round to Jake's house to talk about
it. The whole deal looked really good, apparently. To be
honest, I was more impressed by the fact that Jake's house
used to belong to top record producer Tony Visconti and
had a basement studio where David Bowie's *Diamond
Dogs* album was recorded. That and the fact that Nick
Lowe walked in during our meeting. His band, Rockpile,
had played a Cambridge University college ball the night
before, and he looked the worse for wear because of it.
Nice bloke.

I don't recall us getting an advance from Plangent
Visions, but our thing was 'low advance – high royalty'.

We got £10,000 from Chrysalis when we signed, which was half the advance, the rest being paid when we delivered the album. Consequently, we recouped (paid back the money that was advanced to us) in a couple of months.

We regarded Rick as 'an equal partner' in the band. To give him a managerial percentage of 20 per cent, which was the normal rate, would mean he would be making a lot more than we did. Everything was split eight ways – seven of us and Rick. That way, no one could get shirty about one person getting more than anyone else. Well, at least until the publishing royalties came along.

Our club tour continued. Del with his truck and us with our minibus: Lincoln – AJ's; Dudley – JB's; Bournemouth – Capone's; Aberdeen – Russell's; The Porterhouse at Retford (or was that The Retford at Porterhouse?). Anyway, you name it, I reckon I've played there. The thing started to go so fast, I have only vague snapshot-like memories of events during that time: getting thrown out of a boarding house in Bournemouth in the early hours because Neville brought a (rather noisy) girl back; buying a cassette/radio in Leeds so we could listen to ourselves on the radio (Kid Jensen playing our session); Jerry hurling said radio on the ground in a fit of rage when we wouldn't accompany him to a rather dodgy-looking party after the gig; a Coventry roots reggae band called Hard Top 22, who used to play with us at Mr George's, now fronted by Neol Davies and Pauline Black and calling themselves The Selecter; Neville climbing into the van as we left for another gig saying, 'Me nah sleep yet, y'know'; removing chairs from a club in Chesterfield to sit on in the van (Trevor and Rex had them in their flats years later!); the latest addition to my stereo, a rather old, but very nice, record deck that once belonged in Barnsley Town Hall; the 2-Tone night with Madness and The Selecter – both of whom were going to release their first single on our label – at the Electric Ballroom in Camden (the show was a dress rehearsal for the 2-Tone tour later in the year); 2-Tone now becoming a movement, not just the Specials and their record label; doing a video for 'Gangsters', and finding that Hugh Symonds, who I'd been at college with, was the director; Roddy insisting on smashing some light fittings in the video studio dressing room – some sort of statement I suppose; standing in Virgin Records in Coventry, pretending to browse the racks but really watching people queue up to buy 'Gangsters' . . . pause for breath . . . Jerry spraying 'SPECIAL AKA' in blue across the bridge windows of the M5 services south of Birmingham (it was there for months); Terry rushing on stage to start 'Do the Dog' in Chester, slipping over spilt beer and landing on his arse; getting to Shrewsbury to find that Del's truck had lost its driveshaft outside Luton on the M1 and having to cancel the gig; Lynval missing the M6 turn-off on the way back and driving half-way to Gloucester before someone asked him if he was on the right motorway (we got back just after the pubs shut, much to some people's annoyance); seeing Roland Gift with his own ska band, The Akrylyx (acrylics – an art school band if ever there was one!); going back to some bloke's mansion for a party after playing in Ross-on-Wye; the party turning out to be pretty lame and having to drive the van all the way back to Coventry afterwards (Me nah sleep yet, y'know); playing the Hammersmith Palais with Rockpile and R&B harmonica wiz Lew Lewis; an ill-advised coupling; we played crap (it was not our crowd – a Rick Roger's favour gone wrong – but it prepared us for playing the Palais at least); Sketchley's 'Quick Dry-Clean' service in The Bull Yard, Coventry: get your sweat-drenched suit there for 10 a.m. and it's clean for midday, albeit smelling of something resembling formaldehyde; learning an old Dandy Livingstone tune called 'A Message to You, Rudy'; Elvis Costello turning up at our gigs – generally down the front – at Leeds's F Club and Bourne-mouth's Capone's; being flown to Amsterdam and staying at the enormo-posh Sonesta Hotel to do a TV mime appearance and a whole heap of interviews and then discovering hotel mini-bars (the refrigerator in your room that was stocked with those little bottles of everything alcoholic) – and then having to pay for them.

We returned to Eric's in Liverpool in July, this time with Madness as our support band. We did two shows, an early-evening matinee and the usual night-time show. We met the Mad lads at the Hope and Anchor in Islington (where else!) to confirm the plan. They seemed worried. Lee Thomson sidled up to me and asked if I could give him any advice on a publishing deal he'd been offered. I said I knew of a music-biz lawyer, but apart from that I was no help at all. Our conversation changed tack, and I mentioned our planned trek to Liverpool. 'Yes,' said Lee, kind of nervously, 'I knew a couple of blokes who went there once; they said it was all right.' As if trying to reassure himself, I suppose. Watch out, Lee, north of Watford they eat their young, you know.

Madness hadn't quite got their 'Nutty Boy' thing together then. Chas Smash had only just become a member of the band. The first time I saw them at the Hope and Anchor, he was a larger-than-life member of the audience. Musically, the whole thing was held together by Mike

Barson, who had spent time at music college (a fact that was gently air-brushed out of their early history). Chrissy-boy and Lee had the Ian Dury 'Cockney Cheeky Chappie' thing going, and Suggs was an ex-Sham skinhead, but with suss. Mark Bedford and Woody both looked about fourteen and probably were. Mark very kindly put me up at his mum's flat one night after I had missed the last tube back to Wandsworth. (Thanks, Mark.)

The Liverpool gigs went down well. During the sound check, Terry started complaining about the state of the microphone he was using. The guy who was doing the house PA concurred. 'Yes, mate, halitosis. Johnny Thunders was here the other week.' We agreed with Terry that it would be a good idea if he were to buy his own microphone. The matinee show was not that well attended, but the evening show was a stormer. Somebody 'got one on him' afterwards and hurled a beer bottle through the back window of the van for some reason, thus ensuring a cold, carbon-monoxide-enhanced journey back to Coventry.

I do not remember how much we paid ourselves. I suppose we had money, but I only had the one guitar and the same trusty home-made bass bin and my H/H ampli-fier. I had picked up another cab, which I put on the other side of the drum kit, facing Brad. It was one way of getting Brad to hear what I was playing; if I got any louder, Rod and Lynval, being the noise merchants they were, would just turn up, and the sound would be even more unman-ageable. Thing was, I was always being asked to turn up, by Nev especially: 'Horace, man, the bass *have* to be loud!' Some nights, on a big stage, it worked, but in the little clubs, and we were playing a lot of those, the vocal monitors would be pitifully inadequate compared to the racket coming out of the back line.

I remember Terry saying that, if we had the right clothes, but a shitty PA, he'd still do the gig, but if the reverse was true (shitty clothes and a good PA), he wouldn't play. From a musician's point of view I thought he was barking mad, but we weren't just musicians any more. We were starting to mean more than just paradiddles, octaves and major sevenths; we stood for something that was more than just pop music. It was getting a little scary.

By the beginning of August we'd completed our club dates. It was the end of our Transit van days. A big package tour was being planned for the autumn. The Specials, Madness and The Selecter: forty dates, October to December. Big gigs: town halls, Top Ranks, the same shows we'd done with The Clash, but now we'd be headlining.

'Gangsters' was now in the charts. According to the *Sounds* alternative chart, it was number four on 4 August, and number one a week later. *NME*, who published the MMRB Charts (the *real* charts) put us at number fifteen on 18 August, and number eight the next week.

On 17 August we flew out to Brussels to do the Bilzen festival. It was one of the first 'Chrysalis' gigs we'd done. The European market, as it was called. Well, Belgium, actually. We were way down a bill that included The Pretenders and The Police. Australian heavy-metallers AC/DC were headlining. Adrian Thrills from the *NME* and photographer Pennie Smith came, too. Jerry looked kind of pensive as we boarded the plane at Birmingham airport – he didn't like flying. We got to the festival, and The Cure

were playing – they were the first on. We had to suffer
Bram Tchaikovsky (who?), and then it was us. There was
the stage, then twenty feet of grass and a ten-foot-high wire
fence, then the audience. Steve Dirkin and his buddy Big
Frank came all the way from Coventry to see us, bless 'em.
We went on and killed the place. We rocked. We were
fantastic. About half-way through the set, the wire fence
was pushed over, and the dancing crowd surged forward
to the lip of the stage – we were that good. Trevor had a
photo that someone had taken: we were all (except Brad)
airborne. Well, we would be, we could even defy gravity!
With our tumbled-down equipment, our scrimped-and-
saved-for guitars, our second-hand Gosford Street suits, we
took the whole place by the scruff of its collective neck
and made it dance. The photographs don't do it justice –
how could they! We were the greatest band in the world.
The Pretenders (who followed us) didn't go on for ages.
They finally did and it began to rain – ha! The Police were
tawdry, and even AC/DC, who headlined the show, were a
pale imitation. Everyone knew that The Specials had stolen
the show, had taken on the whole world and showed it who
ruled! I think I did some press stuff; I think I had a crappy
festival-type barbecue meal; I think I got on a coach where
Bon Scott (AC/DC's singer) pissed on the floor of the bus,
and his urine trickled slowly towards the front when we
went down a hill; I think we got to a hotel where Rick
Rogers crawled on all fours through the reception area, he
was so drunk; I think I and the guys from The Cure
stomped on all those stupid pats of butter that were left
out for peoples' breakfasts and that splatted out everywhere
when you stomped on them; I think we charged into a
room belonging to someone from The Cure's management

and disturbed him as he was trying to shag some stupid woman, or some woman stupid – it didn't matter.

Stuff marijuana, fuck cocaine. I had discovered adrenaline. I could fly. I could walk on water. I could leap tall buildings with a single bound. This was everything I had ever dreamt that being in a pop group was – and more. It was indescribable. If I ever told you that I was happier, I was lying.

Del, who brought the equipment over, had pissed off back to England without Trevor, apparently, and we needed an extra plane ticket to get him home. No problem. I was going to London anyway so I gave Trevor my plane ticket and blagged a ride with The Pretenders. James Honeyman-Scott and Martin Chambers were two of the funniest people I have ever met and they had me in stitches all the way to the ferry, and on the ferry, whereupon I purchased a bottle of Pernod, and then all the way into London, where I drank said bottle. I vaguely remember Chrissie Hynde asking me back to her place, but I was too drunk to read between any lines – and may very well have been mistaken!

I headed for a studio in London where Bob Carter was playing guitar on Hazel O'Connor's *Breaking Glass* album. I vaguely remember getting there and waking up the next day feeling dreadful at his and Stella's flat in Wandsworth. I still felt like the proverbial million dollars, albeit with a million-dollar hangover, but this was par for the course. This was rock 'n' roll. I had died and gone to heaven.

Our first appearance on *Top of the Pops* was a landmark, I suppose. Appearing on the television programme that I had watched religiously for the past sixteen years had an unreality about it, but there again everything did back then. It was kind of nerve-racking – the playback we mimed to was nowhere near loud enough, and Terry looked uncontrollably nervous. The camera work was the usual BBC standard: a close-up of Lynval during Roddy's guitar solo. Rod and Brad got slung out of the bar up on the fifth floor afterwards. Alcohol was involved, apparently.

Miming to music was something I had only done in the privacy of my own full-length mirror. To do it in public seemed somewhat daunting. In point of fact, it is a lot of fun – it's the only time I have a drink before a performance. I always liked the subtle stuff some musicians did to ridicule the whole thing: Marc Bolan had the lead from his guitar going into his back pocket; Jean Jacques Burnel from The Stranglers played with no strings on his bass – stupid stuff. We took the piss something rotten, especially in Europe. One time in Holland, we all swapped instruments, and I ended up playing the drums while Brad played bass. Jerry used his Coventry City Football Club scarf as a guitar strap and, using Lynval's guitar, did Pete Townsend windmill guitar poses on 'Message to You'. To be outrageous was a more publicity-grabbing policy, I suppose, but sometimes we crossed over the outrageous line. However, as they say, it's a thin line between clever and stupid.*

The next thing on the agenda was to record an album. We had tons of material. It was all the tunes we played live. We would put on it as many songs as possible, give people value for money. The whole thing was to be recorded during August and released to coincide with the tour we were planning with The Selecter and Madness in

---

* Obligatory *Spinal Tap* reference.

October. Mr Costello was to be our producer. He'd already become a big fan of the band, and everyone got on well with him. I was dying to ask him about the recording sessions for his *My Aim Is True* album, one of my favourite records, but never got the bottle up to do it. Apparently he felt that we would be better off without our punk lead guitarist, a fact that Mr Radiation was not particularly pleased about when being told, but I wasn't aware of it at the time, and it was almost fifteen years later that I found out.

We tried out The Who's studio in Battersea, to see if it was the right place for us, Elvis Costello (or Mr C as we soon came to call him) producing. We recorded an extended dub-style version of 'Too Much Too Young'. It was not my favourite cut on the record; the sounds were all wrong for a band like The Specials – too clean, not funky enough. The studio was cavernous and had a sterility about it that had more in common with a well-oiled business machine than people who would rather die than get old. Perhaps not getting fooled again was more to do with employing the right business managers, but this is the cynical view of hindsight speaking. That and a cheap attempt at getting a load of Who references in the text.

I do not know how we chose it, but we recorded the first Specials album at TW Studios in Fulham, about 150 yards from the Greyhound, where we'd played a few months earlier. It was obviously the studio for us: basement level, small, badly lit, cramped and very funky. On the first day we recorded 'Too Hot'. On the second day we found a *Top of the Pops* backing track that Joe Jackson had done of his single 'Is She Really Going Out With Him'. This was at the time when there was something of a feud going on between our illustrious producer and Mr Jackson. Mr C did a brilliant vocal version over JJ's original. It was mixed down on a cassette – very cool – but I never did get my promised copy.

The engineer for these sessions was a red-haired kid from Barrow-in-Furness, one Dave Jordan. He'd worked on the *Love You Live* album that The Rolling Stones had recently put out and he dug the band. We soon gelled into our own version of a well-oiled machine, and the record was completed in what seemed like no time at all. The performance was relatively easy as they were songs some of us had been playing for nearly three years. The only new tune on the album was 'Dawning of a New Era', which, although we'd been playing it since before our Clash tour days, had not made it into our current set for some reason. It took fifteen minutes to remember it, another half an hour to teach it to Brad, and we took it. I can remember Jerry trying to restrain us, saying we'd need tunes for our second album, but I was convinced we were so amazing we'd be able to write millions of tunes by the time our next record was due. A little over-excited, I think.

Chrysalis provided accommodation for the band's stay in London during the recording sessions. It was a flat on the King's Road. I didn't actually stay there, preferring Bob and Stella's spare bedroom in Wandsworth to what I understand soon became squalor in Chelsea. I realized early on that I needed space and sleep, two things that were a rarity according to the stories that went round.

One morning I arrived at the studio to find our illustrious producer asleep over the mixing desk. He woke up with a start and I went and made him a cup of tea.

I know some people have whinged on about Mr Costello and his involvement with The Specials, how the album sounded weedy and the production was lacklustre. This is absolute crap. Mr C. was a big fan. He loved the music and wanted to interpret it the best way he could. We didn't like the big sound of The Who's studio, we liked the qualities of the Fulham basement. It was claustrophobic, and that comes across somehow on the record. Our producer had some good ideas, too. That's him banging a tin tray on top of the snare drum beats in 'Nite Klub' by the way. To me, the album sounds very 'sixties beat group' and is a very 'British' record It sounded old and new at the same time. It still sounds good.

It was someone who knew somebody who worked for Rick Rogers who put us in touch with Rico. I knew the name, but my knowledge of ska and reggae was not as extensive as Neville's, Lynval's or Brad's, who made out that some kind of second coming was imminent when a date was set for Rico to come down and play on our album. Brad, I recall, seemed disbelieving that he had even returned our phone call.

Rico Rodriguez was (and still is) something of a musical legend. Born in Kingston, Jamaica, in 1934, he was taught at the famous Alpha School in Kingston, where the musicians who created ska from African rhythms and American R&B came from. He played trombone on a host of records in the early/mid-sixties (the original 'Rudi, a Message to You' among them) before coming to London, where he played with Georgie Fame and The Blue Flames. He then returned to Jamaica, where he embraced the teachings of Rastafarianism and recorded the sublime *Man from Warieka* album, quite possibly the best instrumental reggae album ever (well, in my opinion anyway!). He had toured with Bob Marley and The Wailers and, in 1979, he was back living in London. I have never met a more dedicated musician in my life. He was also the first 'true' Rastafarian I had met, and I found him fascinating. He brought with him a trumpet player who he worked with, Dick Cuthell. Dick was born somewhere up near Liverpool, but had a very Queen's English accent. He sported a 'wing commander'-size handlebar moustache and played trumpet, cornet and flugelhorn (which both looked like a trumpet, but a bit bigger . . . or smaller). He was a couple of years older than me. He'd played trumpet in soul and rock bands, but ended up working as a studio engineer for Island Records, where he'd met Rico and ended up playing on most of his recent recordings. They both smoked marijuana – for sacramental, inspirational and medicinal purposes, I'm sure, so they were in with the band's 'herbalists' from the off. Rico and Dick made the band sound fantastic. 'Message to You' and 'Nite Klub' – two of the best cuts on the LP.

The recording of the backing tracks had been completed in August, so I was left to kick my heels while overdubs and mixing were completed. On my birthday (end of August) I decided to go down to TW to add moral support and see what was happening. I decided to begin my birthday celebration with a bottle of Stones Ginger Wine, something of a favourite tipple in those days. I arrived at the studio well fortified by the grape, to find that it was backing vocals time, with Chrissie Hynde helping out. The session was practically over when I got there. On seeing that the normally reserved and sensible bass guitarist was slurring words and making grandiose gestures, everyone retired to the Greyhound to assist with my celebration. I cannot remember what happened, and no one has ever told me! I must have made it back to Bob and Stella's as I vaguely remember waking up in Wandsworth the next morning.

(As an aside . . . I have this theory. It's only a theory, mind you. Some time in 1982, The Pretenders' bass player, Pete Farndon, was kicked out of the band, and Dave Hill (The Pretenders' manager) called me to ask if I would play bass on their next single and 'do a couple of festivals'. I'd just quit The Specials and jumped at the chance. Later that evening, Rick Rogers phoned to tell me that James Honeyman-Scott had died, thus curtailing any Pretending in the possible future. Shame. Anyway, I was in The Pretenders for about eight hours in 1982. Now, my theory is that Chrissie Hynde thought I was this high-alcohol high-octane kick-ass rock 'n' roller type kind-of-guy, as the only times she had seen me was when I was totally plastered (the return from Bilzen and my birthday). It just so happened that the last two times I had been totally sloppy drunk was in her presence. It would have been comical, to say the least, had I been inducted in the ranks of The Pretenders, and then announce that, er . . . actually . . . no, I don't drink that much. Perhaps they would have thrown me out for being too sober. Perhaps it was a stupid notion in the first place. People who mention my Pretenders escapade usually dig me in the ribs and retort with a 'Well, you got out of there just in time' or 'Phew, Horace, you don't know how lucky you were' and go on about life expectancy in The Pretenders. Pete Farndon died soon after of a heroin overdose. Those remarks were not funny.)

We took time out of our recording schedule to play the Hammersmith Palais with London dub poet Linton Kwesi Johnson. It was a benefit concert for The National Council for One Parent Families. Now, charity gigs can be an absolute pain in the arse. The people who organize them like to be seen to be organizing them, but rock 'n' roll is unlike any 'normal' business ('like no business I know'). You are giving your services for free – fine, I have no problem with that – but in order to give your services, whether free or not, you need the proper facilities to do it. Now, I'm not talking about four bottles of Courvoisier Special Reserve and a square yard of sushi in the dressing room. I mean a proper PA and a proper stage. Neither of these were present at the Palais when we loaded in on the afternoon of Tuesday 21 August. The PA crew did the best they could, but we all knew the evening was going to be a disaster as no one would be able to see us on the two-foot-high stage. We had played the Palais before, as support to the Dave Edmunds/Nick Lowe band Rockpile. Then, there was a great big six-foot-high scaffolding thing with boards across it running along most of one side of the hall . . . but not now.

I vaguely remember the organizer leaving in floods of tears, poor thing. The majority of 'people out there' don't realize how much goes into putting on a show – PA, lights, security, a stage manager and crew. All these people will work an awful lot longer and probably harder than we do, so feeding them might be a good idea too. I'm sure most people think you just turn up, plug your guitar into something and the magic just automatically starts, like in *The Monkees*. The trouble is, if you say, 'Yes, we'll do your charity gig, but we want this, and this, and this,' you tend to be treated like you're acting above your station or, at worst, you're a fascist bastard. Don't get me wrong. I think giving your services for free to a good cause is just fine and dandy, and I've done some good benefit gigs, but the best ones are always the ones that have been properly organized.

Anyhow, back to the Hammersmith Palais, and it's about 5 p.m. The doors open in just over two hours time and there's no stage. The plan is to get some staging in and place it on the minuscule revolving two-foot-high stage and hope for the best, so a truck is despatched, and around 6.30 p.m. it arrives back with all this green staging – kind of like big drum risers. Jerry has this idea of extending the risers at the sides, so he, Rod and I could hop up there to make the thing a bit more interesting visually, and to provide a 'second line of defence' if (or rather *when*) the audience decided to join us.

The Selecter and The Mo-dettes turn up, as does LKJ, who realizes he's left his taped backing tracks behind. Hey, don't worry LK, we haven't even got a stage yet! Stage crew, Specials and Selecters all pile in and install the thing. It had an air of desperation that, looking back on it now, was almost like an episode of *Fawlty Towers*. Anyhow, the equipment goes up, lights go down, doors open, and, by the skin of its teeth, the show goes on. Promoter dries her tears and, according to Charles Shaar Murray's review in the *NME*, fun was had by all. 'The Specials . . . The most enjoyable British band since The Members.' Why, thanks, Mr Murray!

6

The Two-Tone Take-Over

The 2-Tone Tour was the culmination of all our concerted 1979 efforts. We had started the year borrowing money to record a single; we ended it with our own very successful record label, an album in the top ten and our names spread across every tabloid and broadsheet in the country. The *Sun* (a newspaper, apparently) hailed us as 'The Black and White Reggae Revolution', whereas the *Guardian* (a newspaper also) frothed at the mouth a little more reservedly: 'Something Special'. They also reported that our songs were written by organist Jerry Bammers [*sic*]. Spelling mistakes would dog us for the rest of our career.

Our tour was to be put together rather like a sixties package tour: three bands, low ticket price, lots of dancing. It was our *raison d'être*. We did what we did best in front of an audience on a dance floor. Our LP was more or less what we played in front of people – it was what we were good at, and now we wanted to put it in front of as many people as possible. There was no talk of budgets, projected profits, tour bonuses, we had no merchandise to sell. Our idealism was without parallel. We had records out, and that was that. It marked an upturn in our work ethic that would not stop for almost a year. It started our 'meteoric rise' and, to continue the analogy, burnt us out.

Forty dates, starting 19 October and running right through until December, with extra bits being added on all the time. Three bands, Selecter, Madness and The Specials, in that order. This was the big time, or as big as time had got so far in our career. We now entered the belly of the beast called Rock 'n' Roll. An articulated truck carried all the lights and sound equipment, a minibus carried the crew, and a forty-eight-seater coach carried the bands.

The coach was driven by a befuddled young man called Alfie. I think he'd been used to taking pensioners to Blackpool and stuff like that. He did not know what hit him when the massed bands of 2-Tone and their itinerant minions clambered aboard. The atmosphere was like a school trip to somewhere fantastic, but with no teachers. Alfie got more or less accepted and did our Europe jaunt the following January. I seem to remember he was very good at getting lost, anywhere between the gig and the hotel, usually after our performance at times when sleep was at a premium, or there was a young lady sitting on my knee, thinking (hopefully) the same carnal thoughts as I.

Ticket prices on the tour were to be no more than £2.50. I don't believe we made any money from the tour at all; in fact, I have a recollection of John Curd, the promoter, wanting to increase the ticket price midway through. I am extremely pleased to say he did not succeed. The Specials were about walking like they talked. If the ticket price was £2.50, that was how much the tickets were. End of story.

We kicked off with what was supposed to be three days

of rehearsals at the Roundhouse in Camden. It turned out to be two and a half days of shopping, and doing a video for our next single, 'A Message to You, Rudy'. I took delivery of a brand spanking new Ampeg bass rig. An '8 × 10' speaker cabinet (eight 10-inch speakers in a huge wooden box) and a thundering great heavy amplifier to stand on top of it. Just like Robbie Shakespeare, according to Lynval. It sounded fantastic. Well, it would, wouldn't it!

The daily business side of things was run by Frank Murray, our tour manager. He had come over to London from Dublin in the early seventies with Thin Lizzy and had just spent the last eight or so years as their tour manager. Looking the part, with a very 'lived-in' face and long, but not too long, hair. He exuded 'blarney', an Irish expression for 'bullshit', which in his line of work was something of a prerequisite. He had recently returned from taking Elton John and his percussionist, Ray Cooper, to the Soviet Union.

I suppose after years of dealing with the drink 'n' drugs intake of Phil Lynott we were a pretty soft touch. He was accompanied by man-mountain Steve English, who we had met on The Clash tour. I believe his job description was that of 'security', but all I can remember him doing was taking the piss out of us and going on about how much cocaine he'd seen famous rock stars take and what part of a female's anatomy they'd taken it from. (He may actually have been tour promoter John Curd's 'on-the-road' tour rep – the very idea of The Specials having a 'minder' seemed ludicrous!) He and Frank Murray soon chummed up – like-minded sorts. I think Rick felt better knowing there was some muscle around to call on if any shit hit any fan . . .

or anything. I have a memory of Steve complaining about how some guy from some appalling US rock band had swiped the rolled twenty-pound note that Steve had provided to snort some cocaine. Ho hum. To some of us, these two characters alluded to a kind of rock 'n' roll that was repugnant – bloated rock stars doing too much coke; but there again, some of us behaved like they'd been waiting all their lives to make their acquaintances. The Specials were starting to pull in different directions.

The tour started in Brighton. We arrived late and carried on arriving late from there on in. After the gig, at the inevitable party in someone's house, I met up with Mike Dempsey, bass player with The Cure. He'd played the same venue a couple of weeks earlier, when The Cure had supported Siouxsie and The Banshees. He said he recognized some of the audience – even though they were wearing a different uniform. Whether we liked it or not, we were still 'pop music', and our fashion stance was as interchangeable as any other commodity. It was difficult to move without seeing black and white check. Pauline Black said that even Evans Outsize were doing it!

The day after our first show in Brighton, we all assembled after the obligatory two hours' sleep and headed across the road to the pebble beach, where one of our more memorable photo sessions took place. Mods on Brighton Beach and all that. All the bands together, 2-Tone en masse, excitement personified, if not a little hung over. According to the *Melody Maker*, the next night's show was lacklustre. I'm not surprised.

As anyone who has ever been to a Specials show will tell you, playing live was the band's forte. I have never experienced such a feeling of utter exhilaration in my life. I've played some pretty spectacular concerts since my days in The Specials and a few of them come close (The Specialbeat gigs in Boston and some of the General Public shows in California come to mind), but they all fail to measure up to The Specials in full flow. We got used to the 'full tilt audience' on the Clash tour, where we witnessed first hand the power that could be generated on a stage. The Clash, for me, had an energy that was edgy, dangerous and, at times, verging on malevolence. The Specials' vibe was different. We played dance music – you didn't pogo to it. It had a happier feel to it. Suggs said that 2-Tone made British males dance for the first time in fifteen years, and I have to agree with him. We had a lot more girls at our shows because of that. We covered all bases. Rhythm-wise it was ska and reggae, the sexiest dance music in the world. It was played with the aggressive attitude of punk, but still retained its 'wind-your-waist' sensibility. Visually we scored too. Apart from our suits, we presented our show tremendously. Every member had their own way of physically interacting with the music, from Roddy's grand guitar gestures to Jerry's Alfred E. Newman style of organ playing. There was always something to catch your eye on stage, even when Neville was stationary. The only choreographed bit in the show was when we played 'Blank Expression'. We all stood stock still. It must have looked extraordinary.

The tour soon established its own momentum, and although Madness, as the youngest band, became the noisier part of the posse, it was interesting to see how we entered the 'rock 'n' roll world' without really knowing it. We went from wide-eyed, open-mouthed astonishment to all-seeing, all-knowing studied cool as we disembarked from our

Trathens coach and shambled through that evening's venue, searching for stale lunchtime sandwiches, or a bottle of beer. There seemed to be a competition going on. Brad had acquired a tiny portable TV. He got it . . . er . . . cheap. You could never get a good picture on it. Then Nev got one. I think he paid top dollar for it. Then Brad got a Haliburton metal briefcase to put his TV in. Guess what Nev did.

I had two suits on the 2-Tone tour, and they were both disgusting, damp all the time, and, by the end of the tour, very smelly indeed. I made do with a Ben Sherman shirt and some Sta-press trousers towards the end. Putting on a suit that was still sodden from the night before was truly horrible. The following year we had a flight case made that would take all our stage clothes. In the end, it just held a selection of damp, putrid, second-hand suits and mouldy loafers and was left outside in corridors because it stank so much!

Madness were obviously aware of the bigger picture. They had merchandise. Three types of t-shirts, one with the unforgettable 'Fuck Art, Let's Dance' logo. Despite my years as an art student, I blagged one. Madness's merchandise was sold by Chas Smash's brother, Brendan Smash, and a little guy called Wandsworth Harry, or 'Wandswer Farry' to use his proper name! They sold their t-shirts for a fiver, and every three or four days, another ten boxes would arrive – they were cleaning up. Fair play, I suppose. We'd never thought about doing t-shirts, and everybody seemed to be doing badges with Jerry's design on it. Nowadays, touring bands survive on what they make on merchandise. The whole thing just went completely over our heads – all we were interested in was playing this incredible, infectious, angry-yet-happy-at-the-same-time dance music, and play it we did.

Our album had been released on the day the tour started, and we champed at the bit to read the reviews. We needn't have champed. The reviews were what you'd imagine, not that we needed any more confirmation that what we were doing was working: a sweat-soaked Top Rank with sticky carpets and condensation running down the velvet flocked wallpaper by midnight was confirmation enough.

Playing wise, The Specials were on top form. The Selecter were learning on their feet and starting to find their own big-stage identity. Ditto Madness; one show in every four of theirs was a stunner. The Specials were just fantastic. All the experience gained over the past couple of years and especially in the last six months made us unstoppable. When Rico and Dick Cuthell joined the band for the last four tunes, the place, which had usually gone wild anyway, went even wilder. Neville threw himself about like a man possessed. Jerry usually ended up away from his Vox Continental organ, doing some loopy dance. Roddy and I were generally inseparable by that time in the show, not that we weren't the best of friends, but our guitar leads had usually become totally intertwined, a big pile of black spaghetti at our feet. My favourite tune on the tour was 'Doesn't Make It Alright' – a real 'lump in the eye/ tear in the throat' moment, with the whole crowd singing along. The message was for you, Rudy.

It obviously hadn't got through to certain inhabitants of Hatfield, when the tour stopped by on 27 October. There was a nasty incident during The Selecter's set. We were away at the hotel at the time and so didn't witness it, but, according to the *NME*, ten people were treated in hospital, eleven people were arrested, and £900-worth of damage was caused by an unspecified group of Neanderthals on that particular Saturday. I remember arriving backstage to find our dressing room being used as a first-aid centre for 'walking wounded'. It certainly didn't dampen the audience's fervour, and the show went on. Mayhem as usual. It was definitely an isolated incident, and there was no trouble on any of the other shows on the tour, but it cast a shadow.

When we reached Blackburn, the message waiting for us was that our LP had gone into the charts. Straight in at number four. This was nothing short of incredible. Madness's Stiff Records debut album, *One Step Beyond*, was twelve steps behind, in at number sixteen. Champagne was produced backstage at the Golden Palms dance emporium by the local Chrysalis rep, and I remember Brad offering a toast to Jerry for making it all happen. I didn't think too much more about it, until show time. Half-way through our set, I looked over to see Jerry push his organ off the riser onto the floor. I wonder why he did that. Too much pressure perhaps? Maybe the champagne wasn't such a good idea after all.

At Leicester, my parents arrived at the stage door, and I took them up the stairs in the De Montfort Hall to the seats that had been reserved for them on the balcony. It was a Kodak moment, to say the least.

Chrysalis, in their wisdom, had decided to release 'Message to You, Rudy' and 'Nite Klub' as a double-A-side, but you knew the radio would never play 'Nite Klub', with its references to girls being like slags and beer tasting like piss. Chrissie Hynde had done such a cool job on the backing vocals, too.

(The record said 'The Specials featuring Rico', which indicated that 'The Man from Warieka' himself was back.)

'Message to You, Rudy' had entered the charts at number twenty-one, the same week as The Selecter's 'On My Radio' (number twenty) and Madness's new single, One Step Beyond', had been released. All three bands were chosen to appear on *Top of the Pops* that week. It was another '2-Tone has arrived' moment. It was also smack dab in the middle of the tour, and we didn't want to cancel a sold-out concert (as most of the shows now were).

The BBC would show The Selector's 'On My Radio' performance of the previous week, but ourselves and Madness would be live in the studio. We would travel overnight from Tuesday's gig (Plymouth) to London, book into a hotel for the obligatory two hours' sleep, then head off to the BBC for 'The Pops' (which was what those well-meaning but somehow slimy record company reps called it), before travelling to Cardiff for Wednesday night's show. Well, er, that's fine – we were used to staying awake a lot by now anyway.

The Plymouth gig was memorable in that during the second song of our set ('Do the Dog'), Roddy swung round in one of his Paul Simonon/James Dean shapes and broke the jack plug off my guitar lead, leaving the end of the plug still in the guitar. I did not have a spare guitar and so I 'mimed' the song until I was handed Mark Bedford's (from Madness) black bass for a couple of numbers until the offending plug bits were fished out. Nobody seemed to notice. Backstage, The Selecter were involved in a moderately furious argument with the local security, and I distinctly remember seeing Desmond Brown attempting to take a bite out of a bouncer. He was held back by several of his band mates so I don't think he succeeded, but I made a mental note to remember to stay on the right side of Mr Brown.

The coach set off for London after the show with Madness and ourselves failing miserably to get any sleep, and eventually arrived at a hotel in Camden at around five or six in the morning. *Top of the Pops* takes all day. It is a meeting of egos. Sullen, surly cameramen who would rather be working with 'real stars' versus jumped-up newly cynical pop groups, sporting the hugely popular 'bored' look. The cameramen needed to get camera angles right so that, when there was a guitar solo, they didn't focus on the keyboard player (they sometimes got it right, too), but the bands would rarely be as energetic on the run-throughs as they were on the actual thing. Luckily, it was difficult to be energetic with a laid-back song like 'Message to You, Rudy'; that, and the fact we were dog tired. Fortunately, we were first on, so we ambled to the stage, did our bit and sloped off back to the dressing room. We couldn't disappear just yet as we had to wait for 'technical clearance', whatever that was, and it could be quite a while.

A couple of hits on a spliff that was circulating and I was soon fast asleep on the dressing-room floor. Some time later I was rudely awoken and pushed towards the studio. 'We've got to do our bit again.' 'Er . . . what?' 'There was some sort of technical cock-up and they need us to play the song again.' Me: 'What song?'

So there I was, standing on the *TOTP* stage with my bass guitar, waking up as the cameras got it right that time, and 'Message to You' was playing. It felt very odd, (if indeed I felt at all), like it was a dream. I had forgotten to put my shoes on, and did the performance in my socks. Phew (as they say) . . rock 'n' roll.

We got a train from London around five o' clock to Cardiff. Jerry refused to sit in the first-class seats that Chrysalis had bought us. I might have joined him, but I was too tired. We arrived at the Top Rank half-way through Madness's set. They had got a plane to Cardiff from London; they had a tighter schedule, and it was a Stiff Records kind of thing to do. (Don't worry, lads, it won't come off your royalties!) The show in Cardiff was one of the best gigs on the tour. Nervous energy, I suppose.

John Peel came to see us when we played at Norwich University. He didn't come backstage afterwards and said in his *Sounds* column that The Selecter's performance was the best of the three bands. Something about having more to prove. Fair comment. I couldn't possibly hold a grudge against John Peel, now, could I?

At The Manchester Apollo, where we had supported The Clash just a year before, the place was rocking, and repeated scenes of chairs being ripped from their moorings took place. We were touring with a PA system that belonged to Island Records. It was fine for a Top Rank or a Tiffany's Ballroom, but for places as big as The Manchester Apollo it was woefully inadequate.

Sound checks became their usual nightmare, with everyone playing at once, and too loudly for the monitor system to cope with. A monitor engineer on the 2-Tone tour had a shorter life expectancy than an English fighter pilot in the First World War. We went through loads of them, and none of them had the nous, or guts, to say, 'The system is under-powered and knackered, and you guys are playing too loud!', because you didn't do that to the artistes; you stroked their egos, gave them cocaine, and, if you were good, they'd tell you about what happened backstage on a Queen tour a friend of theirs did. Some of us fitted into this rock 'n' roll world easily, some didn't. Our road crew, Rex and Trevor, didn't like it. As soon as our gear was away, they wanted to join us in the hotel bar, pick up girls, have a laugh, not haul Martin PA bins into the truck and help disassemble lighting rigs. It wasn't their PA: 'Cha' mon, me look after Special gear and nuttin' else.'

The 'Road Crew Issue', for want of a better phrase, was an indication of where we were and the problems we faced in the business. We now met people who we were on tour with, who worked for us, or rather were (indirectly) paid by us, who we didn't know and who didn't seem to like us very much. Don't get me wrong. Some of the people who worked on the PA crews, the lighting rigs and the trucks dug us. They kept coming back to work for us. Nick Baker, who originally worked for the PA system we were using, became our monitor engineer and went all over the world with us. Lin Scoffin, who did our lights, travelled with us too. The 'crew guys' were a breed apart, lived by their own rules. They flitted from tour to tour and were generally dressed in faded black. Their wardrobe consisted of the tour t-shirts from the previous month and jeans that may have once been blue. Some of them even had tour jackets. They were the true 'professionals' amongst us and had their own mystique. They got excited about equipment, load-ins, get-outs, packing articulated lorries and taking drugs. On the 2-Tone tour the crews all travelled in a fifteen-seater minibus. It must have had a strange vibe about it.

Esoteric road rats mixing with our buddies Rex and Trevor. Madness were in the same situation. Their roadies were two of their mates, namely 'Chalky' and 'Tokes'. They can generally be seen in early Madness videos headbutting one another. Like Trevor and Rex, they played a vital role in keeping feet on the ground. I think they felt the same about Suggs and Co. as our road crew thought about us. We were mates, it was fun. Hard work, but fun. When 'the band' and 'the crew' were separated and we only saw one another backstage, it changed our relationships. It had to.

Me, I wanted the job done efficiently. Whether we liked it or not, a lot of people had put their hands in their pockets to see us, and I thought the least we could do was put on the best show possible. If a 'professional roadie' could tune your guitar better than the lead singer's mate, then tough. It wasn't like we were playing the Golden Eagle with Gordon's van or Ray King's PA back in Coventry. It was the subtle transition that tempted to move us into the 'unreal' world, which was totally at odds with what we'd started out trying to do. These were sideline issues, though, and anyway, we had us a manager and a tour manager to sort all that stuff out, didn't we?

In Stoke-on-Trent, the tour inhabited all the rooms in the hotel. The staff were great and cooked food for us at midnight and thought the whole thing was fantastic – a totally different attitude to most of the hotels we didn't sleep in.

In Glasgow, an early-morning stroll resulted in an encounter with a music store, and a second-hand Fender Telecaster bass with a rather bent neck – £140, a steal. I could easily get someone to sort the neck out on my return to Coventry. A spare guitar was needed, and this one fitted the bill – hey, I saw a photo of Kenny Gradney from the mighty Little Feat playing one. Ultra cool! (The T-bass got its neck straightened out and became my number one bass for the next few months, until I bought another one in New York.)

In Aberdeen, the tour played a small nightclub called Raffles. It was pandemonium, absolute chaos, sweat, heaving bodies, no room, no air. An atmosphere you could cut and put in a box. Fantastic. I still have a tiny piece of the club's plate-glass door. A smithereen even!

Madness left the tour in mid-November. Their plan (or more likely Stiff Records' Dave Robinson's plan) was for them to go to America. This rock 'n' roll one-upmanship did not have a great deal of impact with The Specials. All three bands were linked, all had their salient points, but The Specials were the best. No contest.

The Selecter moved up a place on the bill, and Dexy's came on the tour. Jerry had kept some sort of dialogue going with Kevin Rowland. They had played with us when we visited Manchester a few months previously and not acquitted themselves favourably towards the Factory crowd (Kevin Rowland hit a member of the front row with a microphone stand and their van was subsequently trashed). They were a lot better now. The line-up was, however, not complete. Stoker, their drummer, and later my rhythm companion in General Public, had not been discovered, and the drum stool was taken by a gentleman on loan from The Subway Sect. No one in Dexy's ever appeared to talk to him. He travelled with the band's manager, Dave Cork (another face from The Clash tour), in Dave's car to all the gigs and played stage left, up on Jerry's riser, as far away from the rest of the band as appeared possible.

Now the vibe on the coach changed. Dexy's were very much 'the men with the mission'. They kept themselves very definitely to themselves, all sat together at the front of the coach and all shared the one hotel room (I think there were nine of them). Once the individual members were away from Mr Rowland's vitriolic stare, they loosened up a bit. Pete Williams was a cool guy and a good bass player to boot, and Jeff Blythe, Steve Spooner and Big Jim Patterson were already a formidable horn section. They played on the rest of the tour, including all three London shows. I'm sure Dexy's would have got signed sooner or later, but their inclusion on the 2-Tone tour gave them a kind of 'seal of approval' – there's no denying that.

Other things Birmingham joined the tour, namely a couple of cassettes from Jon Mostyn, our old agent. One was a reggae tape; Brad and Dave Jordan were sitting at the back of the coach, listening and everyone was very impressed by it. 'Channel One,' says Brad. 'Definitely recorded at Channel One.' (These were the very famous Jamaican studios where Bob Marley recorded and Joe Gibbs produced. Apparently reggae snobs could distinguish the different sonic qualities of individual studios.) Dave Jordan was in agreement. 'Definitely Channel One.' The band was in fact UB40 and the tape had been recorded in a front-room studio in Bearwood, Birmingham (England). A few of us smirked 'neath our pork pie hats.

There has been a fair amount of crap written about how UB40 were 'turned down by 2-Tone because they weren't commercial enough'. May I take this opportunity to say a rather loud 'bollocks' to that. The 2-Tone label was interested in bands that played a mixture of punk, ska and reggae, and The Yoobs were a straight-ahead reggae band, therefore not eligible for selection, despite strenuous protestations from Lynval and The Selecter's Charly Anderson. The same thing happened when Elvis Costello was 'in-between labels' and recorded a version of Sam and Dave's 'I Can't Stand Up for Falling Down' some six months later. It was pressed up and everything. Chrysalis must have thought we were mad not to release it, but it wasn't what the label represented. Dreadful business acumen, I grant you, but true to some principles.

The other Birmingham cassette, however, fulfilled all the criteria. A (pre-Saxa) version of 'Mirror in the Bathroom' had us Specials definitely rocking. Rockers' drums played at Motörhead speed, sinewy heavy bass and weedy punk-thrash Velvet Underground guitars. Fantastic tunes, and this Irie Irie toasting over the top of it all from this kid who apparently was only sixteen. The Beat – what a great name. Book 'em Danno!

Whenever we played The Beat tape, Dexy's, who occupied the front seats of the coach, would jeer, boo and hiss. Apparently there'd been a full-scale ruck between some members of the two bands at a party in Birmingham some time earlier in the year, and feelings between the two bands were not good, kind of like West Bromwich Albion and Aston Villa if you will. Sometimes we used to put the tape on just to wind up the young soul rebels, and it generally worked.

As the tour progressed, we tended to meet fans who followed the tour, rather like we'd seen with The Clash. Some of these fans came on board and ended up helping backstage or assisting Rex and Trevor with the equipment. The ones with the 'I'm posing with the pop stars' attitude didn't last too long, but some stayed and proved to be invaluable in 'sounding out' the crowd. So I was grateful we had the immaculately dressed Perry and Gary from London, Kevin, a 6ft 2in skinhead from Derby, and a kid from Doncaster who we called . . . Doncaster. I don't think anyone knew his name, but he didn't seem to mind as long as he had a floor to sleep on and could unwind with us after a show.

There were press-persons on the coach all the time. In one memorable *faux pas*, I asked Robin Denselow, journalist from the broadsheet *Guardian*, if he was a writer from the disposable teen mag *Smash Hits*. Whoops! He was very gracious about it. I'm sure he'd been called worse things than that.

Towards the end of November we bade farewell to The Selecter and Dexy's for a few days and went to Ireland. It was still considered part of the 2-Tone tour, but we were supporting Dr Feelgood, who were in the charts with 'Milk and Alcohol'. (This was post-Wilko Johnson – the Gypie-Mayo-era Feelgoods, fact fans.) The shows were a little bit less frantic – Belfast Queens University and Dublin Olympic Ballroom – and The Feelgoods were very pleasant gentlemen. Back at the hotel in Dublin, the bar ran out of Guinness – 'nuff said.

What with extra gigs here and there, we had been on tour now for almost two months. There were now three London shows, two at the Lyceum Ballroom, where a couple of years earlier we had attempted to awaken a room full of UK Subs/Damned fans, and the Lewisham Odeon (a 'popular ska and blue beat venue' back in the sixties, apparently) in South London, sorry, Saarf Landan. One of the Lyceum shows was to be recorded – we had thought about having a live performance on tape, and this seemed a good place to do it. We also chose to record our Coventry show a couple of days before.

The Coventry show was fantastic – there were 120 people on the guest list! Steve English came backstage and announced, 'There's someone outside from Coventry who isn't on the guest list! Can he come in?' The show sold out months before, and we decided there and then to do a 'homecoming' gig just before Christmas. As it turned out, we did two.

Now, this has always bothered me. Why is it that the most important, prestigious, 'recorded for posterity, rows of photographers down front, can't move for celebs in the balcony' shows, are at the *end* of the tour, when everyone is deaf, knackered, thinking about an alternative career in market gardening, wearing the same sweat-encrusted suit they've had on for the past four shows, contemplating either suicide or, more probably, homicide? The best performances were usually about two weeks in. Did anyone record them? No. Did any press come and see us slay Cardiff Top Rank, Sheffield Top Rank, Leicester De Montfort Hall? No. I could just imagine the press department at Chrysalis: 'Hey, we've got this great band, they've been on tour for almost two months solid, they're cranky, they're smelly, they've got spots, even their hangovers have got hangovers, and they hate everybody! Wanna come and see them?'

If anything in the deep recess of my memory is a blur, it was the last week of the 2-Tone Tour. The Lyceum shows came and went, with a big record company reception/party afterwards. I remember Jerry wanting to get a load of fans in and him refusing to join the party unless they did. I staggered around clutching a rapidly emptying bottle (or two) of wine, leaving with a girl whose name I forget and waking up in her bed the next day somewhere in the suburbs − with a 'last-minute-added-to-the-end-of-the-tour' show in Guildford (or somewhere) to do that evening. But I did it. We did it. We had done it. The most gruelling two months of my life to date had been the two most exciting ones. The Specials rocked and ruled.

There was very little down time. No kicking back in Kingston. No laying low in LA for The Specials. The BBC were doing a documentary on the band and our apparent phenomenon. The plan was to have the band interviewed by *NME* cub reporter Adrian Thrills, film of our Coventry Christmas show and wild and wacky scenes on board a coach heading down to Colchester to do *Rock Goes to College*, yet another TV programme, in which various rock bands played concerts at educational establishments around England. The show itself is memorable for the shots of Terry getting racked off with the security at the front of the stage and eventually hurling a tambourine at them, and the stage invasion, which seemed to be centred on this thirteen-year-old kid with immaculate tonic suit and pork pie hat. The lad was called 'Josh'. I never found out what the hat or the suit were called. While all this audio mayhem and style appreciation was going on, members of the local branch of the National Front lobbed a brick through one of the coach's front windows. It was a cold journey back to Cov. Pity they didn't film that.

The TV show, *The Rudies Are Back*, was broadcast in March 1980, and I thought we came across pretty well. There is a hilarious scene filmed up in Jerry's flat on Albany Road where he sends up the myth of '2-Tone as record company' wonderfully. The rest of us seemed quite

121

embarrassed in front of the camera, but Jerry seemed very natural. Charismatic even.

Rather than release another 'single off the album', it was decided to do a live EP. The A-side was our by now Motörhead-like version of 'Too Much Too Young' coupled with 'Guns of Navarone'. The medley of skinhead standards, 'Long Shot Kick de Bucket', 'Liquidator' and 'Skinhead Moonstomp', which was our 'take no prisoners' encore, and which we decided to call the 'Skinhead Symphony', was on the flip. We didn't know how it would do, chart-wise, but in our drive to do something different, it made sense.

We had some live footage of us playing the song in Coventry, thanks to the BBC and their *The Rudies Are Back* programme, so we based the video around that. Superfans Perry and Gary 'put the word out', and a 150-strong contingent of Specials fans turned up at the sound stage in Elstree to re-create a live gig. We all had to wear the same clothes obviously, to ensure continuity. Unfortunately (or typically) Jerry had lost the oblong white framed sunglasses he was wearing at the 'real' gig and had to make some out of cardboard. If you look hard at the video, you can see him with his cardboard glasses. Perry and Gary are the first two members of the audience to get up on the stage. A great video, but one that I thought set a precedent for stage invading. Not a good move.

Meanwhile, we were not happy about the show we had done in Glasgow. It was in a long, cramped nightclub – hardly anyone could see, and the whole evening was unsatisfying. To rectify this, we decided to go to Glasgow as soon as we could and put on a show that would restore any confidence that had been lost in the band. The evening of 23 December was free at the Glasgow Apollo, so we took it. We also lined up our Coventry Christmas Home-coming do at Tiffany's for the 20th. To keep the whole show on the road, we played in Edinburgh on the 21st. According to the press, it was called our 'Apology tour'. I think that was Rick Rogers's idea. I certainly hope so. We would have the Christmas period off, but would be back to work on the 29th, when I would make my return to the Hammersmith Odeon after four years, to play with The Pretenders and The Who in a series of charity shows for a Cambodian Relief Fund. After that it was Europe in the new year, followed by a trip to America.

Meanwhile, back in the centre of the universe, which in December 1979 was most definitely Coventry, The Specials played two shows at Coventry's Tiffany's. I can honestly put my hand on my heart and say they were the most fantastic shows I have ever played in my life. Coventry, like a lot of industrial cities in Britain during the late seventies, was fraught with problems. Huge factor-ies that had been the mainstays of the city's engineering and manufacturing base since the late 1940s had either closed down (Alfred Herberts), laid off a large percentage of their work force (Alvis, Rootes Group/Chrysler) or had been troubled by strikes (Massey Ferguson). Unemploy-ment was starting to become a way of life for many of the city's skilled and (mainly) unskilled (mainly young) work force. This is probably going to sound really pretentious to anyone who doesn't live in Coventry, but those two shows, just before Christmas '79, turned into a celebration for a city that desperately needed something to celebrate. The atmosphere was even more unbelievable than ever. Playing up there on stage; trying not to get in the way of Roddy's guitar lead; fighting for a chance to get to the front of the stage; narrowly missing a shirtless Neville Staples; attempting to blow beads of sweat off the end of my nose whilst engaged in the wrist-destroying octave runs of 'Little Bitch'; and looking down and recognizing the people in the audience, hair stuck to their heads by sweat, and them grinning up at us. It is difficult to put into words, but I felt as proud of the people in that club as they felt proud of us. I might have cried. Writing this twenty-eight years later makes me feel like I should have.

The shows in Edinburgh and Glasgow were both stormingly good but they never came close to the Coventry shows. This presented its own problems. How do you get a 'high' like that again? I had never taken heroin, but I understood that the first 'high' could only be equalled by taking a larger quantity of the drug, and so on. The comparisons seemed rather frightening.

Christmas came and went and so did The Who. Pete Townshend seemed to be pissed as a fart at the sound check. The Pretenders played first, then it was us. We played for forty-five minutes, which, after the past six months of 'hour and a half, plus encores', was as easy as falling off a log. Neville climbed up a rope that was side-stage during 'Monkey Man' and leapt, Tarzan-like, onto the PA speakers. We acquitted ourselves well, I believe. Then The Who went on. And on, for two and a half hours. God, it was boring. They could have done a cracking hour and a half greatest hits show that would have destroyed the place. The opening chords of 'My Generation' were the high point of the show. I blotted my copy book and stayed sober in the company of The Pretenders. Sex Pistol Steve Jones was there (presumably to ask Pete Townshend what *his* favourite chord was)* and Elvis Costello was also seen backstage with his wife. Just another night with good old rock 'n' roll folks.

Search as I did, I couldn't find my name on the dressing-room wall from 1975.

---

* Just joking, Steve.

7

1980: Europe

If 1979 was the year of acquisition, 1980 was the year of opportunity. We had proved our worth in the UK and were now in a position to do the same overseas. We had always considered ourselves as a strictly British phenomenon and had talked about how difficult it would be to expect French, Germans or Americans to understand what we were about. Most of these countries had only just accepted reggae, and now here was a gang of upstarts from England (*not* Jamaica) who were playing it differently.

Europe did seem to like us, though. During the summer we had been whisked over to Amsterdam, Brussels and Munich, to mime 'Gangsters' on various rather dodgy *Top of the Pops*-type television programmes, and our talent for hamming it up appeared to be having the desired effect. The TV show in Munich was particularly memorable. There were the usual dire Euro-disco acts, ultra-odd new-wave Americans Devo, us and ageing AOR dinosaurs Foreigner. The whole thing was going out live, and two minutes before Foreigner were due to mime 'Hot Blooded', their bass players' guitar strap broke. The clock was ticking, and their roadie, showing great presence of mind I must say, looked around for something bass-guitar-shaped to replace it with. It so happened that his guitar was the same sort as the one I was using.

'Can we use your guitar, mate?'

'Yeah, sure.' I replied. Anything to help out an ageing AOR dinosaur, you know.

Unfortunately, Foreigner's bass player was (and probably still is) about 6ft 4in tall and, in the tradition of AOR dinosaur bassists, played his 'axe' real low, at crotch level (see Guns N' Roses videos for more exact details). Now, although not commonly known as a short arse (5ft 9in), I played my bass quite high in those days, so the chap from Foreigner was handed my bass, which, when he put it on, came down to a few inches below his chin. The opening chords chimed out and there he was.

It made me smile anyway.

After show time (or should that be 'mime time'?), Jerry and I hit a beer festival. Now, that was a mistake. You would have thought I'd got used to hangovers by now.

Our first European tour was to be ten shows in nine cities, a piece of cake compared to the last three months of practically solid road work. In Paris, an extra show had been put in on what was to be a day off, as our first show had sold out. So 10 January saw The Specials leave Coventry in their familiar Alfie-driven Trathens coach, converted to facilitate sleeping at the rear this time, to spearhead 2-Tone's advance on the world. Or something like that.

It was our first experience of long-distance coach travel. We'd travelled from Aberdeen to Coventry and stuff like that before, but this seemed different. You'd take a look on the map and see that you had only moved half an inch since you had set out two hours ago, and there was still six inches to go. I can't remember who were the 'natural' road rats, the members of the band who took to travelling. Lynval was always a 'front seat of the coach' man, me too. Terry and Rod seemed to get bored easily, although I must say that watching Belgium go by is not my idea of teenage fun. I seem to remember a card school was set up, Brad being king card-sharp.

After the Brussels show, we were to drive to Berlin – a long haul (almost 500 miles). Half an inch out of Brussels, the coach's heater packed in. This was the second week of January. Snow, icy winds, below freezing, that sort of stuff. Everyone huddled up near the front of the coach, where the engine was, for warmth except for Rico, who headed for his bunk. Brad had visions of him freezing to death, and us having to carry him, stiff as a board, off the coach.

About twelve hours later, when we finally arrived in Berlin, we were not as healthy as we had been at the beginning of the journey. Most of us had developed colds. I had mine for the next two months, finally shaking it off somewhere in America. Rico did not freeze to death, but was less than enamoured by our travel arrangements. He did not catch a cold, though. This was not the best start to a year where everything had 'pressure' written through it. Nevertheless we continued boldly going where no multi-cultural ska-punk hybrid had gone before.

I seemed to be the band member who did the 'second division' interviews. Jerry was always approached by the music press, and sometimes actually did interviews. Terry and Nev did the teeny mags and the tabloids (the more photogenic, teen-appeal side of things), and I ended up doing the boring local radio, local paper stuff, mainly because I was out of bed pretty early in the morning and could string a sound-byte together. It is very embarrassing to read some of the crap that I came out with. It was not without good reason that I was kept away from the *Melody Maker* and *New Musical Express*. The plus side of doing those interviews was usually that you met the local record company promotions person and could blag stuff like records and t-shirts. If you were lucky, and didn't insult Gerard Haufmanghester from the North German radio syndication network, or whatever, you could get taken out for something to eat or, if you really felt lucky, you could do some sightseeing.

Berlin was a fantastic place. In 1980, the wall was still a reality. There were small memorials with withered bunches of flowers, commemorating some poor souls who had died while trying to get over to the West. It was easy to imagine the East Berliners seeing the bright lights and hearing the sounds of this totally different culture – just out of reach – and feeling like the inmates in Alcatraz must have felt when they could see the lights of San Francisco from their prison cells.

Our show was at The Metropole, a big Studio 54 sort of disco club which had a very impressive lighting display, and it was the first time I'd seen lasers used indoors – very impressive.

Kieran (can't remember his second name), guitar hero from Kettering in my Möbius Trip days, came by to say hello. How he had come to be living in Berlin is another story, but it was nice to see someone from way back when. To think of Dave Linnett and me struggling to play two chords together with him in the youth centre in Church

Lane, Kettering, ten years previously and to now be On Tour In Berlin was good for my self-esteem, to say the least.

We played great in Berlin, but we were playing great every night. There was no such thing as a bad gig in Special-land; everyone gave of their best. It was righteous toil. Thanks to some adept promotion from Chrysalis, we entered Europe as fully fledged pop stars – hit record/ album, the whole deal. We didn't have to do the little clubs/back of a van routine; we went straight into the theatre/large club circuit. The audiences were no less enthusiastic than those in England. Europe seemed to take to us immediately.

Support on this tour was provided by The Urge, Coventry's answer to Joy Division even. They had Squad's Billy Little on drums. He could actually play drums pretty well by then. The band was focused on the vocals of Dave Wankling, a particularly charismatic performer, and guitarist Kevin Harrison's wife, Linda. They'd just signed to Arista and put a couple of very credible singles out in 1980. I've always thought it was important who you took on tour with you. Some record companies insist that you take someone from their roster of acts along, whether you like them or not. Some headlining acts 'sell' the support spot, which means that struggling bands end up paying to play to someone else's audience for three-quarters of an hour if you were lucky, using only half the lights and a monitor engineer *if* you bung him twenty quid a show. I painfully recall spending two weeks of what can only be described as purgatory in 1984 supporting Queen (I was in General Public at the time). We played Wembley and the NEC in Birmingham and felt we were treated like lepers by practically everybody – had to wait until everyone else had eaten to see whether there was enough food for us to get a meal and then 'died like a louse in a Russian's beard' (as Max Wall once said) out on the big stage. We were offered the European dates. We declined. In The Specials we always paid for our support bands' accommodation and made room for them to travel on our coach. It seemed extremely mean-spirited to do otherwise.

In Bremen, we did another Euro pop TV extravaganza, along with Madness, who had just released 'My Girl', Rockabilly rebels Matchbox and the very surly-looking Sugarhill Gang, who, despite their New York cool, were intrigued by some of the scantily clad females who aspired to be Euro-disco sensations.

The best thing to do in these situations is to enjoy yourself. The more ludicrous you are on the stage, the more fun you have and the MORE PEOPLE REMEMBER YOU. We massacred 'Message to You' and joined Madness in a spontaneous display of rockabillying in front of Matchbox, bodging TV cameras and being generally unruly. Oh, what fun to be a pop star!

I suppose we got our coach fixed, as I can't remember any hassles for the remainder of the trip. For the last week, we were joined by some of our 'superfans', namely Perry and Gary, and took possession of a finished copy of our video for 'Too Much Too Young', our live EP, which was being released on 15 January. In Hanover, we played to a barn full of English Army squaddies, who, in true English-youth-abroad style, drank far too much and reminded us how well behaved the European audiences were. After the show a load of them came backstage and expected us to treat them like long-lost relatives. I made my excuses and left. In Hamburg we played a storming gig at the Markt-halle. I know this because some enterprising young Hamburger recorded it and put it out as a bootleg. The first of many, as it goes.

Our road crew had been increased by the inclusion of Rob 'Our Kid' Gambino. This was an attempt to make Rex and Trevor comply with rock 'n' roll professional standards. Rob had joined the 2-Tone tour the previous November. He had 'milk-bottle-bottom' glasses and spoke with a lilting 'oop North' voice which was mimicked mercilessly by the band. He became the band's 'Mr Fixit' and was to figure large in the band's mythology over the next year or so. More later . . .

I have a vague memory of playing a heaving Paradiso in Amsterdam and Frank Murray having to kick a door down backstage to allow us entry, there being a tremendous ticketless crowd round the front. The Paradiso was a building used by the Germans to execute Dutch Jews during the Second World War and was now a rock 'n' roll concert hall. Odd, very odd. Great gig, though.

The last show on the trip was in Cologne, which would give us one day at home before we set off for America. Chrysalis chartered two eight-seater aircraft to fly us home on the night of the gig, giving us an extra day. We were told not to worry, as it *wouldn't* come off our royalties. Jerry refused point blank. He was not happy flying at the best of times, and the thought of a tiny two-engined light aircraft made him look ill. He went on the bus with Alfie. As it turned out, he'd made the correct choice. Over France we ran into some nasty weather, and the limited supply of alcohol provided by the airline was soon consumed. We were thrown around the sky for a good half an hour, and an oppressive white-knuckle silence reigned in the cockpit. If anyone had started singing the 'Dambusters March', I would have punched them in the face.

We landed in Birmingham and swore we would never do the 'small plane' job again. We didn't. At least it never came off our royalties. (Of course it bloody did!)

8

AMERIKA

America had always held a fascination for me. Musically, it was where it all came from. If there hadn't been blues and country music, there wouldn't have been ská, reggae and rock 'n' roll, with all its subdivisions and cul-de-sacs. There wouldn't have been any Searchers, Beatles, Rolling Stones, Kinks or Small Faces to fire the imagination in my pirate radio days. America was where it still lived: Tamla, Stax and, more recently, Steely Dan and the mighty Little Feat. It was almost like a pilgrimage.

Thing was, we were going with an attitude. Our 'punk credentials', which were somewhat dubious, given our mean age, meant that we were supposed to disavow most pre-1977 music from both sides of the Atlantic – 'I'm so bored with the USA', and all that – despite the fact we looked back there for inspiration. It was something that I always felt uneasy about but seemed to be able to side-step in the interviews I gave.

We were at the top of our tree in the UK, the bee's knees, the shark's pyjamas. We had proved our worth over two years of shows and a meteoric rise in popularity. This meant very little to the majority of Americans, save fashion victims and the terminally hip – and I've never

liked posers and hangers-on. I got the impression
(especially in New York) that we were only fêted because
of our high media profile, rather than because of our ability
to reduce full dance halls to heaps of perspiration. Also,
there were those amongst us who enjoyed being fêted by
fashion victims and the terminally hip. A fair proportion of
them were female, and an equally fair proportion of them
had some drugs on them. There was an air of falseness
about it.

I desperately wanted to go, but I didn't know if anyone
would like us. I knew we were good, but I thought the
whole 'wrack 'n' roll' (Foreigner, Journey, Fleetwood Mac)
American music scene would mean we wouldn't make a
dent. That and the enormity of the place.

I kept a diary of our first American tour. I've reproduced it here in its almost original form. Some of the
stuff in it I don't remember at all, but there again there
is stuff I recall that wasn't included when I wrote it. It has
a wonderful naivety about it and, as a book, is one of my
most treasured possessions.

The plan was to start in New York, do our own show at
swanky Hurrah's, then go down to New Orleans, where we
would open for The Police, who were doing a 'secondary
markets' tour, which was basically a diagonal trek across
America, New Orleans to Seattle, taking in Oklahoma,
Denver and Salt Lake City. We would then accompany
Sting and the boys to Vancouver, then Portland. From
there we would go down to Los Angeles and work our way
back east, finishing in New York in early March. It came
straight off the back of the European tour too, but we were
young, we were reckless, we were foolish, we had more
adrenaline per square inch of body space than we'd ever

had in our lives! Adventure! Go west, young man! And we did.

We managed to get one day off after returning from our European trip and flew out on the Thursday (24 January). By that time, I was well into a really horrible cold; Lemsips every four hours. I felt like death. The Coventry contingent caught a train down, and we were hassled by hordes of school children on the way. Nice, but, er, not what I would have liked. We were taking Rex and Trevor (our crew), Lin Scoffin (lighting engineer), Frank Murray, Dave Jordan, Rick Rogers, Rob Gambino (aka 'Our Kid') and John Jostins. John was a friend of Jerry from his college days. He had been to the States before, and we felt it was good to have some 'insider knowledge' on our side and an extra pair of hands. I was glad he was on board. We flew cattle-class.

When we got to JFK airport, I heard a voice over the tannoy announce, 'Would Mr David Bowie please ring fifty-eight,' or something or other. It was like a movie, or a rock 'n' roll movie, or something. It was like something. It didn't seem to be like reality, but as I was full of this cold and a few drinks, it's not particularly surprising. Apparently, the evening we got in, JJ and I went to Max's Kansas City – renowned Andy Warhol/Velvet Underground/New York Dolls kind of club – where we saw The Pin-Ups and Cathy and The Escorts. I have no recollection of it at all.

Friday 25 January: Press conference and first show. Photosession at midday for the soar-away *Sun* (putting a smile on the face of Britain!) and then off to Hurrah's for our press conference, arriving 2.30 p.m. Bit of a farce, as we're more interested in the hired equipment that has been brought in for us. Still, it goes on, but everyone seems to clam up.

The sound check, however, is an absolute abortion. Photographers crowd all over us and start to piss us off. We have hired in some additional monitors for the show, but I think the guys operating them are complete prats. We have *never* had such an awful sound on stage, even when we played at Mr George's or the Heath Hotel. We spend five hours(!) trying to get an acceptable sound, and all our nerves are shot; coupled with the jet-lag, everyone is totally wired. Travel back to the hotel, and I try to get some sleep before the gig. I can't. Luckily, Neville has some Dexedrine tablets, and that seems to do the trick. Our stage time is 1.15 a.m., this being New York, I suppose. A fault is found in the monitor system. (Odd, that!)

I feel like death on stage and have great difficulty putting any effort into it. The sound on stage seems terrible, and Dick and Rico can't hear themselves. Talking Heads soundman Frank Gallagher, who we met in London a month or two ago, is at the gig and he attempts to sort the on-stage sound out. Jerry insists that we do encore after encore. I think this is a mistake, but we do them anyway.

Afterwards, people come up and tell me how incredible, amazing and fantastic we are, while I cough myself stupid. I can't believe them somehow. The gig sucked.

Return to the hotel at 4.00 a.m. and I still can't sleep – the Dexedrine perhaps – but we did it; our first US gig.

Saturday 26 January: New Orleans. Our plane from Newark is an hour late. (Just as well!) We do a 2½-hour flight to New Orleans, clocks back an hour. The difference in climate was the first thing that hit me. It's very humid, and it felt great walking around in shirt sleeves. My cold seems to be disappearing slowly, but there again I seem to have given it to everyone else.

Straight from the airport to the gig, via a couple of rented cars and a night-time cruise into New Orleans. Over the past three days I've had so much to take in, I don't seem to be able to make value judgements any more. The gig is at the Warehouse. We get there as The Police (for it is they who we open for) finish their sound check. Gear on, doors open, no sound check and on we go.

It seems just like the days on The Clash tour, but I get the impression we're too complacent and nowhere near as professional as we can be. Rod's guitar is out of tune towards the end of the set and, instead of changing it for one that *is* in tune, he just turns it up full and makes a racket. I think it's selfish. I'm pretty furious and sound off at everyone afterwards in the dressing room. The gig, however, seemed to go over well. I stay and watch The Police, who do really well, but a lot more rock 'n' roll than they are in the UK. They have the whole audience participation/call and response thing down. I wait with Gervaise, Chris Poole (Chrysalis press officer) and some A&M people (The Police are on A&M Records). Gervais Soeurouge is a photographer, an American, who took photos of us in England the previous year. I don't know whether she is here in a professional capacity, or just hanging out. Eleven o'clock at night on the last Saturday in January and I'm in my shirt sleeves. January – unheard of. I finally reach our motel and check in. The guys from The Police rush past and out into the night. They've obviously been here before. I know that I go on about being ill and all that, but with all the adrenaline, it's impossible to go to bed. In the bar I spend at least twenty minutes drinking a piña colada out of a glass the size of a goldfish bowl.

Bourbon Street is the night life; crowded at midnight, it's full of live music, jazz, blues, country, cajun and people. Gervais is wearing skin-tight leather trousers (sorry, pants) and turns an awful lot of heads. We end up at the Café du Monde, where we get coffee and fabulous French doughnuts . . . Mmmm. I might just wake up any moment now.

Sunday 27 January: it said 'day off' on the itinerary. Everybody gets up at 10.30 a.m., except Jerry, who never went to bed. He arrives back at the hotel some time during the morning and jumps fully clothed into the swimming pool. I have an idea he's waited all his life to do that. Breakfast is paid for by Chris Poole. Chrysalis expense account, aka our money. (Chris is over here with *NME* journalist Paul Rambali and photographer Joe Stevens.) Last night there was a carload of kids who came all the way from Texas to see us support The Police. They said they drove eight hours to get here. They stayed over and came to the hotel this morning. I'm rather humbled. I wouldn't drive 400 miles to see a pop group play for forty-five minutes. It lifts my spirits after all my tirades about 'false' America. I know it's a day off, but we do a photo session. I notice we're staying over the road from the Louis Armstrong Memorial Park. Last night Jerry went to Tipitina's, a famous New Orleans club, and saw Professor Longhair. I bet that was good. I spend the afternoon on a paddle steamer trip up the Mississippi – great. The evening is spent with Rick Rogers and Linda Steiner, who is from Chrysalis in Los Angeles – more expense-account meals. Back down Bourbon Street in the evening; amazing. Bar bands playing Crusaders' tunes immaculately, but looking so bored. I saw three amazing bands tonight, bought a sparkly silver bowler hat and haven't enjoyed myself, felt so good, for ages. I hope we can come back here again.

Monday 28 January: Norman, Oklahoma. Up early. No breakfast. Down to reception, where I forget to hand in my room key – again! I can hear Rico complaining loudly about something. I don't need this, neither does anyone else at this time of day. If you want the breakfast, you have to get up on time. If you want to get up on time ... We scoot off to New Orleans airport and catch a plane to Oklahoma City, via Fort Worth, with micro-seconds to spare.

Arrive 1.15 p.m. and head for Norman (a town just south of Oklahoma City) where we check into a real Holiday Inn! (My first – but not my last!) The Police sold out two shows here but, for reasons I never found out, have cancelled. So, as we're here, we're going to play for free for disgruntled Police fans. 'Now folks, the band you wanted to see isn't playing, but don't go away! Instead, we've got a band from England that you've never heard of, who don't play rock 'n' roll – The Specials!'

This is going to be a peculiar one. Norman, Oklahoma, doesn't exactly sound like the rock 'n' roll capital of the world now, does it? We also have what seems to me to be the world's dumbest PA crew and ineffectual monitors. ('Are they following us around for the whole tour?' I ask Frank. He shrugs and mutters something like, 'That's what it's like out here.' Not the encouraging words I wanted to hear from our tour manager, but, in retrospect, the truth.)

Sound check is a worthless exercise, but guess what? The gig is a stormer! We get a 600-capacity seated venue (surely it was bigger than that!) on its feet and dancing furiously – due mainly to 'Concrete Jungle' (our rock 'n' roll song, even). Brad's playing is great. His improvisation is the most adventurous yet, especially on 'Too Hot'. Somehow he manages to buy a complete new set of cymbals for $350, about half what he'd pay in the UK – jammy bastard. After the gig, Brad and

I end up at a club called Walter Mitty's, which tonight is featuring extremely unpleasant-looking women taking their clothes off. No thanks. Back to the Holiday Inn and bed.

Tuesday 29 January: I have a record at number one!
I'm awakened by a phone call from Rick Rogers, our manager. The 'Too Much Too Young' EP has gone to number one! WHAT! I don't believe it. Last week it was number fifteen, but *this*! It's ironic that we're half-way across the world in a country that hasn't heard of us and have the number-one-selling single in the UK. It would be cool to be in Coventry right now. I don't believe this; the feeling is tremendous and difficult to put into words. Indestructible is the nearest, but it's not really what I want to say. We did a good gig last night, too. Needless to say, the mood is pretty upbeat as we get up and don't have breakfast before our ritual panic-drive to the local airport. We are flying to Denver. During the flight I am sat next to Paul, the *NME* journalist, and, while pontificating, I spill a glass of red wine all over my trousers. I don't believe in fairies, but if I did, I'm sure mine would be sitting on my shoulder, whispering in my ear, 'You're being a prat again, Horace!'

Denver is covered in snow, a radical change from New Orleans, so it's back on with the woolly jumpers. We're staying at a Ramada Inn. Its catchphrase is 'Nice'. They have t-shirts that say 'Nice' on them. Dick is always going round saying, 'Nice.' Dick buys one. Nice. Dave Jordan, Lynval, Frank and I go off for some retail therapy. I end up with two pairs of Levi's for £8.50(!), some Converse baseball boots and, on DJ's recommendation, a compression pedal for my bass. This has cleaned me out!

The TV in America is awful. The programmes are crap, and the adverts, funny for the first couple of days, are now irritating me. So I listen to the radio. It's five years behind – Pink Floyd, Jethro Tull, The Eagles. Radio KBPI plays five seconds of 'Do the Dog' as a trailer advertising our gig tomorrow with The Police at the Rainbow Theatre. We got a telegram from the Madnesses, thanking us for beating them to number one!

Wednesday 30 January: Denver. I spent a day in the wonderful world of interviews. Taped interview with Pete Somebody or Other from KCOG (or something like that) then a live phone-in for another radio station that began with a K. This was great fun as I got to play some of my favourites: 'Roadrunner' by Junior Walker, 'All Down the Line' off *Exile on Main Street* and 'London Calling' by The Clash, and talking to fans on the radio. It would appear some Americans like us after all. Then it's back to the hotel, and Brad and I hold court with Carolyn and Sue from the *Not New Wave News*, a local college paper. We, or rather Brad, puts them straight with a long dissertation on reggae, and, before we know it, it's off to the gig. It's been a good day so far, and a sound check with a competent monitor engineer cools every-one out. The gig is great. We do two encores. The Police don't start off too good (thunder stolen perhaps) but get there in the end. After the gig, a fair proportion of us end up at some artist's palatial loft, where a party is in full swing. I distinctly remember someone saying, 'This is the third-best college in the country to go to if – and it's a big if – you're majoring in Hotel Management.' Hmm.

Thursday, 31 January: Salt Lake City. I'm a bit pissed writing this, sitting on the bog in room 263 at the Holiday Inn in Salt Lake City. We got up remarkably early to get here. The gig was disastrous. Crappy PA, but we manage an encore. The Police start real sloppy, but once they get over the dreadful sound, they start to get better. The rest of our mob leave except Brad and me, who hang around to watch the show. Brad is really tired, but instead of being professional (my favourite excuse for an early night), he stays up. Hey – and me too! We're sharing hotel rooms – perhaps I'm cooling him out, and he's bringing me out of myself. Mr Stay Up Late vs Mr Go To Bed Early. We shall see. Anyway, I do an interview with Barbara Somebody or Other for *Newsweek* magazine. Stewart Copeland drops by and starts talking about politics and the world situation. I'm sorry, Stewart, but to me it was boring, boring, boring. To make matters worse, we have to be up at 8.30 a.m.

Friday 1 February: Seattle. Alarm call at 7.30 a.m. I go straight back to sleep. I don't think Brad even heard it. Luckily there's another call about an hour later from Barbara Wassername from *Newsweek*, thanking me for the interview. Thanks for thanking me – you're welcome. Have a nice day! Guess what! We all get up on time and actually make the 9:35 a.m. flight to Seattle. The Police and their crew are on the same flight. We're starting to get chummy with them. The plane lands in Seattle 11.35, but we have to put our watches back one hour. Time is starting to lose its meaning. The flight in was great. Hughes Air West 727. The view as we get above the first cloud line out of Salt Lake is amazing. The Rockies are there on the left and, as the cloud breaks, a maroon expanse. I thought I was seeing things, but it was definitely maroon. Then the mountains and snow again as we begin the descent into Seattle. I am so tired.

The hotel is the Edgewater Inn, right on the water, where you can fish out of your hotel window. This place is infamous in rock 'n' roll mythology, thanks to Led Zeppelin, and documented in all its rather sordid detail by Frank Zappa (bless him) in a quaint little ditty entitled 'Mudshark'. And we're here in the middle of it. Hard rock Southern boogie boys Molly Hatchet are staying here too, which could be an interesting combination. I am obviously staying on the wrong side of the hotel, as all I've got out of my window is a railway line, which is used to transport stuff out to the docks. The noise of the freight cars, although muse for both blues and country singers, means I can't sleep, despite the dark circles under my eyes. Reminds me of a Tom and Jerry cartoon.

Our equipment was flown here, but not all of it has arrived, so there's a mad panic to hire in the missing bits. Jerry's organ is one of the items missing. Consequently, we are running late, but a combination of 'Well, what's new' and overtiredness means that the band, myself included, don't give a fuck. 'Do you want a sound check?' Frank asks. 'Why?' replies Terry. He's right. We can play these tunes in our sleep, which is pretty much what happens. People come up to us afterwards and tell us we're great, but the mood I'm in doesn't make me appreciate their enthusiasm. I mean, they ain't exactly gonna go out of their way to tell us we're shit, are they? Sting and I talk bass guitars. He has a go on my Telecaster bass and says he doesn't like it as much as his fretless Ibanez (which weighs a ton!). 'Frets – they get in the way.' Jerry is pretty contemptuous of The Police and calls their bass player 'String'. Mr Sumner apparently walked off, snarling. I imagine him thinking, snotty support bands – they get in the way.

Backstage after the show, Lynval and Rick are drinking themselves unconscious – loudly. I head back to the hotel and spend a couple of hours with the guys from Molly Hatchet, who're on tour with ZZ Top. 'Good Ole Boys' in a kind of Dukes of Hazzard style. Beards, big hats and check shirts. Some of the guys obviously don't like me, but I end up talking to Bob, their crew boss, you know, guitars, amps – muso stuff. It cooled me out after the fraught time back at the gig, and it was good talking with different kinds of people. Up to the room, and Brad hasn't come back yet. He's going to burn himself out soon, but he played good tonight, though.

It was sad to see descendants of Native Americans drunk on the sidewalks.

Sunday 3 February: Vancouver. Right! I suppose it had to happen sooner or later. Horace drinks a lot and falls over. I'm attempting to write this in the W. C. Fields bar at the hotel. Kind of appropriate, really.

Yesterday, Seattle, we all got antibiotic shots for our colds from this old doctor, who wore galoshes for some reason. No alcohol for three days. That night, however, Chrysalis were hosting a party for us after the first of our two gigs with The Police in Vancouver. The gig was great: 2,700-capacity hall – sold out. We did two encores. The adrenaline boost, coupled with a few beers after the show and the antibiotics, then the Chrysalis party and all of a sudden, I am indestructible. Number one, Top of the Pops. I can drink anything and everything, and proceed to.

Various Police road crew, Lynval, Brad, a couple of A&M record company guys and I hit the town. I vaguely remember emptying a full ashtray over someone's meal, and hanging out of the back of a station wagon, driving round town singing at the top of my voice. Apparently I got in at 7 in the morning, had five hours' sleep, and I feel dreadful. This is not going to be a regular occurrence.

The promotion goes on forever, and at 2.30 p.m., The Specials are at a record store, signing autographs and copies of their LP. The US cover of our LP is the other way round from the UK version – the back picture is on the front and vice versa. Odd. The 'in-store' as it is called, is nicely low-key, and I'm soon back at the hotel, where I get two hours of uninterrupted sleep. Back to the gig, where we play what in my opinion is our best gig yet on this trip. After our set, Brad and I check out Stewart Copeland's playing from backstage. Brad is a big fan, and I can see why. The effects of my alcohol excess from yesterday are beginning to show, and DJ and I get a cab back to the hotel while the rest of the guys go to appear on a cable TV show and apparently cause mayhem live on air. Gee whiz!

We seem to have caused quite a stir here in Vancouver. Consequently we're playing a hastily organized show on the Monday, at a dance hall called the Commodore. While we were all busy playing and being number one and exhausting ourselves, the logistics side of things is not doing too well. We have three crew – four, if you include John Jostins – and no one knows how to tune our guitars. Rex and ET don't like driving the gear and want to be with Neville, where the action is. This is the big problem. I like the idea of friends being with us. They can usually tell you when you're being a prat, whereas 'professional' road crew guys just laugh and collect their wages. However, if we're going to put on good shows, we are going to need 'professional' crew. It is a dilemma, one which infuriates Frank Murray, who is starting to have less and less time for Rex and Trevor. It makes for an uneasy atmosphere. JJ has a go at looking after the guitars, but you can't expect someone with no experience to just turn up and be a guitar roadie. Rick is aware of all this, but his priority is the band and keeping us on the road and trying to keep our heads above water. The roller-coaster ride seems more like a whirlpool, and we have another month to go.

Monday 4 February: still in Vancouver. Well, at least I got some sleep, and a good lie-in after the previous night's excesses. A trip to the mountains has been planned, but I stay behind with Terry to do an interview. The Commodore is about half a mile down the road, so after the interview, Terry and I take a leisurely walk down to the gig, taking in Army Surplus stores, second-hand shops and a McDonald's.

The Canadians seem a lot more in touch with the UK than the Americans. When they find out you're from England, they ask what part, and how the Sky Blues are doing, and what's going on with the government. They seem to take a genuine interest, rather than all the 'have a nice day' stuff over the border.

Our show at the Commodore is another good one. The audience are real enthusiastic. A lot of them saw us at The Police shows and knew that we needed a dance hall to be appreciated. The club had a sprung dance floor, which was cool for us, but made DJ a little seasick behind the mixing desk. I made some pretty silly mistakes musically. After the show, a TV camera is set up backstage, and I'm doing an interview when Rod, Jerry and Terry come in and fuck it up. Thanks, guys. I seem to do more than my fair share of interviews – usually the crappy local papers – but they're the grass-roots ones, and it bugs me when these people get treated badly by pop stars. Rod, Jerry and Terry never acted like this in England. I thought we were all about talking to people, not taking the piss out of them. Or perhaps I'm taking myself too seriously.

Anyway, Monday's nightclubbing takes place at a club called the Luv Affair, which kinda says it all, really. Terry has picked up an admirer who, despite some withering Hall sarcasm, will not give up. This poor unfortunate is accompanied by a friend. We start to talk. Her name is Bobbie. I think I'm in love. Her friend finally got the message and they both leave. Terry and I order pizza and eat quietly.

Tuesday 6 February: Portland. Up, out of bed, rouse a snoring Brad and off to Portland for our last Police show. At reception there is a message for me. Bobbie has left me her phone number!

The flight to Portland is disastrous. We're late (just for a change) and not all of us get our boarding passes. We are all, however, on the plane. The stewardess wants to see everybody's boarding pass and threatens to chuck us all off and get the cops. Frank leaves the plane to be 'detained', and we're off. To make matters worse, Brad and Rico have lost a suitcase each. Oh no! *Anybody* but Rico, please! He, more than anyone, is not happy with all these early-morning departures. Terry and ET have had their suitcases trashed, but at least they've got them. The plan is to wait at the airport till Frank gets in from Vancouver, hopefully with the missing suitcases.

Quite apart from all that, The Police have pulled the gig tonight. Something to do with Sting's voice being shot. Right. New plan. We're not going to be playing in Portland, as there's no time to advertise a show, and no promoter prepared to put a gig on at such short notice. So we're going straight down to Los Angeles. We hang about the airport, build a fort out of suitcases and pretend to be mental patients (not difficult).

I manage to call Bobbie, and we make plans for her to come down to visit in Los Angeles. This could be good. Brad says, 'I hereby swear that from now on it will be a clean, healthy, well-organized tour.' Honest. He did.

Roddy also said, 'It's fun flying through the clouds,' which seemed odd, as the flight to Los Angeles was very bumpy – I saw a missile being launched, saw the second stage burn out. Pretty incredible. The flight into LAX is spectacular, and it feels good to be back in shirt-sleeves territory. The car drive to the hotel through Beverley Hills – all those street signs that I've only ever seen on TV – and here we are at the legendary Tropicana Motel on Santa Monica Boulevard, palm trees and everything.

The room Brad and I have is real smutty. It has a kitchen but no soap, knives or forks. It's brilliant.

Later on it's up and out with the gang. The Rainbow Lounge – a rock 'n' roll hangout where we meet Sting and Stewart Copeland plus Police crew – and then on to 'Flippers, The Boogie Palace', where Chrysalis have put on a do for us, with a big black and white check cake. A bit embarrassing, really. Not our style at all. The place is a roller-skating rink with a stage in the middle. Music is provided by the rather awful Leroy and The Lifters: 'We'd like to say hi to a bunch of English rockers called The Specials.' Oh Christ, this is the Los Angeles I've read and cringed about. Anyway, Leroy, we're not rockers. If anything, we're mods! I had a go on some roller skates, but was not too successful, although JJ knew his stuff. Anyway, I must have enjoyed myself – I threw up when I got back.

Wednesday 6 and Thursday 7 February: Two days off! I cannot believe this. It is 10.00 a.m. It is boiling hot, the clearest sky I've ever seen, and a breeze to keep you cool. It's obvious why everyone has a car. The heat knackers you if you try walking anywhere. Rick and I head off to Chrysalis, where we meet up with Linda Steiner, who we met in New Orleans and is starting to figure us out. More expense-account lunches. Later, a cruise down Sunset Boulevard, where we stop at the Chinese Theater, check out the film stars' personalized paving slabs (!), and I find that Cary Grant's hands were bigger than mine. Back to Chrysalis, where staff are having a 'promotional party' for the release of The Selecter album. Lots of people going round going, 'Whoo! All right!' Strikes me as weird, but what doesn't? They've got to go out and convince record retailers and radio-station people that this is a great product, sorry, record. It's their job – it pays their mortgage. It's the business side of the music business. They probably do the same thing when there's a new Pat Benetar album. It dawns on me that these people are being paid to like me, to like The Specials. Some of them probably do, but . . .

This is it, isn't it? There's a programme on the TV when I get back to the hotel. It's called *The Guinness Game*, where people try to break stupid world records, and punters bet money on whether or not they'll do it. One bloke caught arrows (from a bow); one bloke ran 100 feet dressed in a suit of armour; another bloke did twenty-six backward somersaults, wearing skis, off a trampoline, and someone else skipped on a tight rope, 33 feet above the ground. There was another programme, called *Real People*, the idea being to show the rest of LA that there *are* some, somewhere. This place is totally out of control.

In the evening, the majority of us head off to the Starwood, which on a Wednesday night (yes, it is Wednesday!) plays host to Rodney Bingenheimer's New Wave Disco. RB is another rock 'n' roll Los Angeles legend. The self-styled 'Mayor of Sunset Strip' has been playing what is hip on the radio since 1976. Recently, he has been playing 2-Tone solidly on his radio shows, and this is Chrysalis's way of paying back – the personal appearance. This evening he's playing wall-to-wall Specials. Now, don't get me wrong. I don't dislike our album. It's just that I dream about these tunes, and even have nightmares about them. The cringe factor is high amongst the band. As I look around, trying to find somewhere to hide, I see a tall bloke standing by himself up in one corner, nursing a bottle of beer. It's David Byrne. Now, I'm a big Talking Heads fan. The guitar figure on the end of 'A Song to Change Your Mind' off the *Fear of Music* LP is terrific, even though it was probably played by Jerry Harrison. I'm a fan again, and get all nervous – David Byrne, wow. Thing is, he looks real nervous, too, standing there, clutching his Budweiser, and would probably clam up if I went over to him. What would I say? 'Hi, I'm Horace from The Specials and I really like your music'? That would sound really crap. So I never said anything. I like to think he would have wanted me not to talk to him. If he had known I was there. Hmm. February 6th. The day I never met David Byrne!

Friday 8 February: a gig! Four nights at the Whisky.
Yesterday, Brad, Rick, Lin, Lyn and I went to Disneyland, 'the happiest place on Earth'. My cynicism rears its ugly head. A patriotic/propagandist funfair where people are paid to smile. They have people dressed as robots, and robots dressed as people. I liked it, but didn't like it, if you know what I mean. I'm trying to put what we do into the scheme of things here, and I don't like the conclusions I'm arriving at.

Tonight we're doing what we're good at: playing music. (Is this what paranoia looks like?) Whatever. Jus' play music! This is what we're here for after all. The Whisky a Go Go is pretty pokey. This stage reminds me of the Nashville in Fulham. Someone from Chrysalis had painted the outside of the club in black and white check. I thought it looked cool, but Jerry hated it. It looks like it could get pretty hot in here. More photo sessions, more interviews – I did three this morning. The deal here is two shows per night – which we've never done before – for four consecutive nights. The first show is *the* show. Record company, media people, press and, if we're lucky, a few fans.

The show is shit, real shit. Monitors completely fucked for Brad, guitars too loud on stage, and I feel like someone has put something in my drink. Really! Afterwards Lynval and I have a slanging match, me shouting that he's playing too loud and ruining it for everyone else, him telling me to shut up and jus' play music, man. DJ backs me up and says, somewhat more diplomatically than me, that Rod and Lyn are too loud on stage. I am in no mood to talk to the media circus that comes by to meet us. The second show is much better, not up to Vancouver standards, but more like The Specials.

The psychological effect of performing two shows is not good. It is impossible to conserve energy while playing this music. Energy is what the whole show is about. To do this once a night – and we're back playing for one and a half hours, as opposed to supporting, when we only played for forty-five minutes – is knackering enough, but to do it twice a night is potentially debilitating. During the encores on the second show, ET sprains his ankle rescuing Lynval, who has jumped into the audience. JJ covers for the next few gigs.

Tonight's (and tomorrow's) support are The Go-Gos – a five-piece girl band. Not a novelty act; they have some great tunes, new-wave-pop-sixties kind of vibe. Their drummer is solid and they can all play real good. Their rhythm guitarist is twenty-one, but doesn't look a day older than fourteen. She has cuteness down to a fine art and plays a lovely solid-body Rickenbacker guitar. Very cool.

I never find out how, but we finally acquire a guitar roadie, a chap called Steve Hutchinson, whose 'regular gig' is with

Pat Benetar (a Chrysalis connection perhaps?). He's a big Texas boy (pronounced bohyy) and he's good at the job, as well as being easy to get along with. Just as well, as both Roddy and Lynval have gone out and bought another guitar each.

Backstage, the *après*-gig thing is pretty desperate. I could have pulled two girls this evening, but they were just so dumb!

'You guys were Great!'

'Er . . . thanks.'

'Where do you get your suits?'

'Gosford Street.'

'Wow! That's really neat!'

'Er . . . thanks.'

I love playing the shows, but all the stuff that goes with it I could do without.

Saturday 9 February: second verse, same as the first. I got back from the gig at 3.30 a.m. I used to think that was late. Or even early. Now it's just 'the time I get in'. Am I losing my battle with time or am I just side-stepping it? Perhaps I can get my manager to order me some more.

'Rick! I want you to get Chrysalis to find me at least four more hours each day!'

'OK, Horace, but it'll have to come off your royalties!'

I do absolutely nothing during the day, but we all get up to the gig early and work on a new tune of Roddy's.

The first show is a good one. Not too over the top – pacing ourselves perhaps. We get the *NME*. There's our picture on the cover and a massive article on the centre pages. Is it nausea, or homesickness? I do an interview with a pretty jerky bloke from UCLA, who seems more interested in his

153

own psychosis than the band. Interestingly, he says he likes living in LA – you can keep it, sunshine!

And then, before you know it, the second show, which starts good, but gets weird when Terry's mike, and subsequent replacement ones, refuse to work. Everything seems to be a struggle as we exchange glances with one another on stage and we start wondering what we are doing here. The audiences have all been great, really enthusiastic – too enthusiastic even. I'm left wondering if every band gets this reception. Paranoia – nah, mate! cynicism more like. I just hope we can keep it together for the next two nights. I end up in the legendary Ben Franks diner with a load of fans who, despite my 'false Californian cynicism', are a lot of fun. Back to the hotel at 5.20 a.m., where Brad and Rod are 'hanging out' in my room with two girls. I'm not in the mood for this and crawl loudly into bed, where sleep beckons. Apparently the soirée (or should that be the matinée) breaks up. They seemed such *nice* girls. Jerry met Captain Beefheart last night apparently. Fast and Bulbous!*

Yesterday was a blur. It was a Sunday, and I slept until 2 p.m. Had 'brunch' for the first time in my life at Dukes, the coffee shop next door, moped around a bit and then did the gigs in the evening. They went pretty well. Afterwards, I ended up in a car with Dick, Rob Gambino and two awful girls who took us to a club which, when we finally got there, was closed. At 3.30 a.m. Dick and I ended up at Cantors, a twenty-four-hour Jewish deli on Fairfax Street. Nice food and a smattering of 'interesting' late-nite Los Angeles people. I think I saw Rodney Bingenheimer.

---

* Captain Beefheart reference. Check out *Trout Mask Replica*, it never did P. J. Harvey any harm.

Monday 11 February: Los Angeles – the last two shows!
More interviews today, Ben Brooks from *Collage* magazine and Jeff Silberman from *Music Connection*. Both asked
exactly the same questions. I gave exactly the same
answers.

Connie Clark, the Go-Gos' roadie, dropped by and very
kindly trimmed my hair. Thanks, Connie. The support spot
for the next two nights will be provided by The Alley Cats.
Dick and I do some shopping. He seems to have comman-
deered one of our rented cars. We hit the second-hand stores
on Melrose Avenue. I buy two bowling shirts. One is too big,
the other is too small – oh well. Presents for somebody back
home.

The final shows are good, the second one being 'extra'
good. Terry does a real good Amerika-type showbiz intro to
'Nite Klub', even down to The Specialettes on 'fancy footwork
and funny dresses'. (These were some fans who'd been to
every show who were invited up on stage.) Backstage, Rico
was talking patois to a little Chinese-looking guy, who was
obviously Jamaican. It was Phil Chen.

Who's Phil Chen, you ask. Well, for a start he was
Rod Stewart's bass player – a giant among the four-string
fellowship. He played on Jeff Beck's *Blow by Blow* album,
which was the bench-mark for any self-respecting muso in
the late seventies. I tried my best not to make a fool of
myself, i.e. kept my mouth shut. Cool, Phil Chen, Dick
and I ended up back at Cantors, and for a moment I
thought I was Jack Kerouac . . . or in an Edward Hopper
painting . . . well, almost. What a relief. Not so much the
end of the two shows a night, but the itchy feeling of being
in the same place all the time is starting to drive me mad.
The Pink Floyd are in town doing *The Wall* (yawn!). Their
crew are staying here and some of them are throwing things

155

and people in the swimming pool, which has brought the police round. Not cool.

Some trivial facts:

i. *Our album is number two in Austria, having sold 592 copies.*
ii. *Our album has gone straight into the Canadian Charts at number eleven, selling 9,000 copies.*
iii. *'Gangsters' has sold 140,000 copies in France.*

Today's quote: 'I'm not some dumb airhead groupie' (a dumb airhead groupie).

It's worth mentioning here that the 'two shows a night' four-night run at the Whisky a Go Go has been mentioned a few times in retrospect by members of the band as the last time The Specials functioned as 'The Specials' – that is, as a unified, cohesive unit.

The band that was now to slog through the interminable expanses of America had changed from the band that had conquered the Top Rank dance floors of England five months previously. We had run out of energy. Tiredness had made us lose compassion, not just for the people we met, but eventually for one another.

LIFE IN THE BUS LANE

Thursday 12 February: we drive to San Francisco in the bus. To bed at 6.00 a.m. and up at 11. It took me nearly an hour to get everything into my suitcase. I don't know how I did it. I'm knackered. I remembered to take my key back to reception this time and, when I handed it in, the guy behind the desk gives me a piece of paper. 'Oh, this came for you a couple of days ago.'

Bobbie had called. Oh well.

THE BUS. Now! I have mixed reservations about the bus. It's a 'Silver Eagle' Greyhound bus type of affair, with two 'living' compartments, separated by sleeping compartments – twelve bunks. There's a toilet that you're not allowed to shit in and a wash hand basin. The front living area has a fridge, a small sink, bench seats and a table. This is going to be our mode of transport until we reach New York on the other side of the country in three weeks' time. It is garish beyond description. Olive green carpeting on the floor and walls and matching Chesterfield-type leatherette seats. Everything is framed in dark wood. It has TV sets that don't work when the vehicle is in motion – not that there's anything worth watching. To say it was claustrophobic would be an understatement. There's eighteen people on the road now and, to make matters worse, two girls that Jerry and Roddy have latched onto are travelling with us. This does inject some light relief, when at a truck stop on the way to San Francisco one of the girls approaches a couple of truck drivers to ask them if she can buy some Benzedrine tablets off them:

Q. 'Got any Bennie's?'

A. 'You can't drive a truck without 'em!'

Classic.

Our bus driver is a black guy, Frank Silar, who for reasons best known to himself prefers to be called Jackson. He seems cool – keeps himself to himself, done this sort of thing before, quite a few times before.

We learn that the 'Too Much Too Young' EP is now at number two, having been toppled by country music singer Kenny Rogers with a tune called 'Coward of the County'. Is America having its revenge on us? This feeling is rein-forced after our arrival at the appropriately named Vagabond hotel in San Francisco, where Dave Jordan is robbed in his hotel room at gunpoint. I think I'd like to be somewhere else.

At 2 a.m., the AM radio news said, 'There are eight honest people in New York.' As many as that? I look on the map. We have travelled all day and most of the night, and have gone an inch and a half.

Wednesday 13 February: San Francisco. Not a good day, this. I slept till 11, then up to do another 'in-store' record-shop type thing. It's held at Aquarius Records on 19th and Castro. From there it's on to the gig. Rick is not happy. The road crew phoned the record store from the club. They are not too happy, and when we get there, I can see why. The gig is at a club called the I-Beam. It has a totally inadequate PA and monitoring system. I am reminded of Terry's hypothesis that if we have good clothes and a bad PA we'd still do the gig. I like to think Terry has moved on a bit from then. If you have a crap PA, and especially a crap monitor system, you can't hear yourself sing, so you shout and mess up your voice for the next few gigs at least. We set up our equipment and try our best, but there is just no way we are going to get it to sound good. The stage is about 12 inches high, and the whole evening looks like an invitation to disaster. When Frank and DJ get there (why the hell weren't they here in the first place?), we attempt a sound check, but it's pointless. We decide to pull the gig. Everyone is agreed, except Brad, who says he's so used to playing without effective monitors it doesn't really make any difference. Yes, fine, but there are people who are paying money to see this. Dick and Rico play acoustic instruments and have to stand up by Jerry and Lynval, who both have amplifiers.

By this time, however, there are quite a few punters

outside. Larger-than-life San Francisco promoter Bill Graham turns up and (surprisingly) sees our point of view. (I honestly thought he would have sneered at us and told us to 'get our Limey asses on stage' or something, but he was right behind us. Good man!) He suggests getting a new PA in, but it's already dark outside, and there just wouldn't be enough time.

So we reschedule the gig for the following Sunday, at a larger venue. Consequently, we have to explain this to the couple of hundred people outside, so Jerry, Neville and I go outside and (successfully) attempt some PR. It works. I'd like to think we came over as genuine. We stayed an hour or so and talked to anyone who wanted to talk to us. If anyone mentioned the words 'guest list', we tried to change the subject. Rick organized a couple of radio announcements to advertise the new show on Sunday, and we go back to the hotel. The phone rings, it's Rick. 'Hey, Horace! Wanna do an interview?' By this time everyone else had gone out to get drunk. Well, I almost got another night off.

Thursday 14 February: Davis. I'm afraid I'm out of it. Two shows in one night takes a toll. The first one, I had some help from Mr J. Daniels, and the second, some Peruvian assistance. It was a peculiar day. I felt dreadful and quite depressed when I woke. Everyone else seemed a lot more together than me on arrival at the gig. A small club. Mr Gambino sums it up: 'I've got a garage bigger than that place there!' I'm sure he's right. The gig reminds me of playing at Mr George's back in Coventry, right up close to the audience, who are very enthusiastic. It was Valentine's day, and apparently, a young lady in the audience was very much into making my acquaintance. No one told me until we were on our way back to the hotel. Thanks, guys.

Friday 15 February: Palo Alto – the doldrums. This is definitely hell on earth. I've completely forgotten what happened this morning. Anyway, we got here, and it seemed just like yesterday's gig. We have the same PA crew. Support band for tonight is SVT – with Jack Cassady, the old Jefferson Airplane bass player. I'm impressed. I remember 'After Bathing at Baxters' all those years ago. It might just be a case of 'how the mighty have fallen', supporting The Specials at Palo Alto.

It's another university gig (like yesterday), and it's two shows in one night. We can't go on like this. We didn't.

The first show is bearable – the monitors are hideous, but no one seems to have the energy to do anything about it.

The second show is dreadful. Somehow, Brad manages to bash his hand while playing and then seems to give up. His monitors are non-existent, and he tells Rex to turn the drum monitors off. The guys working the PA seem to me to be incapable of doing the simplest jobs. The atmosphere on stage is awful, and I just know something is going to happen. We do the 'Skinhead Symphony' as an encore, but when we come back on for 'You're Wondering Now', the PA crew have switched the monitors off and refuse to put any mikes up on the stage. (During the usual encore mayhem, some of them got knocked about, although I imagine some got trashed deliberately.)

Frank has a stand-up row with the PA crew, and Neville has had enough and wades in with his fists. He then grabs a mike stand and hurls it at the half a dozen guys that are still having a go at Frank, over by the monitor desk. Fists fly, but it's soon over, and we retire to the dressing room, where Jerry and Terry destroy furniture, fixtures and fittings.

Nev has lost a tooth and has a nasty gash over his right eye. Rico leaves, never to return, according to Jerry. By now,

Nev is lying on a couch with an ice-bag over his eye. We get back to the hotel in subdued mood only to find reception closed and the crew without their room keys.

This is definitely the worst time of the band's career so far. There seems to be no point, no indication of whether we're progressing or not. This is 'bar-room blues band' country, and, although I don't want to appear egotistical, I can't help feeling that we are achieving nothing playing here in the suburbs. It reminds me of my days in Breaker, playing working men's clubs in Sunderland and dreaming of a record contract. It doesn't work. Two more gigs and we're out of here. The novelty has worn off. It's now a slog.

Postscript: Neville has had four stitches in his head, feels groggy, but is doing tomorrow's show.

Saturday 16 February: Santa Cruz. Over in America, what we call 'charity shops' are called 'goodwill' stores. A trip to one of these after breakfast provides some light relief (some goodwill even). I buy three button-down shirts. One for me, one for Terry and one for Brad; it's his birthday today.

The gig is at a club called the Catalyst. A 'hippy hangout', but nouveau-riche/touristy, as opposed to the place we played in Arnhem on our European trip. A nice long room with a high stage and good house PA and a monitor system. Rico has not left the band and is still with us. 'Here, Horace, have some of this fine California ganja – some of the best ganja in the world.' It certainly is. The sound check is great. Everything is great, in fact. Is it the best ganja in the world, or is it a good monitoring system and a competent engineer? Who knows. The gig is great, and collective spirits rise. Neville is taking it easy tonight, due to the bump on his head, but seems to manage fine.

We play 'Gangsters' a bit slower than usual, which makes

it a lot more groovy. We do 'Monkey Man' as a third encore
and Rico's 'Man from Warieka' as a fourth. Great. Everyone
seems to be restored. Music is the healer, as John Lee Hooker
would have it. This has helped and is a change from what has
been a pretty hideous three or four days. We only played *one*
show tonight too! I get very out of it on the bus back to our
hotel, stumble into the room I'm sharing with Brad and sleep
like the proverbial log.

The weather here in Northern California has been horrible
– the mountain roads are treacherous, on account of the
torrential rain. When that stops, it gets really humid. Our
stage clothes don't dry properly.

Sunday 17 February: San Francisco revisited. Meanwhile,
back at the Vagabond hotel: Check in; lie on the bed; get
something to eat; go to sound check; do the gig; go back to
the hotel; sleep; get up. Us? Zombies? Nah, mate! Our bus
has driven off east towards Minneapolis, where we're playing
tomorrow. (This was supposed to be a 'travel day', but we're
doing our rescheduled San Francisco gig instead. The plan is
to catch a plane to Minneapolis, where the bus will meet us.)

The Wharfield Theater is a small Hammersmith Odeon
type of theatre. Nice big stage. The first four rows of seats
have been taken out, so people can dance. This is a lot better
venue for us, despite the seats. Someone tells me it was where
The Sex Pistols played their last-ever show. There's a fair
amount of credibility resting on the outcome of this show.
We've already pulled one show in San Francisco, so we need
to do a good job here. Supporting us are The Offs, who
sounded good in the sound check, but play faster and louder
during the gig (i.e., they sound dreadful). It's not the constant
touring that gets on my nerves. It's not the strange habits of
some of the band that gets me mad. It's not even the crappy

gigs that whip me up into a frenzy. IT'S SOUND CHECKS! The number of times I've wanted to wrap my bass round someone's head (usually the monitor engineer, but sometimes someone from the band) are countless. Lynval never hits his guitar with the same force he employs during the gig, so it's always too loud, both on stage and in Brad's monitors. Terry never seems to get any volume out of his front wedges, but is it surprising when everyone is playing so loud? I rarely get to hear Dick and Rico on the other side of the stage – especially when Roddy is clanging away beside me. The thing is, I'm usually the arschole who ends up shouting myself hoarse at Lynval, who insists on playing his guitar while Brad is trying to explain to a deaf monitor engineer that the levels on the snare drum need to come up.

I am finding this very difficult. But anyway, I'm happy to say that tonight we delivered. I hope we've got over the California doldrums. The audience are great, and get up on stage for 'You're Wondering Now'. They continue singing after we go off. The stage is cleared, and we go back on and totally destroy them with 'Monkey Man'. Neville, now recovered from his bang on the head, is up on the PA speakers and anywhere else he can possibly get to. Brilliant. Rico doesn't feel up to 'Man from Warieka', so that's that. (I get the impression he'd rather be somewhere else if the truth be known.)

After the show, I'm entertained by a gaggle of girls who run *Idol Worship*, a local fanzine. They take the piss out of me (and anyone else for that matter) mercilessly, and we have a great time. Vicki, their photographer – well, the girl with the camera – is particularly funny. Good. I've missed laughter. Back to the hotel, change and out to the Mabuhay Club, where The Go-Gos are playing. The rhythm guitarist still looks fourteen, but I think Terry has beaten me to it. He must have it pretty bad, as after the show he's helping them load their equipment into their van. He *never* lifted any gear with us!

Monday 18 February (Washington's Birthday, national holiday): The Specials fly to Minneapolis and play at a club called Duffy's. Oh Christ! Not again. I eventually get in at 4.00 a.m, and there's some sort of generator humming away just outside my window so I can't sleep even if I wanted to. You can imagine my state of mind and body when we have to leave at 8.30.

So. It's the usual panic to the airport, get the flight by the skin of our teeth. The take-off from San Francisco was very hairy indeed; lots of sharp banking. Ugh. Luckily there are very few people on the flight, so I am able to stretch out across three seats and fall asleep, waking only to eat a totally tasteless meal.

Into Minneapolis/St Paul, and the temperature change is pretty drastic. From California to 30 degrees F, or 1 degree C. Jackson is here at the airport as promised with the Crass-mobile, and everyone is *real* tired.

Duffy's is a small club and features male strippers early on Monday nights. Neville, never one to miss an opportunity to show off, does an impromtu strip and drives the place wild. What a geezer! The sound check presents its usual problems, but the club's sound system is up to par. The support band is a local reggae outfit, Simba – in the middle of Minnesota! They're good too! It's not a good gig for me. I've reached a kind of emotional cut-off point. I always try to be professional, put on a good show, blah, blah, blah, but tonight everything seems pointless – I'm just going through the motions. Everyone else, I'm sure, has reached this at different times during this trip, but it's my turn tonight. I remember playing a Tamla bass line to 'You're Wondering Now' and Terry saying, 'This one's for Horace, who's acting a bit odd tonight.' About right, really.

I didn't have any feeling to put into the music. Later, after the inevitable interview (same old questions – same old answers), back to the hotel, where Lynval, Rico, Jackson (with some girl – Julie? – he has picked up) and I decide to go and eat. Rico changes his mind at the last moment. He hasn't been feeling too well recently. So, here we are at 2.30 in the morning at Hill's. Lots of strange human low-life. Julie calmly relates to us how she was recently raped. Lynval gets some take-out food to take back for Rico. Compassion still exists somewhere, then. I'm having difficulty coping with this country. Everyone else has gone to a party. I go to bed.

Tuesday 19 February: Madison, Wisconsin, mad city. Time officially has no meaning. Jackson says it's 10. Frank swears it's 12, and no one else gives a toss. I am in a foul mood. I don't understand it. My mid-tour crack-up, definitely. I sleep on the coach and wake up fresh and at peace with everyone, for the moment. At breakfast, Frank had to pull Brad off Rick – but they make up afterwards. The pressure is getting to everybody.

Madison looks a nice place, with a mini 'White House'-looking building in the town centre. Apparently, it won an award for the neatest city. Neat! Cheap Trick come from here, apparently (their bass player and vocalist anyway. Rick Neilsen, the guitar player, lives nearby in Rockford, Illinois).

Tonight's gig is at Merlyn's, a small club like Mr George's, but it looks like they're still building it. Small, low stage, telephone-box-sized dressing room. Support band tonight are called Waves. Musos trying their hand at reggae – almost worked. Nice try, guys. Our set is great – not as manic as usual, and a groove that has not been heard for ages makes a reappearance in a fair few of the songs. 'Nite Klub' especially stood out for me tonight, and 'Man from Warieka' is the best version we've ever played. A short arrangement – it can be a bit boring if it's played for too long. I love playing Rico's stuff. The crowd don't appear to be responsive at the start, but by the end of the night they're jumping. Good singers – they must have sung the chorus to 'You're Wondering Now' for five minutes after we finished. Stayed in key too!

After the gig I found myself talking to a girl called Kathy. Nice hair! Dark red. I'm a sucker for red hair! It's not love, more like self-destruct. Anyhow, we pile off with Dave Jordan and Frank to a very dodgy party, I do some dodgy coke, baking soda and bleach probably, and then it's a cab back to her place. She's a student here and lives in a hall of residence not far from the club. We have very clumsy sex. I do not enjoy it, but Kathy has given me something to remember her by – crabs!

Wednesday 20 February: travel to Chicago. Get back to the hotel at 8.40 a.m. No point in sleeping, and I'm too tired to sleep anyway. I hang around and have breakfast and crash out on the coach when Jackson comes out. We leave some time in the afternoon, but I am oblivious. We get into Chicago about half past seven. We were going to stay in Schaumburg, where our next gig is, but, as it's only 30 miles from Chicago, we decide to base ourselves here (Chicago) for the next three days. The 'Too Much Too Young' EP has gone down to number four in the UK charts. Our album has gone down to number ten. Terry and I talk on the coach about the band's future and reach the very pessimistic conclusion that we will just burn out. The general atmosphere around the band is very depressing. I can see why people take drugs.

Chicago is 'just like I pictured it' – at night it is spectacular indeed. We are at the Ambassador Hotel. I can see the Sears Building – the highest inhabited building in the world – from my hotel room. I'm still pretty tired, but I went out and got a Chinese meal. Had a Zombie cocktail, which is undoubtedly the strongest drink I have ever had. Rick (no stranger to alcohol) apparently had two of them at the Starwood in Los Angeles and had to be carried home; he couldn't remember a thing. (No change there then.)

I get back for an early night – 11.00 p.m., but am woken up by Brad two hours later. He insists on watching the TV, and I'm unable to get back to sleep. Bastard.

Thursday 21 February: Chicago/Schaumburg. So much for some sightseeing. John Jostins calls me from the top of the Sears Tower, telling me how fantastic it is. Thanks, mate! Rick then calls and says we're checking out. Apart from the hotel being too expensive, some of the staff seem to have an attitude about black people. We're all pretty furious about this, but Nev and Lyn take it in a kind of matter-of-fact way. We load up and move to the Allerton, 701 North Michigan, which is not as palatial, but their attitude is better.

So it's off to tonight's gig. We leave at 4.00 and get stuck in rush-hour traffic. It takes us two and a half hours to drive the 30 miles to Schaumburg. The club is called B. Ginnings and is owned by Danny Seraphine, who's the drummer in Chicago (the band!). It looks brand new – the facilities are great. The dressing rooms are huge – presumably planned out by a musician who's had his fair share of changing in rooms the size of double wardrobes. After the sound check, some guys from Hamer Guitars drop by with some samples. There's a beautiful 8-string bass, just like Nick Lowe's, which they can sell me for $1,000. After a bit of haggling from Rob

Gambino, it goes down to $800. I'm very tempted, but I'd like to get another Telecaster bass when we get to New York, so I pass. Nice guitar, though. The show is great. Brad is real tired and plays things a bit slower, which as far as I'm concerned is better. The songs have been getting too fast over the past six months. We all pile back on the coach and head back to Chicago, stopping off at some motorway services, sorry, truck stop, where Jerry and I have a laugh at the t-shirts. 'I'd rather eat shit than ride a Jap bike!' Brad has bought a radio/cassette complete with headphones. I've borrowed it, and while he nods off to Humphrey Bogart on the TV, I fall asleep listening to a local funk/jazz/soul station. Very cool.

Friday 22 February: Park West, Chicago – two shows!
The first job today is to get back to our original hotel and get my laundry. When I get there, I'm presented with a $50 phone tab. For one thing, I never made any calls (Brad!) and secondly, I haven't got $50 to not pay for it with. The nasty little man behind the reception desk will not give me my laundry until this bill has been paid.

Hey, I'm a rock star! I'll phone my manager! Rick eventually comes over and coughs up the money. Thanks, Rick. That's OK, Horace, we've got some interviews to do. So much for sightseeing. As it turns out I do get to see some sights, as FM XRT is right the other side of town, on Belmont and Cicero, which I seem to remember is old Al Capone territory. The interview is the normal stuff, but the staff are friendly. The taxi driver that took us there was complaining about the local mayor – 'If you can't shit, get off the pot.' Hmm.

Meanwhile, back on the promotion trail, Rick and I drop into WaxTrax, a punky record store, who have been promoting

2-Tone in a big way. There's a whacking big display in the shop. We blag some 'unofficial' Specials t-shirts. Rick informs me that Gary Bushell, journalist from weekly music publication *Sounds*, is coming over to New York to do a piece on us.

Tonight we are back with the prospect of doing two shows. Despite the fact that we don't want to.

The Park West is gross in the extreme. It has that whole seventies disco thing going and reminds me of the Playboy Club in London. I don't know why, as I've never actually been to the Playboy Club in London, but I have an idea that it would look a bit like this!

The first show is good. If the crowd is with us and want us to play more, we should. There are 'encores' and there are 'genuine encores'. This was a genuine encore. Perhaps it would be 'professional' to conserve our energy for the second show, but to deny people who have spent money to see us some more music because we have to play again in an hour and a half isn't right. Consequently, some Peruvian assistance is required to do the second show, which Rick says was one of the best shows he's ever seen us do. Towards the end, when it starts to get a bit frantic, Our Kid slips over and bangs his back on one of the monitors. He is obviously in agony and has to be carried off backstage. He is later taken to hospital, where he's told he's dislocated something in his back and should rest. Not that he will, or can, for that matter. He's keeping the crew side of things together. After the gig there are just too many people in the dressing room, which pisses me off. The coach goes on to a club called Tut's via the hotel. I get off at the hotel.

Saturday 23 February: Dee-troyuht. Get on the bus around 1 o'clock to the now familiar sound of Rico complaining. He is finding it hard to get proper Rastafarian food over here and is obviously not enjoying himself. We are mighty late setting off, this plus the fact we do another time zone. Add an extra hour. We've all reached a point where we're too exhausted to care. At one point I'm the only person awake on the bus. We finally get to the gig and have five minutes to do a sound check, which suits me fine. The show is at a club called the Center Stage, and doesn't look like our audience at all. Lots of girls with big hair and men with big hats. There are large TV screens with American football matches being shown. Some of the guys at the bar look like they should be on the TV. The rest of the band go back to the hotel – we're not on till late, but I decide to stay at the gig. I'm glad I did.

Something is obviously weird about tonight's booking. There's this heavy rock band, with loads of amps, loads of hair, all pretending they're Van Halen or somebody up on the stage. Now, I reckon this was their gig originally, and we have been bumped onto it, putting their collective noses severely out of joint. They play two sets – one to the standard yee-haw America-out-on-a-Saturday-night-for-a-beer kind of audience, the second to an increasing number of new wave 2-Tone types who have obviously come to see us. They are called Teezer. They are the funniest band I have ever seen in my life. Every rock and roll cliché, be it musical, be it lyrical, be it posturing with guitars, mike stands; if you could turn it into a phallic symbol, these guys did – but badly. Tears were rolling down my face, and no one else from The Specials saw them. The first set was bad enough, but they started their second spot wearing hooded cassocks and carrying candles. Jerry would have loved it, Terry would have smiled too. The best moment for me was after the five-minute drum solo. The singer shouts, 'D'y'all wanna rock 'n' roll?' to which the assembled Specials fans at the front shouted, 'No!' It was a classic moment.

When The Specials finally get here, they're accompanied

by four kids from Coventry, Liam and Evo, who we have met before, and their mates, Russ and Adam. They're going to be 'holidaying' with us for the next two weeks. It's good to see them. Reminds me that I actually live somewhere. The toilet in our dressing room is blocked, so Rico, who is unaware of what has happened at the gig for the past hour or so, goes next door to ask the support band if he can use their bathroom. They tell him to go away. Hey, there's no need for that. It ain't our fault if you guys are crap.

Right, on we go, and we start playing before the curtains go up – 'The Dawning of a New Era'. Everything looks and sounds pretty good. Towards the end of 'Gangsters', the Coventry contingent get up on stage, but when a local punter attempts to get up, he's manhandled pretty viciously by the club bouncers. We stop the song and walk off stage.

When everything quietens down, we go back on and do 'Long Shot' / 'Moonstomp', and loads of kids get up on the stage – great! Nothing better than making the bouncer thugs look stupid – especially when they are! Off and back on for 'Madness' and 'You're Wondering Now'. The crowd are still going potty, so we go back on and play 'Gangsters' again, all the way through this time. What could have been an ugly situation has been turned into a good night.

After the show, the dressing room is mobbed. I get to meet Wayne Kramer (MC5 guitarist), whom I introduce to Roddy, who doesn't seem too impressed. No matter. Mr Kramer comes over as a great bloke, if not a little drunk: 'You be bad motherfucker!' I think it is meant as a compliment. He's about to form a group with Johnny Thunders. It's going to be called Gang Wars. (I met Wayne Kramer again in 1995, when the reconstituted Specials (without Terry, Jerry and Brad) were in Minneapolis. He was still a great bloke!)

Back at the hotel, check in, and Brad and I go over the

road to a twenty-four-hour coffee shop; my first proper meal for two days. Rob Gambino has done some serious damage to his back and tells of his painful visit to the hospital in Chicago. He needs rest, but the crew, who are getting pretty knackered by now, will fall to bits without him.

Some UK music press gets here, and there's a photo which Brad took of me and Chrissie Hynde the day after the Bilzen festival. The clock says 4.10, 'ten after four', as they say here, and we've to be up at 9.00. Fat chance.

Sunday 24 February: Toronto. No one else can sleep either. Sleep all day, it's the only way . . . We are becoming our songs. Detroit looked like it had been recently evacuated as we drove through it on the Sunday afternoon. Immigration takes hours. Apparently the promoter should have been here with his part of the contract to prove that we really are a pop group that is playing this evening in Toronto.

He wasn't, and consequently we arrive at the gig ten minutes after the doors have opened, and five minutes before The News, the mod support band, go on. We all mill around and try to wake up. No point going to the hotel, it's too near show time. Lynval and Neville both have relatives here in Toronto, and it was great seeing Lynval meet his sister, who he hadn't seen for four years, and Neville with his cousins, whose nappies he used to change (?).

Why is it that gigs with no sound checks give us the best sound? The stage is tiny, bumping into everybody all the time, but the atmosphere is tremendous. We play the whole lot, plus our version of 'Madness' and 'Man from Warieka', Rico playing one of the best solos I've ever heard him play. After the gig, I meet a couple of guys from *TO/84*, a local fanzine, and give what I consider to be one of my better fanzine interviews – only to find that their tape recorder has been taping short-wave radio. The guys, Angus and Dave, are mortified, and we attempt it again. Of course, it's nowhere near as good, and Jerry comes to my rescue and helps me out.

I attempt some creative writing:

> Fetch all the animals out of their cages
> Sit them all down while they set up the stages
> Hassle the manager for advances on wages
> We've been here four weeks but it seems like ages.

Perhaps not ... Stick to playing bass, Horace. It's what you're good at!

9

Downhill All the Way in a Mobile Lunatic Asylum

Monday 25 February: Toronto and beyond. Am awoken at the god-awful early hour of 10.30 a.m. by Rick. There's a journalist waiting downstairs. Hmm. So David (for that is the gentleman's name) and I retire to the coffee shop on the twenty-third floor and do the interview. After that, Jerry and I have a round of press stuff to do.

Oh yes, tomorrow. Jerry has been given some sort of award by The Daily Mirror/Nationwide Rock and Pop Awards or something. It's the Radio 1 DJs' award, apparently – some big simulcast TV thing. Jerry has said he'd only do it if the rest of the band were there (magnanimous, eh!), so the plan is for the band, plus Rick, to fly down to Washington this evening, where we will meet Radio 1 DJ Andy Peebles. We then go on to some TV studio, where the (live) presentation will be made. After which we'll fly up to Albany, New York State, for our gig on the Tuesday night. The bus will have travelled from Toronto and will meet us there.

So Jerry and I stuff our suitcases into the local Chrysalis rep's car and off we go. He'll drop us at the airport after the interviews. This all goes really well. We do a cable TV interview for a show called *Black World*, and Jerry gives what I consider to be the best interview I've ever heard him do. He is obviously dead passionate about his stance on racism, and I have never heard him this articulate. Very cool. Ron, our (Chrysalis) man in Toronto, and a native Trinidadian, suggests an Indian meal. Agreed. But on the way, Jerry and I discover The Greatest Second-hand Shop In The World. It's called 'Flying Down To Rio'. It is incredible. We come out with armfuls of stuff. These zip-up woollen thick cardigan things with ice-hockey players on the back – we bought a dozen of them, enough for the band and crew – bowling shirts and a dark brown leather collarless flying-jacket-looking thing, which is undoubtedly the find of the tour. Second-hand heaven. From then on to Ravi's, our recommended curry house, where we happily tuck in. It is the best meal I have eaten on the whole tour. This is all very well, but there's a plane to catch or, in our case, a plane to miss.

Traffic is dreadful out to the airport, and the usual mad panic ensues, but too late. Thirty seconds too late, as it goes. Some nauseating little idiot on the US Air desk spends two minutes telling us we can't catch the plane. Yes we could, you prat, it hadn't left the whatever it is they call those things they depart from.

There is a not inconsiderable amount of irony in this situation in that the band have gone down to Washington without Jerry, who is the reason they're going there in the first place. Anyway, we have a plan. Jerry and I will catch a plane to Newark in forty-five minutes' time, check into a hotel near the airport and get a Newark–Washington flight in the morning, in time to do this goddamn stupid piece of PR crap that we could really do without at this stage in the tour. We've just over a week left, and I'm counting the days down.

Jerry and I get to Newark with no hitches and book into a Holiday Inn just outside the airport. In the bar we relax and talk about what the band could do next. Jerry seems in a pretty positive frame of mind. The next morning we make our flight no problem and reach Washington, where we are met by local Chrysalis guys. We get whisked to a TV station, where we meet the rest of the band, and before you know it, the presentation's done (It took all of forty-five seconds!). All that rushing around, pratting about and panicking. It hardly seemed worth it. All the Chrysalis guys are slapping us on the back and saying, 'Well done,' and telling us what a great bunch of guys we are, and I wish they'd all just FUCK OFF! I don't know how much more I can give. I suppose I'll find out. We have a couple of hours left in Washington before we depart for Albany, so it's tourist time! Brad and I head for the Smithsonian via the White House, Iwo Jima Monument and Lincoln Memorial. Lovely. Something completely different.

The take-off out of Washington was pretty hairy, but I had a cool view of the Pentagon. We are met at Albany airport by the bus, and from there it's off to the hotel. Doing the TV programme earlier in the day has made me feel homesick, so as soon as I check in to my room I spend all my saved-up money on the phone to my folks and various friends back home, get some local (Coventry) news and feel a lot better. I manage a couple of hours' sleep before Frank Murray drags me out of bed to go off and do a sound check. Only half the band make it down to the club, but that's OK. The promoter takes those that did make it out for a meal – roast beef! Most appreciated. My second good meal in as many days. It appears that Jerry and I weren't the only ones who had adventures. The bus was searched at the Canadian/American border and was detained for trying to smuggle fruit. Yes, fruit. It is illegal to transport fruit and vegetables across the border.

There were apples and oranges that generally get left in dressing rooms, so we have them on the bus. No problem! Apparently, yes, problem. All sorts of palaver apparently occurs, but the bus is here. Back at the club, I discover sloe gin fizzes and the gig is er ... pretty good ... I think. Tonight's support band were called The Units and for my money are the best band we've played with on this trip. I bought a copy of their single; it's called 'Japan'. Terry now looks like he died a couple of days ago. At the end of the show Jerry piles into the audience, somehow cutting his hand badly, and taking part of the low stage ceiling with him. After the show, Neville, two girls and I drive out to a local college radio station, where we take over for an hour or two, playing our favourite records, and, in Neville's case, playing up to these two girls. We got out late and get back to the hotel. The girls disappear with Nev, and I stumble to my room. I've been up for twenty-three hours.

Wednesday 27 February: the Main Act, Boston (well, Lynway Mass., actually!) Leave the hotel at 2.00 p.m. My leather flying jacket is the envy of the bus; me, Mr Uncool – not any more! Jackson, the coach driver, is in a foul mood – he has taken exception to the Coventry Four, who are travelling on the bus with us. He doesn't consider them 'proper' members of the band/crew and doesn't see why he has to carry them. What's it got to do with him anyway?

The gig tonight is in the ballroom of the hotel we are staying in. Or is that: the hotel we are staying at tonight is in the same building as the club we are playing in? Whichever way round it is, it's brilliant. It's always the lesser of two evils, hanging around at a gig between sound check and showtime. Some people like to head back to the hotel and return later. Me, I get too nervous and stay at the gig. Tonight is the best of both worlds. Can we do some more gigs like this please, Rick? All our frustration comes out at the sound check. 'Monkey Man' becomes 'The Monkees'. The monitor engineer (may he rest in peace) is tearing his hair out and goes quietly insane.

The gig starts badly. My amp does not work, but it's coming through the monitors and out the PA, so I bash on. It gets better, but the tiredness is starting to show. Half-way through 'Nite Klub', a fight starts in the crowd over by Lyn and Jerry. We stop and go off. Return and carry on where we stopped. Terry is his usual sarcastic self:

> We only play for dancing, dancing cats.
> Your evening's just been ruined by a couple of stupid
>   twats.

I suppose it was a good gig. In the dressing room I take a good look in the mirror. There are grey/purple patches around my bloodshot eyes. I never thought I would ever look this ill. My watch has stopped too!

Thursday 28 February: New Haven, Connecticut – the Great American Music Hall. Despite a 10.15 alarm call, the bus didn't depart till 1.15, which was partly my fault, as John Jostins and I went to a 'Denny's' to get something resembling breakfast.

The bus is now our 'padded cell' and a pretty smelly one at that. Evo and Adam (two of the Coventry Four), Brad and Rick are having a card game on the back of the bus. I zombie through the day. Roddy has an argument with Jerry over the bunks on the bus. Roddy has 'his' bunk and Jerry's sleeping in it. Because of his lack of front teeth Jerry dribbles in his sleep. I can see Roddy's point. If we all dribbled in our sleep, it would be all right, I suppose.

Arrive at the hotel, and I'm over the road to 'Gino's', a plastic fast-food outlet, where I eat some plastic food, far too fast, and feel sick. Frank comes by at 8 p.m. and drags me out of bed again for yet another sound check. After it, the band head back to the hotel, but Jerry and I stay at the gig and mess around with some new songs and ideas that may appear on the next LP. The 'old' tunes are getting everyone down; we've played them to death. The set goes so quickly now, an hour set seems to last fifteen minutes, and sometimes I've completely forgotten playing some of the tunes I played that night. We need some new material. Tonight's support are called The Elevators, who make a Cars-type of new wave sound, but get a little shirty about the stage ('Can't you move the drums?' blah, blah, blah). Understandable, but it is our gig after all. The show goes OK, I suppose. I can't remember. Lynval has this idea that we're turning into robots. The Golding Theory of Homo-Robotics.

Doug D'Arcy and Roy Eldridge from Chrysalis in England are here along with bigwigs from the New York office to see how their current product is doing. We are fucked, mate, that's how we're doing. The upshot is that, when we've finished in America, we get a fortnight's break. Then we record another single. Then we start writing, rehearsing and recording our next album. I have an idea we might need more than a fortnight, guys. We've been on tour pretty much non-stop since October – that's five months, five gigs a week, and we don't exactly just stand there and play. To celebrate, or drown my sorrows, I can't remember which, I get drunk.

Friday 29 February: not Cherry Hill. Terry's voice has gone completely, so we've had to cancel tonight's show. Fair enough. We're all played out as far as I'm concerned. The upshot is we're going straight to New York for the last two shows. That's right, the LAST TWO SHOWS.

The view from the padded cell as we motor into New York is fantastic. The bridges over the river, over to Manhattan, the city skyline, the tunnel over to the Lower East Side, Harlem, all that stuff. There's amazing graffiti all over the place. Huge tenement buildings – the projects – all very imposing. I feel intimidated by it all. But there's no time for that – we're going shopping. Check into the Gramercy Park hotel (again) and straight out down to West 48th and Times Square where the guitar shops live, and there's three very nice Telecaster basses for under £200 – one just like mine for $275, which is as much as I paid for mine in Glasgow. The Hamer 8-strings retail for $1,395, and I could have picked one up for $800. Hmm. I now have to see what I can afford, and whether I have to blag some money off Rick.

So, what do visiting English punk rock stars do when they're in New York? They go and watch other English punk rock groups! The Inmates and The Jam are playing the Palladium Theater. Rob Gambino – now strapped up and coping OK – is transport manager. So he and I, Steve Hutchinson, Roddy and two of the Coventry Four pile into a rent-a-car, and off we go. We get there to see the last two Inmates tunes. The Jam don't impress me. It's the first time I've seen them, and they don't seem to do it for me. The lighting is great, though – mainly white. About half-way through they kind of get going, but by then Rob, who has the keys to the car, says he wants to go, conveniently saying his back hurts. I conveniently bump into Barbara Wassername from *Newsweek* and I put forward the idea that we meet up to go see some New York bands next week – she seems keen. I mention to Rob about the Hamer bass guitars, and he has the factory phone number. He agrees to chase them up to see what we can do about me getting one of those 8-string basses. Cheers, mate.

Back at the Gramercy, and the night, though not necessarily young, is definitely not over. I end up in the bar talking with some English guy who's over here working as a recording engineer on the new Joan Armatrading LP. Brad has got a fair dose of the flu, just being run down. There's only so much excess you can do, I suppose. Frank Murray actually gives me some money! *The Avengers* – Patrick McNee and Diana Rigg – is on TV.

Saturday 1 March: New York, You Nawk. I slept late and woke up feeling somewhat peculiar. I seem to be running a temperature. Perhaps I've caught what Brad's got. There's nowhere to get breakfast at 2.30 in the afternoon, but I end up somewhere. One thing about this place – you can always get something to eat. By the time I get back to the hotel, it's time to get off to the gig. A day went by, and I hardly noticed it.

Tonight, we're at the Diplomat Hotel. The gig is a 1,000-capacity ballroom, very chintzy, not unlike the Lyceum in London, with 'boxes' round the side. There are all these 2-Tone-looking posters outside going on about how Ron Delsener, the promoter, is charging too much money for tickets and how The Specials intend to give away 500 free tickets. The posters give the impression that we printed them. I don't understand this and never get to the bottom of it. It's either a bad practical joke or promoter envy. Garry Bushell, from *Sounds*, plus photographers Ross Halfin and Jill Furmanovsky arrive, accompanied by Chris Poole, from Chrysalis UK.

A TV station is filming the sound check, which is a pain, as we have to change into suits etc. The stage is pretty small, but the gig looks like it has a great atmosphere. The New

York Dolls used to play here regularly, and Iggy Pop is scheduled to play next Tuesday or something.

Everyone else heads back to the Gramercy, but I hang around to 'talk to the press'. I have some brandy – it's medicinal, you understand, for my fevered brow. Needless to say, when the guys get back for the show I'm a little worse for wear.

The gig (I have it on good authority) was good. Frank says the first number ('Dawning of a New Era') was amazing – full of nastiness – but the show went downhill from there on in. I kept shouting, 'It's too easy,' during the encores to no one in particular, probably pissing everyone off. I know I didn't go to the dressing room afterwards. I felt it best that I stayed away from the rest of the band. I felt very violent and quite mad; just briefly, but quite mad. I changed in a corridor. At that moment, Nick Edwards arrived. He's a guy from Coventry, a friend of Jerry (went to school with him, I think). He had a PA system we used to borrow from time to time years back. It's good to see him. It's good to see anyone who isn't involved in this circus. It cheers me up and pisses me off at the same time.

After the show, Chrysalis insist on taking us to a club called Privates, where we have a 'reserved area'. Ian Hunter is there with his wife, Trudi; he looks at us with a sneer. If I was (a) sober, and (b) in a better mood, I would have fallen at his feet and told him how Mott the Hoople had been one of my favourite bands when I was learning to play, how I watched him side-stage when I was eighteen and could I play on his next album, but his scowl put me off. That and the 'roped-off' area that we are ushered to. UFO, another Chrysalis band – heavy rockers from the East End of London – arrive and get all 'rock 'n' roll' all over the place – loud, 'look-at-me' kind of behaviour – and I want to go home. So does Roddy, Dick and Gambino. We leave, get a cab and head back to the hotel, where Dick and I find a coffee shop round the corner. Good old Dick. Nice, man. Nice.

Apparently, Bruce Foxton (Jam bass player), David Bowie and Mick Jagger were at our gig tonight. I'm afraid I couldn't care less.

Sunday 2 March: Speaks, Long Island. The last gig! Today was spent in and out of stretch limousines and in the company of photographers. We did the World Trade Center and the Statue of Liberty. I kind of perked up for it, but Jerry looked as miserable as sin. Our 'Rude Boy' image had not survived the past six weeks, and I am sure Jerry was not happy with our return to a mix-'n'-match style. I wore my 'coolest jacket in the world', and Nev was wearing a US army helmet, which I'm sure didn't help matters. There had been a 'closing down' in the band. I know I was just 'hanging on in there' and had enough to do to keep myself together, quite apart from worrying about anyone else. The tour had reduced us back to seven individuals.

The last gig on our first American tour was at a club called Speaks out on Long Island. It was going to be at a club called My Father's Place, but the ticket demand was so great that they moved it to a bigger venue. Debbie Harry and Chris Stein from Blondie are here with us and gee us up. Ms Harry looks as stunning in real life as she does on a record cover. She comes over as a lot more intelligent than her 'punk Barbie' image suggests. Chris Stein seems a cool guy too. The show tonight is a three-band bill. First up, roots reggae outfit Monyaka, who are great, followed by rockabilly types Levi and the Rockats, some of whom are English. Smutty, their stand-up bass player is covered in tattoos and is definitely the coolest person backstage. Roddy definitely thinks so. They do good, too, and the atmosphere is electric by the time we get to go on.

Debbie Harry goes on to introduce us, and the whole place goes nuts. It is one of *those* nights. All the stops were pulled out. It was the last gig in the world. We played like demons, destroyed the place. Incredible. Lynval spent most of the last number being pulled out of the audience, then pulling his amp over and mashing up Brad's drum kit. 'Madness' was exactly that, and 'You're Wondering Now' was hardly the soft ballad we once heard on *History of Ska*, Volume 2. We played 'Man from Warieka', but by now we were finished, and it wasn't a brilliant version. It did serve its purpose and cooled the audience down. They still wouldn't let us go, so we did 'Monkey Man' again. Neville and Lynval threw me into the audience. Neville stripped off and threw his black and white check suit into the crowd. Rick Rogers and the Chrysalis people were all beaming. It was great. We had done it! Total euphoria. The relief that we had finished was palpable. Back on the bus for the last time.

Monday 3 March: the day Debbie Harry made me a tuna fish sandwich. Wake up and the TV is still on. Brad is out for the count. The phone rings – interview with *Time-Life*. Interviews before breakfast, interviews over breakfast, interviews in the morning, interviews over lunch, interviews in the afternoon, interviews after sound check, interviews before the gig, interviews in my sleep. Whaddya wanna know?!

Anyway, off to West 48th, and I get myself a lovely sunburst Telecaster bass, just like the one I've used on this tour, but with a far nicer neck: $318 – a bargain in anyone's language, with a nice case too. Back to the hotel in time to see everyone else leave. See you in a couple of weeks. I'm staying over for a couple of days. I don't think I could cope with sharing a flight home with sixteen nutters. I'm taking the opportunity to be in my own space for a while and do what I want to do for a few days. The evening was spent relaxing at Debbie Harry and Chris Stein's flat on West 58th Street. It feels great to be in someone's house (well, flat) compared to hotels. You get the impression touring that everyone in America lives in hotels. So it's me, Jerry, John Jostins and Rick cooling out in the Blondie front room. Chris Stein has a huge record collection and a penchant for god-awful records. I tell him about the support band in Detroit, and we have a good laugh. This is just what I wanted. There's a black guy called Steve in attendance and he's got some rap records. We are transfixed. This stuff is great – where can we get some? Steve tells us about who to get and where to get it. JJ and I decide to get up early tomorrow and search out some of this. To make a good day perfect, Debbie Harry makes me a tuna fish sandwich. This is great.

Tuesday 4 March: the day after the day Debbie Harry made me a tuna sandwich, and I go home. Brad has gone home, so I'm sharing a room with JJ. We're both up early and off to Harlem via 'the ride', the freeway up to the north side of Manhattan. Up to 125th Street, and there's a record store open opposite the famous Harlem Apollo, where Funkadelic/ Parliament are doing a week-long residency next week. Now *that* would be cool!

I pick up three 12-inch singles, Grand Master Flash and the Furious Five, The Funky Four plus One More, and a dubious looking dub album, *Dub Out her Blouse and Skirt.* JJ gets a load of stuff, too. We buy up and get going. Outside there's some guy yelling, 'Get all the whites out of Africa.' Hmm. Is this how Lyn and Nev feel? So it's a cab back to Downtown. Tourist time. Peggy Guggenheim Museum, Empire

State Building – the view was brilliant, all over Manhattan, Bronx, Brooklyn, Queens. Then it's back to the hotel, pack and get off to the airport.

The film showing on the flight was *Electric Horseman* with Robert Redford and Jane Fonda. The sun rising over the wing of the airplane was beautiful – the dawning of a new . . . day. I almost cried when I got back to Heathrow. Train to Coventry, cab home and bed. I slept for eighteen hours.

Looking back now, the first American trip was a landmark in the band's career. We were at our best, and we were at our worst. We had been seduced by the great god rock 'n' roll. Some of us had welcomed her gladly, some of us refused her point blank. Me, I wasn't sure. I had this notion that if you wanted 'the big time', 'superstardom', and all the trappings that went with it, you lost everything you had before and lived in a fragile world full of yes-men, ego-strokers and people who would charm you to work for them. Being fêted by the young and beautiful had its short-term benefits, obviously, but wasn't rock 'n' roll all about living for the 'now' anyway? How did 'seasoned campaigners' cope? They changed their goals. I wanted to be a musician, and obviously I preferred success to obscurity, but I did not want to be cast adrift in the rarefied atmosphere of superstardom. Never mind that, I didn't want to become dependent on touring. It was hell. The sacrifice that I had to make to play this music seemed too much, especially as our tour went on and ground us down. I was touched at my optimism when I reread these pages; I never lost hope in the band, but I did become aware of how brittle the band became when under such a gruelling schedule.

It was obvious that we would never 'crack America'. The record company said their biggest headache was that the record retailers did not know what shelf to put our records on. We didn't belong in the reggae section alongside Burning Spear and we didn't play the same music as the new wave acts. We were not compartmentalized, which I was extremely proud of then, but in terms of translating to the business it was our nemesis. That, and the fact that, during one interview, Jerry said he had a better time on a school trip to Russia than he did touring the States.

Although the tour was the hardest and most demanding thing I had ever done in my life, I thought the country was incredible, so different from state to state. I had made some good friends over there.

When I got home I distributed a case-load of presents to my Coventry posse, then went to see my mum and dad. Good food. It appeared that the amount of money that it cost us to do the American tour was just about made up for by the number of records we sold. If you looked at it one way, we went all that way, and did all we did, for nothing. It was difficult, looking at it that way. I preferred to think that we'd 'laid the foundation' for a profitable career in America. Well, you've got to be optimistic in these situations, and after all, we were The Specials, and we were back in the UK and it was 1980.

10

Working for the Rat Race

While we were in America, an interesting little sideshow had been developing in England. Reggae journalist Eric Fuller had written a piece in a February edition of *Sounds*, where he insinuated that the 2-Tone bands were carrying on the well-documented tradition of ripping off black artists. Admittedly, he went on to describe the veritable minefield of publishing houses, three of which claimed to own the same song, but there was an injustice being done by someone who should have known better. Our single 'Gangsters' deliberately had no writing credits on it, as we did not know how to get money, or how much money, to Prince Buster for the 'Al Capone' section of the song. 'Too Much Too Young' featured the riff and vocal section 'Oh, no, no, give me no more pickney!', which was taken from a skinhead obscurity called 'Birth Control' by Lloydie and The Lowbites. (We used to play the tune 'Birth Control' – I remember it from the Clash tour.) Lloyd Charmers (Lloydie), who wrote the song, was credited on the record, and Plangent Visions (our publishing company) was currently tearing its collective hair out trying to find out who *really* owned the publishing. To get criticized by tabloid journalists was almost expected, but having a dedicated reggae journalist who seemed not to have done his home-work get shirty with us was very weird. It is lucky we weren't around at the time to respond. As it was, Chris Poole from the Chrysalis press office penned a wonderfully worded reply, which put the record straight.

We were knackered. Adrenaline and nervous energy (and varying amounts of Bolivian marching powder) can only keep you going for so long. The cumulative effects of six months' touring were beginning to become apparent. Not just me. I was practically teetotal compared to some of the guys. It was obvious that we could not sustain this level of energy – but we had a schedule. We were part of 'the music business'. The fact that 'we owned our own record label' was irrelevant. Chrysalis wanted a second album, Europe was clamouring for us to tour there again, Japan was on the touring schedule, America needed 'following up'. We were musical flavour of the month in England. All sorts of dodgy deals, big concerts, a feature film, TV programmes hurtled our way, needed to be discussed; decisions needed to be made, and all we wanted to do was sleep. We didn't have any choice. We had to learn to enjoy the ride or get off, and nobody wanted to get off! I would have liked it to have gone a little more slowly, though.

A trip to Paris to play at the formidable-sounding 'Pavillon Baltard' turned into a fraught performance, inter-spersed with fights between travelling Specials fans and French skinheads. To make matters worse, my bass was tuned wrong by some trainee guitar roadie Our Kid had brought along. I had to suffer the indignity of tuning the thing by ear over by Jerry's keyboard, while the whole world, it seemed, watched. To make matters *even* worse,

Adrian Thrills was accompanying us to do an article for a new rock/style magazine, and we were going to be on the cover. As it was, the *Face* came out in May 1980, with Jerry, complete with plastic grin and fetching spot between his eyes, on the cover. The article detailed our lacklustre performance and showed how knackered we were. Great! When it came out, we were recording *More Specials* and Jerry had a blazing row with Brad about Brad's idea for a 2-Tone review, mixing ska, soul and reggae. Don't know why – it seemed a good idea to me.

A next single was required, and a tune of Roddy's that we'd been working on in America was going to be it. 'Rat Race'. Rod had not exactly shone at school and had spent evenings down the Lanchester Polytechnic (probably when Jerry or I were down there) drinking the cheap beer and clocking the students. The song, Rod has since told me, is not an anti-student rant, more a song about privilege, how these guys (and girls) would spend three years pissing it up at college, knowing full well that Daddy would get them a good job when they left no matter what. The best thing you could hope for in Coventry working men's circles was to get a job at 'the Jag', as the Jaguar car factory was called. Rod was railing against the people who bought them. We took Linton Kwesi Johnson's tune 'Me Wan' Fi Go Rave' as our musical starting point. Rockers' drums, walking bass, a cool Dennis Bovelle production. The tune came together pretty quickly, Jerry putting a touch of John Barry (the plucked piano intro) into the tune, pre-empting our foray into muzak, and Nev put some bongoes over it.

We had to sort out a B-side. At rehearsals Lynval was playing harmonica, and he and Nev were doing this 'Rude Boy dem a come' thing which sounded shite, but no one had the bottle to tell them. Hey – I could write something for that. The result, 'Rude Boys Outta Jail', was my first foray into song-writing. I never wrote anything else for The Specials. The tune took about ten minutes to write. Jerry sorted the bass line out, and the arrangement was done by consensus. It was not exactly 'Desolation Row', but it was the B-side to 'Rat Race' and was credited to Golding/ Staples/Gentleman. Rico always said it was one of his favourite Specials tunes. Perhaps he was just being polite.

We recorded it back in Coventry at Horizon, where we had cut 'Gangsters' just over a year before. It was a good exercise to see if the studio was still any good and whether Dave Jordan could cut it as a producer. A yes for both of those, and the path was kinda clear for the next album, which was scheduled to be recorded in the summer . . . as soon as we'd got the tunes. We didn't have any tunes . . . yet.

Brad, on the other hand, not being content with being the drummer in the best band in England, wanted to record a solo single, a cover of an old Northern Soul tune, 'Sock It to 'em JB' (by Rex Garvey and The Mighty Cravers, apparently). The 'JB' on the original was James Bond, but we thought it could be a reference to our drummer, John Bradbury. Whatever. He had been sweet-talking a studio in Tulse Hill to get some studio time, and we all piled down there, learnt the song in twenty minutes and recorded it. The original sax player on the session couldn't cut it, but the backing track was sound. The whole thing seemed a waste of time, but the tune ended up on *More Specials* – and became one of my favourite cuts.

We had been offered a chance to appear on NBC's *Saturday Night Live* programme in New York. It meant national exposure on US television – more exposure than six weeks on a bus could bring – which begged the question: 'Why did we do a tour, when a TV programme gave more exposure?', but hey, rock 'n' roll, phew, etc.

As it turned out, it was a terrific performance. Jerry was in a foul mood. He hated the extravagance of staying in expensive Manhattan hotels and let his feelings be known to anyone in the vicinity. By the time we got set up in the NBC studios on the eighth floor of the Rockerfeller Center, we were all wound up as tight as springs, pissed off and angry, and all this came out in our performance. I only got to see the thing (it went out live) in 1995, and it is a chilling piece of live television. We are all cramped up on a small stage – no room, and snarling and spitting with real rage. Roddy especially looks like he could rip someone's head off. It looked fantastic. And it got repeated . . . and repeated. It passed into mythology in the growing US ska scene. Touring almost twenty years later, I was still accosted by people telling me they'd seen The Specials on *Saturday Night Live*. I was amazed at how influential our performance was.

During a break in rehearsals, a little wizened old man with wild hair and a 'lived-in' face came up to Jerry, gave him a big hug and said something like, 'Love your record, mate.' It was Keith Richards. Dave Jordan had sought him out and brought him along. Everyone lined up like you do when you meet the Queen or something, and 'His Keefness' bestowed his blessings upon us, gave Lynval a delay pedal and Rod a graphic equalizer. What a nice bloke. He handed me a spliff, which I declined. 'Wow, you *have* got a problem,' was his reply, which, coming from him . . . Mr Richards was accompanied by a pale girl, whose job seemed to be to laugh at his not-very-funny jokes, and a gentleman who was obviously the 'bag man', whose eyes darted around furiously whenever anyone spoke to him.

Brad was in paroxysms of rock 'n' roll ecstasy to be in the company of such exalted a person as Keef himself. Me, I didn't think I'd like him looking after *my* house while I was away on holiday. He obviously inhabited an atmosphere a lot more rarefied than mine. I kept my distance but dined out on 'the day I met the remains of Keith Richards' for a considerable time afterwards. I understand he's a lot better these days.

The Hamer Guitar rep who we'd met earlier in the year showed up back at the hotel, and I got a lovely 8-string bass, just like Nick Lowe's, for a splendidly knock-down price. It's on 'Rich Girl' and 'I Can't Stand It' on *More Specials*. I sold it in 1982, when the rent was due. Guitars come, guitars go. Be nice to have it back now, though.

I can't remember if there were any specific rehearsals for our second LP. I do remember us congregating in Horizon Studios in Coventry with Dave Jordan, deciding the sound wasn't 'live' enough and going to buy two dozen sheets of corrugated iron to build a 'shanty town' vocal booth and to put round the drums and amps to 'brighten up' the sound. (At the very end of the session, I took the sheets over to my parents' house. My father used them for a new shed roof. He was very appreciative.)

We had been playing around with the riff to what became 'International Jet Set' since half-way through our American trip, and 'Stereotype' was just starting to take shape. Lynval had a three-chord reggae tune with the chorus 'I'm just living in a life without meaning', which was to become 'Do Nothing'. Roddy had quite a few songs,

193

but only a couple – 'Hey Little Rich Girl' and what was to be called 'Holiday Fortnight' – were chosen. This friction between Jerry and Rod over song-writing was to get worse. Rod had always made it clear that he wanted to have his own band, so he could play his own rockabilly-tinged rock 'n' roll. Jerry was moving in a 'fake jazz/muzak' direction, which was poles apart from Rod's quiff-a-billy stance, especially since rockabilly stylists The Stray Cats had started to make waves in London.

Such was the setting, then, for the making of the second Specials LP.

The recording sessions were also dogged by the outside world. I remember we were just about ready to do a 'take' of 'Rat Race' when someone from the front desk popped her head round the control room to say there was a journalist in reception to see the band. Various members of the band traipsed off to see the journalist, and the 'vibe' for the song was lost. I was furious. Talking about yourself had obviously become more important than playing the music.

Jerry had taken delivery of a Yamaha home organ and was generally to be found giggling over the pre-recorded rhythms – especially the Latin-American ones. The 'cheesy organ' tone was the real deal when it came to his 'muzak' vision. He used it on stage for the remainder of the band's career. We used it to record in a 'one instrument at a time' fashion as opposed to the 'ensemble' recording we had done for our first record. The drum track and keyboards were put down first, I put the bass on, Lynval did the guitar, and so on. It gave a totally different feeling to the music. It sounded 'soulless', which is kind of what muzak is.

The material slowly started to come together. We dredged our old repertoire and used a tune that used to be called 'Rock and Roll Nightmare', but ended up being called 'Pearl's Café'. 'I Can't Stand It', too, was a blast from our Heath Hotel past. It was recorded in the 'one instrument at a time' layered fashion, like 'Stereotype' and 'International Jet Set'.

Terry presented his first Specials lyrics for 'Man at C&A', to which Jerry added a second verse and the killer tune, with a horn arrangement inspired by Nelson Riddle or somebody. Rico and Dick took to it straight away and made it their own. It is one of my favourite Specials tunes and was fantastic to play live. Brad stuck some syn-drums over it. These were generally linked with dreadful disco tunes, but they made those 'explosion' sounds on 'C&A'. Luckily, Brad was keen on new gadgets, and his interest in the new technology stuff was a good foil for Lyn, Rod and me, who preferred recording live like our favourite records were back then. I was originally very sceptical about recording individual instruments at different times. It is interesting to note that nowadays this method of recording is generally standard – if musicians are used at all, that is.

'Enjoy Yourself' was learnt and recorded in about forty-five minutes and sounds like it. (I did hear that the original late-forties swing version was banned on the armed forces radio in Europe – Cold War paranoia and all that.) We, naturally, lifted it from a ska version by Prince Buster. Lynval's rabble-rousing at the end of the tune still makes the hair stand up on the back of my neck; the frustration is audible. The even-more-cynical version at the end of the album was done with the help of The Go-Gos, who had played in town with Madness earlier that evening. It becomes a chilling end to what is, to me, an uncomfortable record.

Brad's Northern Soul foray, 'Sock it to 'em JB', was brought up to speed with the help of Paul Heskett's saxophone, which added an extra bit of sixties kitsch to the proceedings.

Although other members of the band are credited as songwriters, it was Jerry who masterminded the sessions. He put an extra chord in Lynval's tune 'Do Nothing' and wrote at least two of the verses, although the song is credited to Lynval. Terry and I wrote a new verse (the last one) for Roddy's 'Hey Little Rich Girl'. 'Pearl's Café' was just an instrumental when I left the sessions, as was a 'calypso' version of a tune that Roddy had written. (It remained an instrumental and was called 'Holiday Fortnight'.) My favourite track on the record is 'International Jet Set'. It is as spooky as hell and, up until then, was the best bass playing I felt I had recorded in my life. The horn parts were fantastic, and Dick Cuthell's soloing towards the end of the tune was brilliant.

The whole record, to me, was laced with a 'beyond cynicism' vibe. It was dramatically different to our debut LP, which had a vibrancy and a 'positive anger', if there is such a thing. *More Specials* seemed angry at its own impotence. It didn't seem to care.

Roddy's rant 'Rat Race' was released on 17 May 1980, complete with video shot in the main hall of the Lanchester Polytechnic (now Coventry University), where Jerry and I had studied, and where I'd seen all manner of bands in the previous eight years. (Presumably it was where Roddy prowled, too, while writing the song.) For the video we all dressed up as teacher stereotypes: Lynval – track suit, Nev – gown and mortar board, Rod – art teacher, Terry – bow tie and glasses, Brad – science teacher, me – obligatory tweed jacket with leather elbow patches, and Jerry as the headmistress from hell. The video was banned due to Jerry's cross-dressing, which was ludicrous considering Danny La Rue was prime-time Saturday-night viewing. We also used a load of 'extras', students who thought it'd be fun to be in a video. (It wasn't; some of them got really pissed off and couldn't wait to get out of there.) A lot of the crowd camerawork featured Brad's girlfriend, Emily (the one in the lime-green blouse). Like most of the videos I've been involved with, it was not a pleasurable experience. The single entered the UK charts at number eighteen the next week and went up to eight, six, or four the following week, depending on which chart you looked at.

It was obvious the album was going to take a lot longer than was originally planned, so we had to leave the studio to fulfil various commitments, which was good really because we got a break to do something different. The Pink Pop festival in Holland was a good example.

The big European outdoor festivals were generally pleasurable affairs. A couple or three days abroad, a whacking big stage and loads of people to play to. The audiences were nowhere near as partisan as English ones. The bill, when we played Pink Pop in 1980, was: Garland Jeffries (Brooklyn singer/songwriter with reggae overtones), The J. Giels Band (American blues rock), Joe Jackson, The Specials, Van Halen and The Jam. In England, that running order would have been disastrous, but over in Europe, everyone seemed equally appreciative of all the acts. This, however, didn't stop us having to calm down a certain section of the audience halfway through our set, which, because of our recent studio confinement, was not up to its usual standard. The Van Halen crew put the word out that they wouldn't stand for any skinheads invading *their* stage. They must have been worried. The Van Halens were hilarious. Dave Lee Roth arrived with a big plaster across his nose; he'd broken it a couple of nights previous jumping too high and nutting a mirror ball. Twit. The band – dwarfed by walls of speaker cabs, and a huge drum riser – never actually seemed to finish a song, but broke down into what I can only assume was 'spontaneous' delight: 'Wow, you're such a fuckinfantasticaudience!' The crowd went wild. Me, I laughed a lot. This was pure showbiz, and, great players though they may have been, the music became a dreary second to their 'rock 'n' roll' vaudeville.

Joe Jackson was very cool indeed, if not a little paranoid of photographers backstage, and The Jam were surly and miserable, but they did play 'Start' (this was before it was released – a fantastic tune, Bruce Foxton wielding this lovely black semi-acoustic Epiphone bass guitar – ooh, I was jealous).

For me, one of the main attractions of these festivals was the certain amount of anonymity that you got, both backstage and out the front. You might get recognized as 'someone in a group', but there were so many bands on they rarely bothered you. It became a hassle when some rabid Specials fan latched on to you and asked to come backstage, whereupon they usually made total berks of themselves and drank all the backstage alcohol, familiarity breeding contempt in generally about fifteen minutes. Jerry and Terry were very much in favour of letting fans back-stage, but I was starting to feel they were an unnecessary hassle when you were trying to work. The whole audience/band thing was never resolved. I didn't like the idea of being 'separate' from the audience – it was what punk was all about anyway – but I did not appreciate eight drunken skinheads from Romford largeing it up in the dressing room straight after a gig, and then expecting you to sneak them into the hotel and have them spend the night on the floor of your bedroom. I needed the space; they needed to grow up.

During the summer of 1980, our road crew, Rex and Trevor, decided to throw in the towel. They formed their own band, 21 Guns, with vocalist Gus Chambers, who had replaced Terry in Squad. Rex had been tinkering behind Brad's drums for a while, and Jerry had been showing Trevor some basic keyboard stuff. Whether they left because they didn't like being our road crew any more or because they wanted to get what we got, I don't know. I was pleased they had their own band. Neville was talking about setting up his own record label (as was Brad, naturally!) and was going to release their records. It was a shame they had to leave. Two remnants from 'the old days' gone. Their replacements were a couple of Rob Gambino's buddies from 'oop North', Rob Stalker and Jim Salter. Both solid, dependable guys, but . . .

The whole question of 'what 2-Tone was' was never far from our lips. Jerry had talked about it being a collective of fourteen people (us and The Selecter), but I also remember Bernie Rhodes pontificating back in 1978: 'Never 'ave meetings! Never 'ave meetings!' and we rarely did. I never felt that any issue was ever resolved. On a good day, people would agree to differ. On a bad day, we'd just sulk. Rick Rogers was more of a facilitator for Jerry's ideas than a manger in the traditional sense. The idea of having an HQ with a club and a recording studio was an idea several of us had. An old cinema in Gosford Street (the Paris) had recently closed down, and a costing exercise was carried out by the president of the Lanchester Polytechnic students' union, one Peter Hadfield. We were very impressed by his efficiency and thoroughness. We passed on the Paris, but kept the messenger. Pete Hadfield would become our tour manager. Someone not yet infected by rock 'n' roll.

Romance loomed large for me during the summer of 1980. I hadn't had any 'serious attachments' for a year or so, but I had started corresponding with a girl I had met when we played at Exeter University the previous year. Jackie was in her final year at the university. She came from Cheltenham, not exactly plummy, but a Girls' grammar school type. We started seeing one another during my stay in Coventry while I was recording *More Specials*. Exeter would become something of a rest and relaxation destination for the next year or so and contributed to my gradual withdrawal from the group.

During our confinement at Horizon Studios, I got a call from Rick's office in London. They had received a letter from the mother of a teenage boy who had been in some kind of accident; he was in intensive care in Gateshead. The letter said that the lad was a mad keen Specials fan, and a message of encouragement would help enormously. I said I'd see what I could do, but the vibe at the studio was not conducive to brotherly love, and the plight of a distraught mother seemed to be a different universe compared to the 'I don't see why Jerry says his songs are better than mine', or 'We should make decisions as a band, and not have one person calling the shots' rubbish that people were starting to come out with. I got some more phone calls from our office over the next couple of weeks asking if I'd done anything about it, and I eventually got a cassette of rough mixes together and wrote a few lines of encouragement. I sent the thing off and returned to my role of failing miserably to pour oil on troubled waters and starting not to care whether the maracas were in stereo or not. A while later, I got a letter back from the mother in Gateshead, thanking me for sending the tape, but she had buried her son a fortnight previously. The tape had arrived too late. (I have never told anyone in the band about this and, try as I might, I can't find the letter for any more details. It has not been easy writing this.)

This had a deep impact upon me and made me question an awful lot about who I was and what I was doing with my life. I was part of the most influential pop group of the day, I was doing what I had only been able to dream about a few years ago. Now, I was helplessly watching it unravel in front of me, seemingly unable to do anything about it. It also got me thinking about a bigger picture. Perhaps it was unfair for a mother with a son in intensive care to look to her boy's heroes to save his life. Could a cassette of rough mixes and a scrawled few lines have done anything? The fact that it arrived too late meant that I would never know. The whole thing made me feel sick. Sick and very angry.

It would be easy to get very melodramatic about the whole thing, but here was something that put what we were doing in a different perspective entirely. The Specials, whether we liked it or not, was becoming more than just a pop group. I felt tremendously proud of our collective stand against racism and the fact that we 'stood for something', rather than just being another pop group, but being looked to as the 'spokesperson for a generation' was not something I (or anyone else in the band for that matter) was prepared for or able to handle. The responsibility that was being dumped on us was more than I wanted to cope with.

I kind of closed down after that. I finished my backing tracks and went down to Exeter. The different environment down in the West Country helped to mellow me out. The talk among Jackie and her friends was of a self-awareness course they had done in London recently. They were all fairly ecstatic about it, and about how they had become more self-assertive. They did seem to enjoy life more and were demonstratively positive about things. I was naturally dubious, but I thought if there was one thing I did need, it was to be more self-assertive and positive. The next 'seminar', as it was called, that I could do was at the end of August. I decided to do it. It was called the Exegesis Programme . . .

As The Specials attempted to 'do things differently', it was decided to do a tour of English coastal resorts. Our 'Seaside tour', 4–19 June, took in such salubrious venues as Barrow-in-Furness Civic Hall, Skegness Sands Show Bar and Margate Winter Gardens. There were fourteen dates in all, including Aylesbury and Leeds, both of which are nowhere near the sea! Support for the tour was new 2-Tone signing The Bodysnatchers, an all-girl ska band from London and, from Los Angeles, our old buddies The Go-Gos. It wasn't until I was on the coach that I realized we were on tour with two girl bands! Oh well, off we go again.

I enjoyed the fact that we weren't travelling the usual

rock 'n' roll circuit and were playing quite a few places that weren't on the touring map. Consequently, the shows in places like Barrow, Yarmouth and Skegness were real good. (The hydraulic stage collapsed at the end of the Skegness show and we had to hightail it out of town pretty quick as the club bouncers were after our blood!)

The Bodysnatchers had only been together for a number of months and were learning to play their instruments on stage. Sax player Miranda Joyce was seventeen and looked it. Rhythm guitarist Stella Barker (who had formed a romantic attachment with Neville Staple) was older — mid-twenties I'd guess. They made a joyous racket, however, and fitted a punk stereotype by being 'only just' able to play their material. Musically they were held together by bass player Nicky Summers. Their visual presence was provided by vocalist Rhodar Dakar, who excelled herself night after night with outrageous mini-skirts and tall hair.

The Go-Gos had a pretty rough time of it; they weren't ska, and our (mainly male) audience wasn't keen on their snappy power-pop tunes. Audiences still spat at groups in those days. Despite all this they seemed happy to be on the road with us. They did the first week and then went off to go on tour with Madness (The Go-Gos had signed a single deal with Stiff, Madness's label). Terry continued his friendship with rhythm guitarist Jane Wiedlin, and they would generally be seen in one another's company, causing not a few nudges and winks from assorted Specials. I don't know whether they were making sweet music together and it is none of my business, but they did write a song. The Go-Gos' IRS album, *Beauty and the Beat*, went to number one in the American album charts and contains the rather wonderful 'Our Lips Are Sealed', a Hall/Wiedlin composition.

The lyrics could easily be taken as a withering comment on Terry and Jane's status on the Seaside tour.

> Can you hear them?
> They talk about us
> Telling lies
> Well that's no surprise!
>
> Can you see them?
> See right through them?
> They have a shield
> Nothing must be revealed
>
> Doesn't matter what they say
> No one listens anyway
> Our lips are sealed
>
> There's a weapon
> We can use
> In our defence
> Silence
>
> So just look at them
> Look right through them
> That's when they disappear
> That's when we lose the fear
>
> It doesn't matter what they say
> In the jealous games people play
> Our lips are sealed*

The Fun Boy Three did a somewhat turgid version of it on their somewhat turgid second album. Terry probably made more money from his liaison with Jane Wiedlin than with Jerry Dammers. Me? Jealous? Nah!

---

* Hall/Wiedlin. Published by Plangent Visions/BMG.

One major up-turn in our fortunes during the Seaside tour was that for the first time we had SINGLE ROOMS. How fantastic is that! Not to have to trip over someone else's suitcase, or get woken up by someone barging into the room the worse for drink at 2.30 a.m., was luxury indeed. Privacy, my own space. Fantastic! On the rather badly photocopied tour itinerary that had been sent out to the hotels, my name got changed from Horace Panter to Alice Pinter. I got a t-shirt printed. It said: My name is Alice Pinter.

Bridlington Royal Spa Pavilion saw a surprise stage invasion during The Bodysnatchers' set by members of Bad Manners, who were ... er ... passing through. It sounded like Terry was trashing the dressing room after the show, Rick Rogers standing guard as glass shattered behind the door. What was all *that* about? The Bridlington date was also memorable for its 'day off', when a massive 2-Tone pub crawl took place. There was a drinking contest between Sean Carasov, our t-shirt guy (hey, we got merchandise!), and Margo Olaverra, the Go-Gos' bass player. The poison of choice was vodka and orange. Margo won hands down. We had to carry an unconscious Sean back to the hotel.

Not staying up boozing had its benefit in Leeds, where an early-morning visit to a second-hand shop yielded up a 1975 Fender Telecaster guitar, just like Lynval's, for £120. Bargain or what! I took it with me on the coach, where it was coveted furiously by Selecter guitarist Compton Amanour, who was 'escorting' Bodysnatcher Sarah-Jane at the time.

The house was definitely rocking in Hastings, the pier moving on its foundations for The Specials and their

1,500-strong mad-for-it audience. They came, they danced, they limped home happy.

I was looking forward to returning to Friars in Aylesbury. It was where we did our first show as The Specials, supporting The Clash almost two years ago. Any fond memories were short-lived, however, as the gig was beset by crowd problems, and, despite a hefty barrier, a horde of people got on stage towards the end of the show. The promoter explained that he was in danger of losing his use of the hall because of crowd trouble and vented his spleen at us after the show. Terry and Roddy told him to fuck off. Gigs had been put on at that venue for at least fifteen years, and it had a nice vibe about it, apparently until we came along. Rather than changing anything, we just seemed to be responsible for closing things down. Chrysalis Records execs had turned up at the show politely enquiring when our next album would be ready. If I remember right, they were treated with the same respect as the promoter.

It was clear to anyone with a brain that things were not happy in Special-land. *Melody Maker*'s Paolo Hewitt witnessed Roddy hurling empty beer glasses and threats in anyone's direction. I suppose if anyone was not coping, it was Rod. It was plain to see he had difficulty handling being a Special and he'd try to blot out the problems with alcohol, which temporarily turned him from a likeable lad to an unpredictable and angry young man. During the show in Colwyn Bay he smashed a beautiful Gibson Les Paul guitar over Jerry's keyboard. We had difficulties keeping guitar roadies. Two of them quit because they couldn't stand Roddy trashing his instruments. We ended up with a guy called Cedric. He and Brad got on very well together (I think they both lived in the same part of London). Cedric

Cool shot of Lynval, with E.T. in the background. Lyceum, 2 December 1979.

EUROPE

◎ Just before the big freeze. Left to right: Frank Murray (tour manager), Rob 'Our Kid' Gambino (crew boss), Alfie (bus driver), 13 January 1980.

◎ Rick Rogers and me at the Berlin Wall, 14 January 1980.

AMERICA

◐ New Orleans,
27 January 1980.

◑ Denver Airport,
31 January 1980.

The Specials on tv, February 1980. Here's Rico, the 'Man from Warieka'.

The Mobile Lunatic Asylum and its lunatics. Left to right: Brad, Dick Cuthell, John Jostins, Jerry (with E.T. hiding behind), Nev, Dave Jordan, Rod and Lynval.

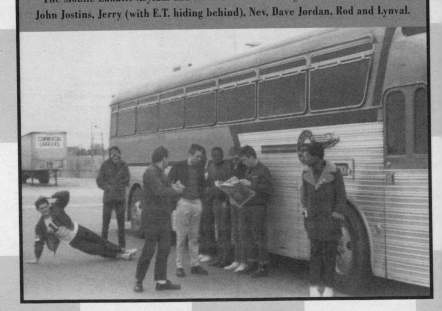

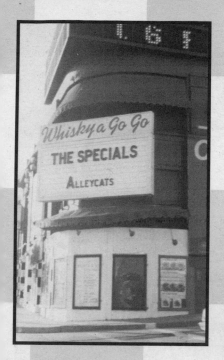

◖ Ah! My name
in lights on Sunset Strip!
The fateful Whisky a Go Go,
10 February 1980.

◖ New York.
A slightly more fateful photo,
2 March 1980.

◖ Jerry, the perpetual tourist.
Brussels, June 1980.

The coolest jacket in the world has its photo taken at Horizon Studios during the *More Specials* sessions, April–June 1980.

Japan. Complete with sceptical fan, 29 June 1980.

Me, Terry and the back of a bus in . . . er . . . Amsterdam. Pink Pop, 1980.

Sound check, Ireland, January 1981.

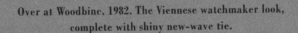

Over at Woodbine, 1982. The Viennese watchmaker look,
complete with shiny new-wave tie.

would work for us until the band finally split. Lynval once said that The Specials was like a marriage, but we never got counselling! About sums it up really. Things seemed to get swept under carpets and ignored. A very British trait, stiff upper lip, keep soldiering on and all that. Sometimes, the atmosphere in the band was horrendous and it had started to surface on stage. A year ago we could strip paint we were that good. Now we didn't have to be. We could play crap, tardy, soulless, far-too-fast versions of our tunes and the crowd would still go bonkers. As long as we finished off with 'Gangsters', big trombone solo and Neville going mental across the front monitors, the business, as far as the punters were concerned, was done. The music almost came secondary to 'seeing' the band. We were The Specials, a 'band to follow', a movement. A monster of our own creation.

The departing Go-Gos were replaced for the last remaining dates by Coventry's Reluctant Stereotypes. Originally an 'art-rock' kind of ensemble (a departing offshoot became indie heroes Eyeless in Gaza), they had recently taken a ska leaning, signed a deal (with EMI I think) and had a Roger Lomas-produced album out. Their vocalist was Paul King, who went on to front Coventry's version of The Bay City Rollers a few years later, but King, as they say, is outside the scope of this book. What The Reluctant Stereotypes did possess, however, was guitar player Paul Sampson. He and I shared a predilection for all things Frank Zappa, although his knowledge was a lot more comprehensive than mine. We had a hoot being very esoteric and dropping all sorts of Zappa-isms ('Hello Teenage America!') all over the place. A couple of times after gigs, we'd sit up on the back seat of the 2-Tone coach, its passengers increased by various Romfords, or

Catfords, and sing the *We're Only in It for the Money* LP all the way through, from 'What's there to live for, who needs the Peace Corps' to 'If it doesn't show, think you'd better know, I'm another person', which wasn't exactly the last track, but the end cut was 'The Chrome-Plated Megaphone of Destiny', which didn't have any lyrics . . . or tune. What fun. Hey, look at me, I can be annoying too!

I'm trying my best to think of any one thing that caused the Specials to fall apart. It's difficult. It was lots of small things. For me, it was Brad's blustery, aggressive manner and wind-ups; Roddy drinking; Jerry drinking; Terry's self-defensive cynicism; Rick Rogers trying to placate everybody at the same time and failing; me singing Frank Zappa tunes in the back of the bus; cocaine, and the money. Ah yes, the money! We had started to get royalty cheques. The Specials recouped very quickly. Twice a year, April and October, we would get statements and a cheque for our mechanical royalties (the number of records sold) and the publishing royalties (paid to the writers of the tunes).

Our statements were all individually broken down, and there was a lot of bad feeling when it was seen that Jerry, as the main songwriter, copped a considerably larger sum than other members. Personally, I thought (and still think) that Jerry deserved every penny he got. Whether we liked it or not, we wouldn't be in the enviable position we currently found ourselves in without him. Some 2-Tone bands had agreed to split their money equally. (The Beat, if I remember correctly, did this for a while, as did The Selecter, although Neol Davies, who, like Jerry, wrote the lion's share of the tunes, says he felt some pressure to divide the money equally.) Money has always caused problems in groups, especially lots of money. It makes people greedy. 'I do as much work as him, why shouldn't I get as much money?' 'You're supposed to be a socialist, why don't you practise what you preach?' I thought it pathetic. I began to lose faith and trust in people who, two years ago, I would have emptied my pockets for. Now, it was the rise of the Pop Star as Greedy Bastard.

The Seaside tour ended in chaos in Portsmouth. I remember after the show Lynval sitting on the edge of the stage, talking with a kid who had a British Movement symbol shaved into his already cropped head. It was one of those 'I wish I had a camera' moments and woke me out of my cynicism. There was an awful lot of good that The Specials could do, and there were times, if I wasn't blinkered or could get out of my current malaise, when we did.

The hotel in Portsmouth was taken over by Specials fans. The management threw their hands up in horror and went to bed. The band's London contingent (Brad, Rick, Dick and Rico) left for the capital that night. I went to bed amidst all the mayhem, got up early the next day and headed back down to Exeter. Next up, Japan.

11

The Specials Go to Japan and Don't Enjoy Themselves

Japan was somewhere that even the most cynical of us wanted to go. The fashion side of the 2-Tone empire had taken off big time in the land of the rising sun. Toshiba/ EMI, who sold our records over there, had been doing a big promotional campaign, and all the signs were very favourable. We could be 'big in Japan'! We were scheduled to do seven shows, but, as you will see, it turned out to be eight: four in Tokyo, two in Osaka and one in Kyoto. The only other 'new wave' acts to have visited Japan were Generation X and The Boomtown Rats, both pretty straight-ahead four-to-the-floor rock (albeit with safety pins attached). So what they would think of our take on ska-with-everything was anybody's guess.

I kept a tour diary of our trip to Japan, the entries being generally made last thing at night, with me sometimes the worse for wear from drink, but usually just high on adrenaline. This was 1980, remember, before Glasnost and the dismantling of Communism, so we couldn't fly over Russia. It was Heathrow to Anchorage (Alaska), refuel and then on to Tokyo. Up, over, and down again, so to speak.

The touring party was the band plus Dick and Rico, Rick Rogers, Dave Jordan, Chris Christie (Selecter's guitar roadie) and Rob 'Our Kid' Gambino as 'the road crew', lighting female Lin Scoffin and Nick Baker, monitor engineer, making a posse of fifteen. The diary starts here and, although not as concise as my American journal, gives a reasonable account of our failed attempt to appreciate a foreign culture.

Monday 23 June over the top and down the other side. I'd spent the week in between the seaside tour and our trip to Japan with Jackie down in Exeter. It was from there that we left at 7 a.m. Monday morning and arrived at Heathrow ahead of schedule at 10.30 a.m. Everyone slowly assembles, and the mood is quite melancholic. Jerry looks the worst. He is not a good flyer, and this is going to be some flight – eighteen and a half hours in the air all told. Girlfriends and wives are kissed goodbye; we do all the boarding nonsense and get gone; the flight departs at 1.30 p.m.

One day soon, I'm going to work out just how many miles we've travelled so far this year. It'll be pretty staggering. I might come on a bit blasé about flying these days, but it doesn't lessen the thrill of taking off and crawling up into the sky. When you watch it take off, a 747 seems to hang almost motionless in the sky, not really sure if it's going to make it or not. When you're on board, however, there is no doubt. It is a tremendous feeling, the take-off.

Everything I've ever seen from the air pales into insignificance compared to the ice floes on the Arctic Ocean, followed by the Greenland land mass. This must be the most desolate place on Earth. Sheer white. We fly somewhere between the 'true' pole and the 'magnetic' pole, right over the top of the world, before we stop off at Anchorage to refuel. Flying over millions of square miles of snow and seeing nothing but our shadow with accompanying vapour trails chasing us was incredible.

One of the many things that baffle me on this planet is the time-zone thing. We left Heathrow at 1.30 p.m., arriving in Anchorage at 12.30 p.m.: a trip of eight hours has us arriving in Alaska one hour before we set off. Now, the journey from Anchorage to Tokyo takes nine hours, when all of a sudden it's 2.30 p.m. on Monday afternoon. We've been in the air for seventeen hours, and it's supposedly one and a half hours since we left! Unfortunately it's 6.30 a.m. on Tuesday in England. I am confused. Having been awake for nearly thirty hours, I'm not surprised.

Anyhow, it is an understandably weary ensemble that eventually lands in Japan. We're met at Narita airport by Massy, our promoter, and various henchmen-looking types, who stuff our suitcases and instruments onto a bus, and off we go. Before I realize what's going on, we're in Tokyo. Everything as far as the eye can see is populated. Flimsy packed-together houses and Le Corbusier-style apartment blocks, Frank Lloyd Wright roofs, ziggurat blocks of flats and, wherever possible, trees. Even if it's a six-foot-square plot at the back of a house, it's got a tree in it. Roof gardens too, six storeys up. What a fantastic place! Out comes the camera.

Finally we arrive at the Shiba Park hotel. Our rooms are small but uncluttered. Single rooms, too! The bath is 4 feet long (two-thirds of a 'normal'-size bath), and there's a kimono for me to wear. My body clock has thrown in the towel; I'm so tired I can't sleep, so I'm going to stay awake as long as I can, to try to adjust more quickly. I haven't been outside yet, but after a shower and several cups of strong coffee, I'm going to take a stroll. We appear to be here!

Tuesday 24 June. I finally got to sleep some time in the evening. I slept for at least twelve hours. Woken up at 10.30 a.m. by someone delivering five guitars to my room. Hmm! Things are looking up! I wonder if everyone has had five guitars delivered to their rooms? So here I go, clothed in my hotel kimono, sorting out this freshly delivered Yamaha bass guitar, when there's a knock on the door. 'Sorry, the guitars were delivered to the wrong room.' Damn fiendish, these Japanese. They should have gone to the promoter's room, and here's me thinking my luck was in. Never mind. It's too late for breakfast, so it's out for another look round.

Street-wise, the place is built American-style, in blocks, and only the main streets have English subtitles (so to speak). To save getting totally lost, I walk up the road, and then back down on the other side. Not particularly adventurous, but it enables me to experience the local colour. The old and the new are linked together. Traditional wooden-built craft shops housing tailors, shoemakers and so on next to concrete-block stores. All gaily coloured decorations, very festive. Unfortunately I really do feel like a stranger in a strange land, and repair to a symbol of the West for something to eat, namely a McDonald's. Kinda dumb, really, to come all this way, see all these sights and end up with a quarter-pounder with fries!

Back to the hotel, and the pop business has started already. I sit in on an interview with Terry and Jerry.

Rick Rogers and Dick Cuthell appear, clutching recent photographic purchases. Rick's got a second-hand Nikon camera in brand new condition for the equivalent of £150! In the afternoon, we are all taken to the Tsubaki House, a disco/nightclub (where some of the guys ended up last night) for a press conference, which ends in chaos. Very reminiscent of the one we did at Hurrah's in New York earlier in the year. The questions asked range from the vaguely interesting to the mundane, but The Specials just come across as ignorant, rude and insulting to the Japanese journalists, who just take it and smile. Inscrutable. Rico is plainly embarrassed by our behaviour, and so, I'm afraid, am I.

If people have taken the trouble to set up these interviews, the least we can do is answer their questions civilly. Terry comes over as the main culprit: 'We're all gay,' he says, and 'All Japanese girls are slags.' The rest of the band guffaw and throw cigarettes at one another, but I don't think it's funny.

After more interviews, and a painfully awful TV spot, where we come across as ignorant buffoons, we are taken back to the Shiba Park, where Massy takes us all out to a tiny restaurant for a meal. The food is fantastic. We sit around a circular bar-type construction, with the chef in the middle. The food, thin strips of meat with vegetables, is plonked in a pan for thirty seconds, then put straight in front of us. My deftness with chopsticks leaves an awful lot to be desired, but I muddle through without making too much of a fool of myself.

After the meal Dick and I venture out and end up in a jazz club called Misty, where we are entertained by a piano/bass/drums trio with the promise of a girl vocalist later on. The piano player, according to Dick, is too flash, the double bass player is dire, and the drummer had great difficulty keeping the whole thing together, that is to say, they went out of time a lot. We stayed for about an hour, leaving during the second of the guest vocalist's songs. (God, she was awful!)

Wednesday 25 June. Now this is odd. Monday night I slept for twelve hours straight, but last night I only managed three. I remember the second day in America as being the worst one as far as readjusting went. Luckily, tonight's show starts at 6.30 p.m., as opposed to the horrendous half past one in the morning that saw us finally appear in New York.

So, it's 4.30 a.m. here in Tokyo, and I'm ready for anything . . . not that there's anything to do, mind. I decide to write some letters home. At 1 p.m. The Specials head off to prepare for their first concert in Japan, the Konen Hall, to be precise, a large Hammersmith Odeon type of theatre with a huge stage. Audience capacity is 2,000 and we've done 1,800 advance tickets. It's looking good.

The rented equipment we are using for this tour is great. Brad is over the moon with his all-black Pearl drum kit. The Yamaha guitars don't sound as good as they play, which is a drag, as we're constantly pestered by a Yamaha rep, who extols the virtues of his company's products at every opportunity. Chris Christie and Neville put the hustle on him and try to get him to part with a couple of 6-strings, but no deal. Inscrutable. The gig opens at 6.00 p.m. and The Specials go on stage at 6.50 p.m. This is how the concerts work in Japan. Show starts early; show finishes early. Everyone goes home to bed. Good night's sleep. Up bright and early and fit for work the next day.

The gig started off very odd: low background music, the atmosphere similar to that of a church. Polite clapping, which turned to moderate applause as we went on stage. The first few numbers were greeted with polite applause, and the front four or so rows of punters stood up. It was very difficult to know how we were doing, and there were some odd glances exchanged between the musicians. When we started 'Too Much Too Young', the place seemed to get going, and most of the audience vaulted over the seats and surged down to the front. The gig suddenly seemed like a good idea. 'Gangsters' goes down a storm, and we're straight back on for 'Nite Klub', when the audience join us on the stage. Now, as far as the

UK is concerned, I do *not* like stage invasions. The people who get on are usually drunk and have become pig-headed morons who sing football slogans and get shirty when you ask them politely to get off. There in Tokyo, they were all sober, having a great time, and they all got off at the end of the tune. All of them. It was comical really. The atmosphere was now one of a great big party. After 'Nite Klub', we do a rousing version of 'Moonstomp' and we're off. The crowd are still going bonkers, so it's on for 'Enjoy Yourself'. Whether we didn't play long enough, I don't know, I got the feeling we could have played the whole show again – they could have been dancing from the first tune. We do 'You're Wondering Now', and again we're off. Thank you very much.

Far from it being a wild celebration backstage, Massy is very crestfallen. He has had a severe dressing-down from the hall owners, who have been having the Japanese equivalent of kittens concerning the behaviour of the audience (?). They have decreed that he'll never be able to use their hall again, or any other hall in Japan for that matter.

Meanwhile, back out in the hall, the crowd are *still* clapping and shouting, so The Specials go back on and play their final, final encore, 'Long Shot Kick de Bucket', and that is very definitely that. Good night.

The promoter is off apologizing profusely somewhere, and Rick is rubbing his hands together with glee, saying this will probably be our last gig in Japan. 'Specials kicked out of Japan' – just think of the press mileage we can get out of this! I hope he's not serious. Rico, who didn't have a particularly good show (bad stage sound) has met a Japanese Rasta (?) who will be providing all herbal requirements. Good. I was wondering how 'Our Man from Warieka' was going to cope in traditionally herb-free Japan, but 'Rasta always find a way'. It's still really early, about 9 p.m., and I volunteer for a *British Top Twenty* radio interview backstage.

After that, it was a cab back to the hotel with Chris, Dick and Neville. It is 10.30 p.m., and I have been up since 4 o'clock this morning. Sleep – the final frontier.

Thursday 26 June: Tokyo to Kyoto. We travelled from Tokyo on the famous bullet train. It was very impressive. The train ride was very comfortable, despite the fact we were travelling at over 100 mph. The scenery, buildings mainly, and the people on the train – everything was a new experience. It took three hours, and everywhere we passed through was built up. There are 12 million people living in Tokyo, so Brad tells me. The view from my room in the International Hotel in Kyoto is breathtaking. The Old Palace (Kyoto used to be the capital of Japan) is over the road, with undulating, forest-covered hills stretching way into the distance, with a few clouds rolling off them.

The room itself is fantastic. A paper screen in front of the windows, and the room done out in soft cream and brown. There's recently been some rain, so the view is clear, and the air is nice and cool, unlike Tokyo, where it was hot and humid. The 'Old World' Japan seems more appealing than the new 'America-plus' consumer Japan that we've just come from. So – pour myself some green tea, sit cross-legged on my sofa and relax. Nice.

Off to the gig, and there's no Jerry. He's not feeling very well, apparently. 'Anyway, sound checks are quicker without Jerry,' says Rick. They'd go even quicker if we didn't bother doing them, sunshine. I detest sound checks, they go on, and on, and on. The sound is never the same when the gig starts, and I always seem to be the stupid bugger who ends up trying to get it to run smoothly but gets on everyone's nerves. Terry can hardly ever hear himself. Perhaps that's why he's got his poker-faced angry-young-man look. If I had two years of trying to sing without hearing myself properly, and having Brad's ferociously loud drum monitor mix deafening me, I wouldn't exactly be Mister Happy.

We get everything working, play 'Man at C&A', once, twice. Everybody 'appy? Good. Off. This gig is an outdoor affair, 1,500 capacity, and looks like photographs I've seen of the Hollywood Bowl, but a lot smaller. The sound system seems up to the job, but it looks like rain, which is causing Massy today's headache.

We have a support group tonight, 'the number one group in Kyoto', so I'm told, called The No Comments. Er . . . OK, then. Crap name, but a great band. Wacky striped pyjama-type suits with a Japanese Barbie doll-type girl thing who sings in an incredibly squeaky voice and plays alto sax (probably squeaky as well). They remind me of Deaf School and start their sound check by playing a rocking version of 'Monkey Man'. We take it as a compliment . . . I think. They were great to watch and had some great tunes.

A shot of brandy (or two) loosens me up for the gig. Jerry arrives, looking like he's been dead for a fortnight, cursing about how stupid this all is, how he wants to go home, and has anyone got any Alka Seltzer.

It's show time, and the gig is great, better than last night. A real stormer if you'll pardon my lack of modesty. Four encores, the final one being 'International Jet Set'. The brass comes in too early on one bit, but nobody notices. It sounds fantastic. We end it with each individual member of the band stopping playing and walking off one at a time, leaving Brad alone on stage to finish it. Tremendous. Hit me with music!

The audience were great. Older than last night, but very

receptive. 'Stereotype' is better tonight. Everything is better, in fact, even Jerry, who seems to be all the better for one and a half hours of adrenaline. We hand out autographs through the dressing-room window afterwards. People give us presents – sweets, bracelets, all kinds of stuff – and are all far too polite. You wouldn't get the Catford skins giving you a tube of fruit pastilles after a gig, that's for sure.

We head back to the hotel, not knowing what to do really, so I hang around the bar a while and get myself invited out with Massy, his assistant (Tora?) and two guys from Toshiba/ EMI. Some more superb food. Low table, legs crossed, shoes off. Memo to self: must remember to change my socks after gigs in Japan. Great end to a great day. The record company paid the bill too! (Yes, I know. Royalties!)

Friday 27 June. I'm feeling a lot more refreshed and acclimatized. I manage to get up in time for breakfast. I discover there's a short sightseeing tour which starts at 9 a.m. from the hotel. It lasts for three hours. We're not scheduled to leave until 1 p.m. so I reckon I can do it!

The tour takes in the Hiro Castle (Shogun Dynasty), the Golden Temple and the Old Imperial Palace. Lots of camera. A great way of using a spare morning. I'd wanted to do 'regular' sightseeing, get out of the rock 'n' roll thing for a while, and this is just right.

Also on the trip is Carol, a lady from Bournemouth, who works for a UK company that makes printed circuit boards. (I never got to know her second name, or the name of the firm she worked for. I suppose she was in her early–mid-thirties). She's over here working and, like me, has got some free time to go sightseeing. She's been to Japan before and is due to be in Tokyo later in the week. We swap hotel telephone numbers and agree to meet up to do some Tokyo sightseeing next

Monday, when we return there. Great! That's half the problem solved as regards being a tourist – finding someone who knows where to go and how to get there.* I have to admit that I took one of the hotel's towels. I mean, the International Hotel, Kyoto – how cool is that down at Coventry baths!

Meanwhile, in Special-land, it's back on board the bullet train. We leave Kyoto for Osaka, check into our hotel and an hour later are off to the gig. We're scheduled to play two nights at the Expo Hall, a big sixties exhibition complex. It looks like a science fiction movie set. Visions of Utopia and that sort of thing. The gig is definitely not Utopia. Another seated venue, a football-pitch-sized stage, with a hydraulic orchestra pit at the front, which could be raised to the level of the stage if desired. Word of our 'exceptionally rowdy' concert in Tokyo has obviously reached Osaka, and the people in charge of the hall are looking apprehensive to say the least. After a lot of discussion, it is agreed that fifty members of the audience can occupy the orchestra pit. I can see this is going to cause problems. Show time arrives, and we troop on stage, and the gig is far from full (a polite way of saying it's practically empty). By the time we get to 'Monkey Man', the orchestra pit is heaving with kids. It looks like being a great show despite the poor turn-out. The hall manager is having a fit, though, as his hydraulic orchestra pit is bouncing up and down alarmingly.

There are big gaps between numbers where Jerry is yelling at Rick and Massy to stop the security staff, who by now are attempting to manhandle the audience back to their seats. They (the security staff) are starting to get heavy and get an ear-bending from the stage. Things are starting to get

---

* Remember, this is a long time before the *Rough Guide* series of books came out!

ugly. Jerry lets off a backstage fire extinguisher (I really don't
know why – frustration?), and by now, we are all starting to
get pretty mad.

Listen! The band are having a good time. The audience
are having a good time. What's the problem? During 'Stereotype', the house lights come on; we stop playing and walk off
in disgust. The bouncers are continuing to get heavy with the
audience. Terry hurls a couple of mike stands over, and Jerry
does the same. (The PA company, who own the mike stands,
have nothing to do with the hall, its management or its
security staff, but this fact is overlooked in the heat of the
moment.) Unfortunately the mike stand that Jerry knocks over
falls on Dick's cornet, putting a sizeable dent in the bell.
Dick is less than pleased.

After five minutes spent shouting and sucking our teeth,
we go back on to finish the show with the house lights still on.
We owe the fans that much. A ferocious version of 'Gangsters',
followed by 'Moonstomp'. The crowd go berserk. We finish
with a monstrously cynical version of 'Enjoy Yourself', which
has the majority of the audience on the stage. Neville is in his
element, top class, total chaos. Everyone clears the stage, and
music comes over the house PA. It's not very loud, so we
return to do 'You're Wondering Now' ... what to do, when
you know this is probably the last gig we'll ever play in Japan?
As soon as the song finishes, the power is switched off.

Backstage it is pandemonium. Massy has been hauled
down the local police station, Rick appears to be close to
having a nervous breakdown, and we are coming to the
conclusion that this whole trip is a waste of time. The hall
owner in Tokyo has banned Massy from putting any more
shows on at his hall for a year. Even ballet! I'm sure the
people here at the Osaka Expo Hall aren't too happy either.
Not only are we putting a promoter out of business, we're

diminishing the number of halls that bands can play. I can't see how any compromise can be reached. The whole thing is just becoming pointless. Again.

Great, eh? Just think of the press: 'Specials Destroy Japanese Touring Circuit'. Fan-bloody-tastic. The Specials need to play DANCE HALLS. Hello! Is anybody listening?

I now fully understand why people trash dressing rooms. I didn't trash one, mind you, but I can see why some people would. We eventually calm one another down. Jerry is very embarrassed about damaging Dick's instrument and apologizes profusely. He promises to buy him a new one when we get back to Tokyo.

Incredible. We go from the high of last evening's show in Kyoto to this mess in Osaka – all in twenty-four hours. It's exhausting.

Saturday 28 June. Dick joins me for breakfast, and here we all are again, ready for another day's catastrophe. Apparently Massy was released from the police station after an hour and charged with allowing 800 Japanese kids to dance!

Along with Lynval and DJ, I manage a couple of hours snooping round Osaka. I buy a hideous Hawaiian shirt and an appalling t-shirt which bears the legend (in English): 'I'm Special – come with me, let's make love'! Waaaaugh! Not my most essential purchase. I think Lynval bought one, too.

So, back for more of the same at the Expo Hall. For this evening's performance, forty 'policemen' have been called in to provide extra security. This is not on. We have a big meeting with Massy, hall staff and security people, and eventually a compromise is reached. The security staff don't wear uniforms, we'll give them Specials t-shirts to wear. They'll sit at the front of the stage in the orchestra pit, so no one can get up on stage (fine by me). The trade-off is that the audience can get as close to the stage as they want, there being no restrictions as far as the hall is concerned. Terry is disgusted, calls us all 'weak' and accuses us of 'not having any beliefs' (?). Point taken, Ted, but, as usual, we're over a barrel. If we don't play, the people who'll lose out (apart from us) are the people who've bought tickets to see us, and if we do play, the security will piss us off. Anyway, show time comes, we go on, and I'm half expecting Terry to throw at least a tambourine, if not a tantrum.

As usual, I needn't have worried. The band are definitely back-pedalling. There are longer gaps between numbers, and we're not putting so much energy into the music. The audience (bless 'em) are very responsive, despite the row of Specials-shirted-with-ear-defenders-on guys sitting right in front of them. The band, however, seem to just get down to playing, and, as usual, the power of the music prevails. It is a great gig. The tunes are as groovy as reggae should be. You couldn't help but dance. Neville hurls the front wedge monitors off the stage in 'Gangsters', and the crowd go barmy. I have fears that the encore will end in a riot, but on 'Enjoy Yourself', The Specials invade the audience. Lynval and I go down to the orchestra pit (our guitar cables just about reach) while Nev, Terry and Jerry go right to the back of the hall and wave at us. Very cool. We play a storming version of 'Nite Klub', with new extended intro, and finish with 'You're Wondering Now' – the band going down to audience level for the a cappella ending, Jerry handing over his microphone to one of the security guards – nice touch.

The audience is *still* shouting for more, so we do what turns out to be a pretty mediocre version of 'International Jet Set', then off. The crowd are still not satisfied, and we return yet again for what I can only describe as an amazing version of 'Man at C&A'. That's it, the end. Finish. What I thought was going to be a nightmare has turned out to be a brilliant show. Backstage, Massy is going round shaking everyone's hands and sighing with relief – he was really apprehensive about this evening's performance, and the possibility of another night in the cells!

Brad, however, appears to have lost £700 which he had brought over to buy recording equipment. (Why he had to keep it in his back pocket, I don't know, but who am I to say? He ended up buying some recording gear so perhaps he found his wallet after all. Whatever. He made a big fuss anyway.) Today's show started at 4.30 p.m. in the afternoon! So there's a whole evening to kill. The Japanese fans, especially the girls, are the weirdest. Here in Osaka, about a dozen of them have booked rooms in our hotel. Now, I know what you're thinking, and if this were America, you'd be right. But this is Japan, and all these girls want to do is 'hang out' – just talk. Nothing else. One girl gives me a necklace with a little fan on it – just gives it to me! I'm very touched. Everyone congregates in the hotel bar, and a contingent retires to a nearby club. I'm staying put. I haven't been eating particularly regularly and feel like I need some food. I manage a meal and end up in Dick's room with Gambino and some particularly strong Japanese beer. Eventually I start to make less and less sense and stagger off to my own room around 1 a.m. I have a nightmare: *The Fog* (John Carpenter) meets *Alien* (Ridley Scott) on an old deserted ship. The main bad guy looks like Stewart Copeland. I am about to be eaten alive when I wake with a start. I eventually go back to sleep.

Sunday 29 June. Well, whaddaya know? Alarm call at 9, and it's raining. I instantly get homesick.

9 a.m. Sunday morning in Coventry, I'd probably be

awake, but still in bed, thinking about getting up soon, who can I visit that can feed me, and what did I do the night before. However, if it's Sunday 29 June, it must be Japan. Osaka to be exact. This morning we are travelling back to Tokyo, doing an in-store record-shop appearance thing (always good for a laugh) and that's it. No show. No interviews. Almost a day off.

The train ride back to Tokyo is very funny. A fair proportion of the guys have bought these new Walkman cassette machines, which have headphones. When you're listening to music with headphones on and you talk to somebody, you tend to talk louder. Also, sometimes, you can hum along tunelessly to the music without realizing it. This, coupled with the fact that I'm reading *Getting Even* by Woody Allen (whose only regret in life is that he's not someone else) makes for a hilarious train ride.*

Back at the Shiba Park Hotel, and some photos I left to be developed are waiting for me – very cool. Brad shows me some photos that he's taken with a self-focusing camera that he bought here when we arrived. The prints are loads better than mine. I'm going to have to get one.

The 'in-store' is a massive department store place that doubles as a record store and music shop, which is cool, apart from the Yamaha rep, who is very much in evidence. The autograph session goes off well. I get presents from fans, all sorts of great Japanese toys and badges. Everyone is wonderfully polite. I love it. While the signing is taking place, the building kind of wobbles – well, either that or I am having some sort of seizure. No you weren't, Horace, that was an earthquake. Just a little one. Everyone giggles, says sorry

---

* This is 1980, remember. The only time we'd ever worn headphones was in a recording studio. This was a long time before iPod etiquette.

(for the earthquake) and carries on. I've never been in an earthquake before. Very strange – they should include it in the tourist brochure (no Japanese holiday is complete without your very own earth tremor!).

After the autographs it's upstairs to the music department with various fans in tow. Dick tries out trumpets and cornets, Rico tries out trombones, Neville tries out everything, and I am taken with a double bass that I can almost play. Off to the 'electric' section, and they will not let me have a go on the £12,000 Alembic bass guitar. Inscrutable.

There is no way we are going to do this Yamaha guitar deal. The guitars aren't top-of-the-range models, and the terms are too restrictive. (We have to use *only* Yamaha guitars for live work and recording for one year). Nah, mate, my Telecaster bass knocks spots off the Precision-style Yamaha that's on offer. Lynval and Rod agree. Roddy, however, leaves the store clutching a deep orange Gretsch semi-acoustic rockabilly type of Stray Cats kind of guitar. Very cool, and very, very expensive. Guitars, especially vintage American ones, are far more expensive in Japan than in England (where they're more expensive than they are in America), but, as they say, love is blind.

Back at the hotel, and one very expensive meal later, I'm talking with Dick and Jerry and generally hanging around. I'm sightseeing tomorrow, so it's an early night. Rick has obviously been in touch with his connections in the press. UK tabloid the *Daily Mirror* gleefully reported on 28 June:

Pop group face boot from Japan after fans run riot
Top pop group The Specials face the boot from Japan today following a concert riot. They were being detained at their Osaka hotel last night after a wild stampede by fans at

their show in the city. Police threw the group's Japanese promoter into jail.

Thanks Rick. Great for the reputation!

I telephone my parents to tell them I'm not in a Japanese prison and am OK. They hadn't seen the story but were pleased to hear from me. The phone call used up all my money I had saved to buy a camera!

Monday 30 June. Today is my sightseeing day. Breakfast, followed by a cab to the palatial Hotel New Otani, where I meet up with Carol, and off we go. A tube train (a novel experience in itself!) to Asakusa Kannon, a Buddhist shrine, then on to the Menji Shrine, which is Shinto. Both places are out in the suburbs, a different pace to the teeming city centre. Buddhist shrines are very ornate, gaudy and brightly coloured, lots of red and gold. Shinto shrines are very austere and aesthetic. Minimalist even. Both very beautiful. A nice morning spent in the company of someone who wasn't rock 'n' roll. Thanks, Carol.

This evening's show is just up the road from the hotel, the Shibuya Hall, with another audience-unfriendly hydraulic orchestra pit. Here we go again. The pit gets raised to the level of the stage, but it leaves a huge space between the band and the crowd. That's OK. We'll just move our back line 10 feet forward and problem solved. No way. Our back line will be in front of the PA causing feedback problems, and the hall manager says no. Total no. There's a big 30-foot-wide space between us and the front of the stage. The gig, however, passes off without incident, rather flat, as far as I'm concerned, but Rico is well pleased. He's been playing really well lately. The encore is our extended intro version of 'Nite Klub', which works terrifically well tonight.

My gut feeling is that we just got down to playing music and still managed to reach the audience.

Yes, I. Jah be praised! The power of music, as Rico say! After the gig, it gets fun. Lynval, Our Kid, Dave Jordan, Dick, myself and two local girls that Lynval has brought along go out in search of a mythical curry house. We eventually find it. It is closed. Never mind, there's a pizza place round the corner, so that's our destination; decent meal time. That's not to slag off Japanese food, but a change will do me good. Camaraderie prevails, and I end up paying for the whole thing (everyone pays me back the next day . . . Or eventually). Back to the hotel. Easier said than done. We must have spent thirty minutes trying to flag down empty taxis. What's the matter? We're not Japanese, that's the matter. Dick does it in the end. We thank the cabbie profusely, and retire to the Our Kid suite where I indulge in some 'thai stick', a rather strong type of marijuana. I am not a frequent dope smoker, so when I do partake, it doesn't take too long for a desired effect to be reached. Fifteen minutes later and I am blotto, to coin a phrase. Apparently, it's 2 in the morning. Me gahn!

Tuesday 1 July. We are back at the Shibuya Hall again tonight, with our 'invisible' barrier, and a row of security in each aisle. This is getting unbearable. During 'Stereotype', the bouncers start manhandling some fans. We stop playing and walk off. We refuse to carry on playing until these goons have been removed. We win, for once, and the gig carries on where it left off, but at full tilt, all the anger and frustration coming out in the music and the dashing around. The crowd go crazy, and we get a stage invasion, albeit a polite one, on 'Moonstomp'. Another jazz-intro to 'Nite Klub', which I muck up! 'Enjoy Yourself' is hilarious. Jerry seems to have lost his braces, and his trousers are round his ankles. He has this habit of invading the audience these days. Either that or he was after borrowing some braces. Final encore is an under-powered version of 'Jet Set'. I am knackered. Physically and emotionally.

I think The Jam were at the gig tonight. I hope they fare better than we did with their audience.

Back to the hotel, where I join Brad in an extremely verbose interview which bores me to tears. I make my excuses and leave. A fan gives me a present. A kaleidoscope. Thank you. I think my opinion of the Japanese is changing. Tonight I met a young lady from Brighton (England) who is over here working for the International Volunteer Service, or something. Her job is to teach English to Vietnamese refugees, before they get shipped out to America. Her opinion was that the Japanese are a very racist nation, who look down with contempt on anyone from the Asian mainland. They tolerate English people and kow-tow to Americans. They've just voted in a conservative government, too! The Vietnamese workers get the equivalent of 60p per hour in the factories whilst Japanese workers doing the same job get an hourly wage of £4.50. Out of the kindness of their hearts, they have agreed to let 300 Vietnamese settle in Japan. Roddy says the Japanese are like ants, just obeying and not thinking.*

I finally get off to sleep, only to be awakened at 2.30 a.m. by a very pissed Rick Rogers shouting up and down the hotel corridor.

Tomorrow's show at the Sun Plaza has been cancelled (can't imagine why!) and an alternative venue has to be found in about eighteen hours. Poor old Massy, and he brought us all 'happi coats' (kimono-type dressing-gown things) today as

---

* Rereading this over twenty-five years later, it seems a very narrow and naive worldview, considering the globalization that has taken place since.

well. He looks like he's aged twenty years since we got here. I dread to think what it'll be like if The Clash ever get to play over here. (Ah lilly worship thah Crarsh!)

Wednesday 2 July. Down just in time for breakfast, and the news is we're to play two shows tonight at The Tsubaki House. OK, then, Tsubaki House it is. At least it's a dance club. So, get my suit cleaned (the hotel does a dry-cleaning service) and off to do some shopping with Terry, Rick, DJ and Dick. On our return to the hotel, the news is that the gig is to be at the Carnival instead. This is a larger dance club, and did I want to go to see it? Well, not really, if that's where we're going to play! Massy seems fairly insistent, so Neville and I go over with one of his guys to this club. A half-hour drive through Tokyo and we're there. Yes, it's bigger than The Tsubaki House, but not as expensive-looking. Like a little Top Rank (that's not meant to be a compliment).

There's a largish drum riser affair, but no actual stage. By now, our equipment, the PA and the rest of the band are here. We insist on some sort of stage. We've done this sort of thing before. Anybody remember the Hammersmith Palais? Some staging arrives ten minutes before doors open, and we all pile in to put it and the gear up. We just about make it, but I'm exhausted already and I have two shows ahead of me. The plan is to do two forty-five-minute shows, one at 7.30 p.m. and the other at 10.00 p.m. This seems a bit cheap. Everyone agrees to play two one-hour spots.

The first show goes well; it's being filmed for Japanese television, apparently. I saw the cassette afterwards. We played too fast, though. Rico is struggling. He hasn't eaten much lately. He orders rice, and they put pork in it! Rasta does *not* eat pork! He doesn't blow his usual style this evening. Kids invade the stage for 'Nite Klub', which staggers a bit, but we've done it. The second show doesn't have the same feeling. We're all tired, exhausted and annoyed over the fact we've been dicked around. It's not the way I would have liked the tour to end. We're jaded and, unfortunately, we sound it. Same old story: two shows a night don't work for 2-Tone. I recognize a few faces from previous Tokyo shows, and this cheers me up and makes me try harder. A massive 'UK-style' stage invasion accompanies 'Moonstomp', and for the first time on the tour, it gets hairy. Brad's drums get knocked over, and a girl gashes her arm pretty badly. He (Brad) felt sick about the whole thing, especially as the girl kept saying, 'Sorry, sorry!' with blood pouring out of her arm. Nev trashes the set of congas that he has been using on the tour. It makes me mad. The guy who we hired them from is still paying for them! It's not like they're from some big instrument rental firm which can easily swallow the loss. Nev 'chas' and sucks his teeth a lot and says he'll pay for them. Our Kid is pretty pissed off with this, too. He'd got a good rapport going with the Japanese crew, and this soured it.

Sorry. I'm in no mood to party. I found myself sitting in Nev's room, listening to the cassette of the first show. Some of it is OK, but most of it is too fast.

That, you might think, was that. We'd finished our shows here in Japan, but we were now going to glorious Belgium for two festivals, and then down to Switzerland to appear at the Montreux jazz festival. International Jet Set or what!

Thursday 3 July. A free day, even. We give ourselves a Y2,500 clothes allowance and go out and buy The Specials' 'new look': the perpetual tourist, fashionable but ultimately naff. Or is that naff, but ultimately fashionable? Depends on who's wearing it, really. We have to be back by 5, as we're leaving tonight. Terry, Jerry, Dave Jordan and I, plus a

Japanese girl/tour guide, set off in a taxi and end up near the Menji Shrine I visited the other day. Our tour guide takes us to punk rock shops. Wrong. We want the *ordinary* clothes shops. There are a few nearby, so purchases are made. I get three startlingly loud jackets and four slightly more restrained polo shirts. I'd rather be exploring on my own than waiting for other people (especially Jerry) to buy stuff. Mr Dammers has turned prevarication into a fine art. I bid my fond farewells and am gone! By now, I think I've got the hang of the railway system – bit like London underground – and I get the nearest 'tube' back to the hotel, leaving Terry and Jerry to giggle over printed jackets and funny sunglasses.

Luckily, I recognize the local stop, and within five minutes I know where I am. Meet Dick and Rick in a market-place/mall. I manage to buy my father the zoom lens he wanted for his camera, which cleans me out. Rick lends me Y10,000, and shopping continues furiously. I love the toy robots and buy half a dozen.

Our departure is a rather sad affair. Several girls congregate, have their photos taken with us and give us presents; some of the fans are in tears. Do we really mean that much to them? Rico says he's never had such a 'sad to go' feeling. I admit it's touching to have people come and see you off but, to tell you the truth, I'm glad to be going. This place is starting to depress me.

John Hasler (he used to manage Madness), when asked what he thought of New York, said, 'It's like Camden Town on speed.' Tokyo is like New York on speed.

Looking back on all the Japan stuff, it was a good tour for us. The seated venues, bouncing orchestra pits and inflexibility of the touring circuit made us pull together and we seemed to get back a sense of purpose. We played good, too. The music seemed to become important again. The tempos were more or less spot-on, the groove, which had disappeared during the Seaside tour, had re-emerged, and I remember being elated by some of the performances, especially the concert in Kyoto.

We were also out of the UK limelight, with all its responsibility and sycophants that tended to circle round, waiting to brush an ego and be admitted to some kind of rarefied inner-circle atmosphere. And there wasn't a Romford Skin in sight.

The projected tour of Japan by The Selecter was cancelled.

12

The International Jet Set

One totally disorientating 'back over the top of the world' flight later, and we're in Belgium: home of . . . er . . . the Belgians and the scene of our two festivals. It's the same bill both days, but the second day's location is in a different part of the country: Tourhout, just west of Brussels, then on to Werchter, which is east of Brussels. The Kinks are headlining, so it's a chance to see first hand if all those stories about the Davies' sibling rivalry are true. The Kinks deliver, or rather, are delivered by two large black limos. One contains Dave Davies and the band, the other, true to form, contains brother Ray, complete with matching Chrissie Hynde. Also on the bill are America's Mink Deville, big-in-Belgium UK new wavers Fischer Z and that relic of sixties psychedelia Kevin Ayres, with whom Brad forms an unlikely friendship.

During our set, Roddy's equipment, an old 8×10-inch cab of Lynvals with a 50-watt amp on top, starts cutting out. True to form, Rod kicks it over. However, behind it is The Kinks' big electric piano. The amplifier lands squarely on the keyboard, shattering keys all over the place. Rod plugs into a spare Marshall 50, and The Specials thunder on regardless of the death threats that are being hurled around backstage. I remember, out of the corner of my eye, seeing Rob Gambino handing over a large wad of Belgian francs to a Kinks-type roadie. Hush money, perhaps. It didn't seem to dampen the audience's enthusiasm. The Davies brothers seemed larger than life, prowling up and down their own individual ego ramps out into the crowd. I have no recollection of the second show at all.

1980: Montreux, Switzerland

After that, the plan was for everyone to go back home for a couple of days, then come out again to play at the Montreux jazz festival in Switzerland. Jerry and I decided that we may as well stay over in Europe, make our own way down to Montreux and meet up with everyone at the weekend. A kind of tour decompression if you will.

Montreux is chilly. Everything looks very clean and tidy, and the locals all look as though they have a Bentley at home in the garage. The hotel we've been allocated is right out of town and far too posh. Jerry and I decide to relocate the band to a cheaper hotel, which, apart from being a lot more friendly, is situated just down the road from the gig. *Melody Maker* inkaholic Allen Jones and photographer Adrian Boot are in town too, and we meet up for a chat and a drink. Our 'loud tourist' look does not seem out of place at all. In fact, we look surprisingly normal.

I ventured down to the casino on the Friday night to see Van Morrison and B. B. King. Now, some people genuflect at the mere mention of his name, but Van the Man doesn't do it for me. I've mellowed a bit towards him, probably with the onset of age, but in Montreux, July 1980, he honestly looked as if he wanted to be somewhere else. B. B. King, on the other hand, knew exactly where he was, as did his fifteen-strong pink-suited orchestra, which put me off for a start. It looked too much like a Las Vegas revue, but the benefit of hindsight has changed my opinion of a man who recently cut down his road schedule to 250 gigs a year! At Montreux, I couldn't relate to it, even when tears rolled down his face during the show-stopping 'How Blue Can You Get'. At that time I loathed show business, and his pink-suited posse got in the way of the music. It's interesting to look back and see how narrow-minded I was about music, and especially its image.

The day of the show, and the band and crew arrive. Lynval looks dreadful. He had been to see the The Mo-dettes at the Moonlight Club in London, and on his way back he was followed by three guys who hurled abuse at him and beat him up. He was treated in hospital for cuts and bruises and was on some pretty heavy-duty pain-killers for the show. Bastards. A racist attack, pure and simple. The incident was the starting point for the song 'Why?', which was released on the 'Ghost Town' single.

Let the music retaliate.

The show (we headlined over the Q-Tips and Jo-Jo Zep and the Falcons) was great. It was being televised, too, so there was more to perform for. I've seen the footage, and it is really good, very exciting, very funny. At one stage Neville jumps off the front of the stage and lands, cat-like, on top of one of the quarter-of-a-million-pound TV cameras. The TV crew have a fit, and Rick, who was in the control room, says the technical bods all had seizures on the spot. Allen Jones said Neville had a smile on his face that was so big you couldn't put it in a shopping bag.

Summer 1980: Coventry

August, for me, was down time. The album was being mixed in London. Recording can be a very exhilarating experience, but I'm only really interested in my performance and the overall 'feel' of a track. Sitting in a badly ventilated control room listening to guitar overdubs and backing vocals drives me to distraction. I am in total awe of people who can last anything up to fourteen hours at a time and still be objective in a recording studio. My attention span is usually about four hours. If the bass and drums are solid and rocking, the track is going to be great anyway. Mixing, for me, is the nearest thing to purgatory I've ever experienced.

I left them to it. Any attempt at moral support would have rapidly deteriorated into boredom, and there were already enough people down there giving their opinions. I felt I could be more help by not being there. I really felt that other people in the band could have been more help by not being there, too. Just let Jerry and Dave Jordan get on with it. The plan was to get the album ready and then go on tour, some time in September.

I was arranging a holiday for after the tour. I'd made some friends in America and was planning to go back there some time before Christmas, do all the touristy stuff I never had time to do when the band was touring. Los Angeles, San Francisco and New York were to be my ports of call, and Jackie was going to come out for some of it, too. Royalties had started to come in, and money was waiting to be spent.

Although not exactly Liverpool of the sixties, Coventry

was a pretty rocking place to be in 1980. There were loads
of local bands, and a lot of the city-centre pubs put them
on. Three, sometimes four nights a week you could see a
local band play, with 'name' bands (I always thought that
was a funny description – every band has a name, doesn't
it?) playing at the weekend at the Polytechnic or at the
General Wolfe.

The Targets, The End, Urge, God's Toys, Eyeless in
Gaza, Criminal Class, the mighty Squad, The Clique, Team
23, Solid Action . . . And a load more. Some of these bands
only lasted a couple of months, some went on to release
records. Criminal Class were in on Gary Bushell's 'Oi' movement and got a lot of press space in *Sounds*. Solid Action's
bass player, Karl Shale, went on to play with Terry Hall in
The Colourfield and later joined The Candy Skins.

Fanzines were abundant too: *Alternative Sounds*, *Adventures in Reality* and the hilarious *Dead Yampy*, who were a
band as well as a fanzine. My favourite local band was
called The Mix. Sometimes a four-piece, sometimes a
trio, always great. They were led by a kid called Dave
Gedney, who always seemed to get a great sound out of
whatever guitar or amplifier he was playing. He wrote some
very good pop-rock tunes – great hooks, terrific choruses.
I could sing you the words to 'Insect Life', 'Dead Boy' or
'Taxi' even today. On a good night they were as good as
any band I had ever seen. I was a regular at Mix gigs,
especially as a female friend of Dave's girlfriend was
beginning to catch my eye . . . More later!

At the end of August, I did my Exegesis seminar. This
looked like something that would do me good. I did not
like the blustering, rowdy, big-headedness that emerged
every time the band got together, especially around alco-

hol. We became bullies. Like the 'hard' kids at school who everyone tried too hard to be friendly with, but were really intimidated by. We can behave like pigs and get away with it because we're The Specials. I didn't like it. Leaving the band was furthermost from my mind. At the end of the day (so they say) it was still a fantastic emotional high. I just handled it differently.

The Exegesis seminar promised to increase my confidence, raise my self-awareness, and make 'more' of who I was. It sounded just what I needed to do. The whole thing had been started in the early 1970s by one Robert D'Aubigny, who, by the time I did my seminar, was in his forties. The organization had grown to incorporate an administrative staff, and plans were afoot to sell its services to business. People paid to do the seminar (it was £230), which took place over a weekend in a hotel in London. We were put up in graduates' (as those who had done the seminar were called) houses in London in the evenings and congregated early the next day. Friday night, all day Saturday, all day Sunday.

It is difficult to describe the seminar. The nearest I can get to it is a 'mental boot camp': exposing your 'stuff', the things that governed your personality, turning them from negative to positive, and changing your attitudes to ones of success, rather than failure. It all sounds very ridiculous but involved a lot of group therapy/gestalt therapy and quasi-religious techniques that are commonplace in what are now called 'life-affirming strategies'. The sessions were intense. We had 'processes' to do: humiliating tasks to perform in front of the group (there were about fifty of us), which, after you'd done them, didn't appear too humiliating at all. It was all about being afraid, facing fear and (hopefully) overcoming it. We hardly slept the whole weekend, giving the whole thing a very dream-like quality.

By the Sunday afternoon the whole vibe of the group was terrific. We would all be friends for life. I didn't mention that I was the bass player in The Specials, just 'a musician', but what I was didn't seem to matter, it was *who* I was and who these people saw me as that counted. The Sunday-evening grande finale was a very emotional moment. Jackie and all her Exeter 'graduate' friends were there, and I felt like I had been inducted into this new brotherhood of 'humans plus'.

Exegesis continued to grow for the next few years, moving into its own premises in Queens Park, London. A Bristol office was also set up. The business side became 'Programmes', a telephone marketing company. To this day it still runs corporate business training for many major companies – household names in banking, commerce, transport, etc.

It would be fair to say that my involvement with Exegesis was a contributing factor to the decline of relationships within The Specials. The 'solid', dependable Horace (Sir Horace Yes Man, as Roddy once described me) was replaced with this new person who made a lot more noise but ultimately was unable to change anything. All the stuff that was later written about 'Horace giving all his money to a cult' is rubbish. As I've said, the original seminar cost £230. I did other seminar series that they put on, for which I paid, but their cost was nowhere near as much as the original one. Exegesis would become a real bone of contention later, but I'm getting ahead of myself.

The More Specials tour

Rehearsals started for our next tour. The LP was to be called *More Specials*, with a cheesy out-of-focus sixties photograph on the cover, taken in the bar of the Regent Hotel in Leamington Spa (it's now the Travelodge). The album was due out in the second week of September, which is when our tour started.

Jerry was not around for the first couple of rehearsals, which was not a good sign. He'd done all the album sessions at Horizon Studios and all the mixing sessions in London and was exhausted. The tour was supposed to start the next week.

My evangelical Exegesis zeal was treated with raised eyebrows by the rest of the band. Lynval said, 'Horace have a new head on 'im shoulders.' I said to Neville that it was like taking your head to the dry-cleaners. He replied, 'Yes, Horace, and your bank balance too!' Terry said I just shouted a lot more. Jerry didn't say anything.

Our new show consisted of most of *More Specials*. We didn't do 'Holiday Fortnight' or the 'Enjoy Yourself Reprise' and cut out stuff from the first album that had gone past its sell-by date: 'Little Bitch', 'Blank Expression', 'Do the Dog' and I suppose a few more. I know we kept in the show-stopping 'Too Much Too Young', 'Stupid Marriage' and 'Concrete Jungle'. We were also featuring a Rico single, 'Sea Cruise'. It was a big show, lasting a good two hours in length, and it started in St Austell on 13 September. Support was to be from new 2-Tone signings The Swinging Cats (Jerry's buddy John Shipley on guitar, and soon-to-be Fun Boy Three and Colourfield's keyboard player Toby Lyons). Also on the bill, all the way from New York City, were The Stray Cats. Only they told us a week before the tour started that they weren't doing it. A good career move, I suppose. Who wants to spend three weeks travelling round England having abuse hurled at you by skinheads anyway? The story went that they had met Keith Richards and had been invited to his South of France domicile to hang out. They were on all the posters too. Little shits. It would have been a fantastic bill.

Our single 'Stereotype' / 'Jet Set' was released the day the tour started. The album was released the next week. The critics went barmy. Vivien Goldman in the *NME*, Mike Gardner in *Record Mirror*, John Orme in *Melody Maker* and Garry Bushell in *Sounds* all frothed at their collective mouths about what a bold step it was, breaking away from a mindless safe-ska stance, redefining dance music for the eighties (dance muzak for the eighties, to be precise) and all that stuff. It entered the album charts at number nineteen. Not bad.

It has taken me about twenty years to be able to listen to it without squirming. For me it was the sound of a band breaking apart. I bought it recently on CD and must confess to being totally knocked out. 'Man at C&A' is fantastic, as is 'Jet Set', although I prefer the almost-instrumental version on the B-side of 'Stereotype'.

So, 13 September. Abyss, this way please. I am trying my hardest to think of anything positive, uplifting or happy to write about the More Specials tour. It is difficult. Rob Gambino arrived with a huge box of drumsticks, a hoard of percussion instruments and two very nice conga drums. He'd done some sort of deal with a drum firm. We also had our soon-to-be-foetid wardrobe flight case.

We also had 2-Tone cocaine mirrors. Honestly! 2-Tone cocaine mirrors! They had the Walt Jabsco logo on them and a 3-inch groove cut out of them on one side – from where you snorted your 2-Tone cocaine, presumably. I don't know where they came from, but I made sure they were binned at the earliest opportunity.

St Austell, in the south-west of England, was close enough to Exeter for Jackie and her posse to attend. The band's hotel was miles away, but I got a room at a small hotel near the gig. The plan was for the coach to pick me up the next day. Now, I've gone on about not liking to sneak people into hotel rooms, but on that particular occasion there was Jackie and me, two of her friends and two American girls who turned up at the gig and said they had nowhere to stay. All six of us managed to get some sleep sooner or later, but the hotel sussed, and I got charged double for the room. Grrrr!

Jerry arrived and said he didn't want to do the tour, but by then it was too late. There was nothing anyone could do. The halls were booked, the trucks were unloaded, the equipment was set up, the tickets were sold, the press were here. The inevitability of it all was, for me, very frightening. I coped by keeping myself to myself. On the previous year's 2-Tone tour the band seemed to consist of three separate tribes (Hedonists, Herbalists and Sensiblists). Now we had seven. Or ten. Dick and Rico were there, of course, but they were now complimented by Paul Heskett, who was to play saxophone on 'Sock It to 'em JB', 'Hey Little Rich Girl' and on our over-the-top encore 'Nite Klub', where Paul proved he could 'over-the-top'-it with the best of them. He was, up until a week before the tour, a member of our support band The Swinging Cats but said he had been sacked (along with vocalist Jayne Bailey) by band leader John Shipley. Paul found it embarrassing at best and strained at worst to be on the coach with the band that had just fired him. As it turned out, his tenure with The Specials was longer than it would have been with The Swinging Cats, who split up some time in 1981.

The high point of the tour? Doncaster (oop North again!) and probably the two nights in Liverpool. Both of these venues were clubs, rather than cavernous municipal halls, or worse, characterless sports centres, where the sound clattered round the place like a badly aimed squash ball. I distinctly remember this enormously fat kid who would come to our gigs in the north. He usually got up on stage for the last couple of numbers, although how he did this was difficult to say. He was the size of a small car. He was a lovely bloke and genuinely thought the band was the greatest thing since the pop-up toaster. I have a fond memory of him standing on the side of a recently 'danced to death' stage (it may have been Doncaster) after the gig. He'd managed to get one of the microphones and he was standing there, sweat pouring out of him, repeating, 'Specials, fookin' magic. Specials, fookin' magic,' as the crowd queued to leave the building. Presumably the crowd were of the same opinion, but it didn't stop our new public relations division from chanting his mantra as the hall emptied. It was a wonderful moment.

The power went off half-way through our Edinburgh show. We never left the stage, we just sat there and gave the audience the soggy sandwiches and beer from our dressing room. Hey, I did remember something funny after all!

A feature film was being made around live footage of all the 2-Tone bands currently touring, and the Leicester and

Liverpool shows were filmed for what would be released as *Dance Craze*. 'Concrete Jungle' and 'Man at C&A' from the Liverpool shows are fantastically exciting, but played on nervous (and probably chemical) energy. There is no groove there at all. More Motörhead than Marley.

Almost everywhere we went there was crowd trouble, usually accompanied by a journalist from one of the music papers, pondering on whether the 2-Tone bubble was about to burst or something along those lines. The stage was now being invaded about half-way through the show. The whole flow of the performance stopped, and the atmosphere became very icy at times, as we tried, usually unsuccessfully, and always temporarily, to remove drunken oafs off the stage. The music seemed to come second. I found it impossible to relax on stage, when, at any minute, a tanked-up member or three of Swindon's finest were going to lurch across the stage and trip over my guitar cable. A year before this we never did a bad show. Now we hardly ever completed one without having to stop the music, then trying to reach the point where we left off. Skankus interruptus you might say.

We didn't want rows of bouncers between us and our audience, and a few people on at the end was not usually a problem, but 200-plus kids during the last number meant chaos with the PA and stage equipment. The lighting rigs nearly toppled over at the show in Bristol apparently. Anarchy is freedom with responsibility. No one told the audience about the responsibility. In Glasgow there was a massive ruck between the bouncers and some fans. Admittedly, the fight may have had its origins a fortnight previously somewhere else in the city, but that didn't make me feel any better, standing up there, on that vertigo-inducing Glasgow Apollo stage, attempting to play songs that talked about living together in harmony.

The wheels were turning, however, the machine was in motion, and, as much as we wanted to, we couldn't get off. I do remember Jerry, Lynval and I all shaking our heads in disbelief at the end of some debacle or another and vowing that we would never tour like this again. This tour didn't have the sense of purpose that our first tour had had. Back then, it was Specials/Selecter/Madness – a new music, a new movement. This time it was 'just' The Specials. We were adrift in a sea of our own celebrity – promoting our new product. We obviously meant a lot to a lot of people, but there was something different about what we were doing, compared to our tour of a year ago. I have thought about this a lot during the past twenty-odd years. Groups form with the intention of 'being famous', i.e., playing their music to numbers of people, being musicians for a living and making records (CDs if you really want to be modern about it!). This is all very well and good, but there are subtle changes that take place during this process that can end up clouding an original vision. Although I loved 'being famous', it was not the main reason for wanting to play a bass guitar. I wasn't as militant as Jerry, who wrote 'Don't wanna be rich, don't wanna be famous', but I was very aware that we had become detached from our original moorings. I look at bands who have stayed together in their original line-ups for over twenty years with awe (U2 spring to mind). What changes have had to take place in the relationships between those people to enable them to stay together and still be creative?

The Specials were able to handle the 'rise' of their popularity but were unable to make the transition to a stage where we became a 'mainstream' act. There again, The Sex Pistols had ground to a halt and The Clash were in the process of asking themselves the very same questions that we were. It wasn't like we had any role models, and we refused point blank to take advice from anybody older than us. But hey, the hotel bar's still open, and I've just got thirty quid from the tour manager!

There has been a lot written about the National Front and the British Movement in relation to The Specials. Some articles have been written about 'a sea of Seig-Heiling skinheads' at our concerts. This is rubbish. I can honestly think of only two occasions when a group of people in our audience started giving us Nazi salutes, and both were near London. Bracknell is a small town to the west of London, near Reading. Its sports centre played host to The Specials two weeks into the tour. There were a lot of skinheads there from different towns and different parts of London, football teams being the identifying factor. This in itself seemed a recipe for disaster, what with British youth's predilection for a fight on a Saturday night. During the show (which was going pretty well, as it happens), a group of not more than two dozen skins started to give Nazi salutes. We quickly stopped playing. Terry, who by now was an absolute master of the acidic tongue, got them to stop. We carried on playing, but a dozen or so of the meatheads carried on Seig-Heiling. The band stopped playing and, led by Jerry and Terry, jumped over the barrier and into the crowd, where the aforementioned meatheads were chased from the building by the artists they had presumably paid money to see. On our return to the stage, the crowd went crazy. I met a guy a few years ago who was at the concert and he said it was the most amazing thing he'd ever seen, the band jumping off stage and taking direct action like that. He wasn't a skinhead, he was just a punter who liked the music. I thanked him very much, but took pains to explain that it was everyone in The Specials except me who jumped off the stage. Perhaps I wasn't angry enough. Perhaps I was scared stiff! The concert continued, with a bit more optimism from the band. The following Monday's *Reading Evening Post* had the banner headline: 'Skinheads on the Rampage: Nazi salutes – then fans invade stage'. Great. Apparently, the same thing happened a week later at Brunel University, although I have no recollection of it.

The tour sank to its all-time low in Cambridge. Our concert was to be held in a great big tent on Midsummer Common. Cambridge has this image of academia: dons with college scarves punting down the River Cam quaffing Pimms. Er . . . wrong. Since the closure of the Corn Exchange, Cambridge had been bereft of any live music venue. The council had put up this 'super-tent' (3,500 capacity) for a country and western festival. A proposed Motörhead show there had been cancelled, but we got to play there instead.

There's a kind of etiquette at rock gigs. The audience at, say, Newcastle Mayfair, will behave in a certain way towards different bands. The security staff will know their limits (hopefully), and the crowd will be aware of this. You behave yourself, you have fun. You misbehave, and something else happens – generally something you don't like. These are unwritten rules. This is why venues like the Newcastle Mayfair keep putting on shows. There is a system. It works.

Now. Cambridge Super-tent was a 'new' venue. They'd

only ever put on a country and western show. Their
security was totally unprepared for all the local skinheads
(a sizeable contingent), all the kids from the surrounding
area – Peterborough, Bedford, Luton, Ipswich – all trying
to be harder than the rest, all wanting to get on stage with
Terry and Lynval.

It was a disaster. Team 23, a promising Coventry new
soul outfit we'd taken on tour for the last week's dates,
lasted two songs. Chris Long, the Swinging Cats' singer,
was punched out by some local Neanderthal pretty much
as soon as they got on stage. And this was even before
we'd gone on. The local security were overwhelmed. Faced
with a 3,500-strong crowd, a fair percentage of whom were
in a pretty belligerent mood, we basically played background music for fighting (headbutt muzak?). It was appalling. We stopped playing three times during the show. At
the third time, after some altercation in the crowd over by
Lynval, Terry berated a bouncer, who turned on him. Terry
picked up a mike stand, but it was taken off him before he
could use it as a weapon. We left the stage, Terry screaming at the promoter. After five minutes we went back on
and finished our set. The stage may very well have been
invaded, but I can't remember, and by that stage in the
proceedings I don't suppose I cared. After the gig, I
attempted to calm down in the Portakabin dressing rooms.
Everyone had got on the coach – just Jackie, Jerry and me
left behind. The promoter came into the cabin with a
policeman, who arrested Jerry. I'd never seen anyone
arrested before. It was surreal. Jerry heard the news, didn't
say anything, finished off his half-bottle of whisky, put
his hat on and left with the police. I went and told Rick,
and he and Pete Hadfield went off down to the Parkside

Police Station, where Jerry (and Terry) were charged with 'behaviour likely to lead to a breach of the peace'. Jackie burst into tears. Poor kid, she'd been looking forward to touring with the band. Coaches, hotels, backstage, celebrity lifestyle, high jinks. Sorry.

At the first of two surprisingly uneventful shows at the Lanchester Polytechnic in Coventry, my Telecaster bass, the one I bought in New York, got stolen.

The tour ended at the Birmingham Odeon on 16 October. We'd been on the road just over a month. *More Specials* was now at number nine in the charts. Wowee! And just when you thought it couldn't get any more weird, The Specials went to Barcelona.

Our concert in a bullring in Barcelona could be used as a working definition of the word 'fiasco'. We got the gig via The Urge (Coventry band who came on tour with us in Europe – you remember!). Some concert promoters they knew in Amsterdam wanted to put on a show in Barcelona, and did we want to do the gig? The plan was we'd truck our 'back line' to Barcelona, fly out on the Friday, do the gig on the Saturday, go home on the Sunday. Job done. The whole thing seemed perfectly feasible.

Suspicions were aroused when we met the promoters, two men and a woman, black leather trousers (in that heat!), black everything in fact. One of the guys was behaving very erratically and very quickly took everyone into his confidence. He said that he would offer £5,000 to anyone who could get his car from out of the police car pound. (To my knowledge, no one did.) Later on the Friday evening, I went with him and representatives from the other bands playing the following night (The Urge, an early version of The Thompson Twins, and The Boys, a '77 vintage punk rock outfit) to a local radio station to do an interview advertising the show. As we were entering the studio, our erratic promoter produced a bag of cocaine and asked me if I would care to join him. I declined, and he disappeared into the toilets. He was practically vibrating when he finally returned during the interviews. This did not look good. I'd seen people do coke before, but I'd never seen anyone look as bad as this. What was in the boot of his car, I wondered, and why would a Dutch concert promoter decide to set up a gig in Spain, with all the currency regulations and bureaucracy stuff?

The gig was at a bullring where, the previous year, Bob Marley and The Wailers had played to a capacity crowd. Ticket sales hadn't been too brisk, but our promoter friends were expecting a large 'walk-up' – people without tickets who would pay on the door. The place was indeed a fantastic building, if not a little agricultural in odour, and I could imagine Bob Marley having a good time here – everybody getting up, standing up and fighting for their rights.

The organization was pretty *mañana*, that is to say, the lighting rig had only just been delivered, and the stage wasn't finished. A rat, along with a lot of other things, had been smelt, but after the previous months' bludgeoning, nothing could phase The Specials now. We had to just ride it out. Our promoters needed 8,000 people (about one-third capacity) to break even. As it turned out, about 2,000 people turned up. There were worried glances exchanged between Pete Hadfield, Rick Rogers and the crew – contingency plans, worst-case scenarios. In the absence of women and children, it was 'band and their instruments first'. Our promoters, even the less erratic ones, were showing visible signs of mental collapse, but, hey, it's show time.

The Specials took to the rather wobbly stage, looked out over the vast eighteenth-century bullring, which reeked of history and smelt of bullshit, and played what I thought was our best gig for ages. The whole situation was so ludicrous we all had grins on our faces, even Terry, I suppose (when he turned his back to the audience). There was no 'pressure' from the crowd, and the whole show was played with a finesse that reminded me of some of our concerts in Japan.

There was very little time to congratulate ourselves afterwards, though, as our gear was packed away double quick and put into the truck. The owners of the place, and the local organized crime representatives, were searching the place, looking for our buddies from Amsterdam, and the fear was that, if they couldn't get their cash, they'd impound or, worse, sell our equipment. It all became high farce. A few chairs were broken to provide us with clubs, should they be needed, and a discussion took place as to whether the lorry carrying all our equipment had sufficient power to batter down the huge wooden doors that were our exit. All very Hemingway.

We needn't have worried. We got out fine, leaving our promoters cowering in a locked office somewhere, with the local heavies pounding on the door. The night passed in the usual gay abandon that generally happens when more than one pop group stays in a hotel that someone else has paid for, and we all buggered off the next day. The promoters were later spotted back at the hotel, asking anybody and everybody if they could get a ride to Amsterdam. They had not only lost their shirts on this gig, but their entire wardrobe. And their car.

1980: My American holiday fortnight

Our only other commitments that year were two charity gigs at London's Hope and Anchor pub, to raise money to buy blankets for local old people. Loads of bands were doing it – The Selecter, Madness, Ian Dury and The Blockheads, Bad Manners, The Damned – and we kicked the whole two weeks' worth of shows off at the end of October.

It was great to be back in a small, sweaty basement, but we were now a ten-piece band, and there was never any room at the Hope and Anchor anyway. The stage had been extended, using the good old rock standby, plastic beer crates. We played too loud, too fast and were generally crap. I know I keep going on about this, but it used to sadden me no end, especially when I knew what we were capable of. Towards the end of one of the shows Terry got his foot stuck in one of the beer crates and had to wear it like a big yellow overshoe for the rest of the set.

To mark this momentous occasion, our second LP went up to number eight in the charts, and the next week I left the country.

The month I spent in America during October/November was just what I needed. Hiring one of those silly little Pinto cars and pootling round Los Angeles was great. The county museum down by the La Brea tar pits had a brilliant art collection. Frank Stella, Morris Louis and some enormous Kenneth Noland paintings. I'd seen them all in books, but the real things were spectacular indeed. I did rock 'n' roll stuff as well. My LA posse, David Kendrick (he was the drummer in Sparks) and his girlfriend Catherine, took me to some very groovy places, but we never did the swanky 'I'm a famous pop star' stuff. We paid for our own drinks. I got to see a pre-Henry Rollins Black Flag at the Starwood. A very tense show, with lots of mean-looking Los Angeles skinhead/punk types. The band was great. We also took in the Whisky a Go Go, which was still painted black and white in honour of our residency there in February. We saw Social Distortion, who reminded me of Grand Funk Railroad, and Christian Death, who were just stupid. We even saw the emergence of a ska scene, a band called The Box Boys skanking reasonably furiously at the On Club, and I heard about a new band called Fishbone. Hey, trendsetter or what?

Jackie came out the second week. Her plan was to stay over for a bit longer and look for some work in the new year. I took the train up from Los Angeles to San Francisco – right up the coast, in one of those big old observation carriages, with a steward who'd come by every now and again and give me coffee. Wonderful.

In San Francisco, I stayed in a house up near Haight Ashbury with the gang of kids who ran the *Idol Worship* fanzine. Again, a great vibe. Vicki Berndt, their photographer, later came to visit in England in '81. In the guise of fanzine proprietors, we went to see Siouxsie and The Banshees, who I'd never seen before, and they were pretty damn good. We got backstage afterwards and I immediately noticed the tense atmosphere. Siouxsie hid in the corner, and Steve Severin looked suicidal. We made our excuses and left. Our backstage vibe, even during the worst times on the More Specials tour, was nowhere near as bad as this. A couple of nights later, we went up to Berkeley and saw The Slits. They were brilliant. The drummer was Bruce Smith from Rip, Rig and Panic, avant-

garde muso Steve Beresford was on guitar, and Adrian
Sherwood was doing the sound. Tessa Pollit, their bassist,
was really solid. They sounded like a 1970s Studio One
reggae band and played this really funky, sexy music. I
was in awe. The music they played was fantastic, and
made what we in The Specials were doing sound tame.

From San Francisco I flew to New York to stay with
journalist Stella Kramer and her boyfriend, Harry. They
lived in a tiny one-room apartment down by the World
Trade Center. Their bed was on this kind of mezzanine
affair, and I had the couch at the other end of the room. It
was November: to someone coming straight from the West
Coast the temperature drop was brutal. It was freezing. I
did my usual 'art-tourist' stuff, as well as checking ESG
and Bill Laswell's Material at Hurrah's. Cool. I was glad to
go home, but the break had done me the world of good.

1980: *Top of the Pops*

Back in the UK Chrysalis had decided to release 'Do
Nothing' off *More Specials* as a single. Jerry put some
dodgy synthetic strings on it, using Paul Heskett's dodgy
string synthesizer, and the single, featuring the Ice Rink
Strings, complete with our tribal-sounding version of Bob
Dylan's 'Maggie's Farm' on the flip, was released in the
first week of December to less than favourable reviews in
the music press. This didn't stop it selling, and, a fortnight
later, we went down to *Top of the Pops* for the usual day
spent miming and hanging around.

Luckily for us, The Beat were on the programme too,
so a chums' club was quickly set up. We had never toured

with The Beat, and there was a lot in common 'good-cause-wise' between the two bands. The royalties from their 12-inch single 'Stand Down Margaret' were to be donated to the Campaign for Nuclear Disarmament. We decided that our people would talk to their people to see what we could come up with. In the meantime, there was the problem of how to enliven a tedious day spent at the BBC.

I don't know if anyone has ever done this before, but Beat bass player David Steele and I decided to swap roles. I would get to mime The Beat's new single, 'Too Nice to Talk To', and David would get to do his funky shuffling on 'Do Nothing'. At least I wouldn't have to wear one of those dreadful Christmas jumpers that Jerry had bought us all for the occasion. As I'd done all The Beat camera rehearsals, nobody from the programme twigged (or cared less). The fans at home would notice, though. Very cool. The two performances get repeated every now and again. David Steele, complete with awful Christmas jumper, getting in Terry's way, and me with my thirteen-quid 'mime bass', attempting to dodge the meandering Andy Cox. Very funny. 2-Tone – One; BBC – nil.

1981: The Specials go to Ireland

The new year did not get off to a good start. On 10 January, Terence Edward Hall and Jeremy David Dammers were each fined £400 with £130 costs on top for conduct likely to lead to a breach of the peace at Cambridge Magistrates Court. Despite affidavits from professionals (a doctor and a lawyer) who were actually at the concert, the judgement went against them. Against *us*, really. Jerry said: 'The

3,000 people at the concert will recognize the injustice of the decision.' It was sick. I'd only once had a run-in with the police (Alfreton, you remember?) and I still had this notion of 'law and order' and 'a fair trial', but it seemed once again I was proved to be stunningly naive. The powers that be closed ranks, and that was that. It added to my feelings of powerlessness.

On a more pop-tastic note, that week, The Specials new single, 'Do Nothing', entered the singles chart at number nineteen. It would peak at number three later that same month.

A series of Irish dates with The Beat had been organized for the middle of January. We would do four shows together, the profits from which would go to charity organizations, like HELP, which took both Catholic and Protestant children on holiday together. Four dates: Belfast, Dublin, Galway and Cork. One coach, two bands. Dave Wakeling and I would fly to Dublin to do a radio interview advertising the tour, and the rest of the guys would do the ferry journey over to Belfast for our first show.

Jackie was back from California, and she and I met Dave Wakeling and his girlfriend, Dominique, at Birmingham airport. Dominique's family lived in Dublin, so we would stay with them overnight and take a train up to Belfast the next day. The interview went over well; Dave and I complemented one another. It was a fortuitous meeting. I would work with him and Ranking Roger when they formed General Public in 1983.

In Belfast, The Specials all seemed in good spirits, except for Dave Jordan. Dave had a recurring heroin habit, and at the time of these Irish dates, he was going through some heavy withdrawal symptoms. He looked dreadful, his eyes were grey, and he just stared, hating everybody, demolishing a half-bottle of vodka before sound check. I suppose it would have been pertinent to talk about this with other members of the band, but there seemed to be a kind of *laissez-faire* situation. Dave knew what he was doing and was obviously capable of carrying out his sound-mixing duties. Heroin eventually killed him in 1994 in Paris, when he was on tour with Shane McGowan.

The Belfast Ulster Hall was rocking. The Catholic skinheads may very well have been downstairs, while the Protestant skins were in the balcony, but the whole place was jumping, a tremendous show – no need to preach, just play. After the gig, the majority of The Beat's merchandise – 'Stand Down Margaret' t-shirts – was nicked during the load-out, along with Roddy's 'piano-demolishing' amplifier. Thanks, guys, nice of you to welcome us to Belfast. We checked into the Europa Hotel, the most bombed hotel in Europe, apparently, through metal detectors and very tight security, and hit the downstairs bar.

The location, coupled with the charity-based righteous-ness of our being there, seemed to bond the band back together again. Crusaders for a public good and all that. Or it could have been the Guinness. The next day we got on the coach to head down to Dublin. As I left the hotel, an army patrol was coming down the street. Armoured Land Rover with soldiers, guns at the ready, peering up at the buildings. It was a sobering sight, if not a little surreal. We'd raised over £2,000 for our worthwhile causes the previous night.

Dublin's show was at the Stardust Ballroom, a run-down old dance hall in a run-down part of the Dirty Old

Town. The Beat's set was well received, but trouble flared during our performance. Rival gangs, apparently. Terry, according to the press, handled the situation with 'sensible aplomb'. The 'Cambridge decision' was still a recent injury. Despite our pleas for calm, during the encore, a massive fight broke out which spilt out over the stage between gangs, security and PA crew attempting to defend their equpiment. The stage-right PA stack toppled over, breaking some poor girl's jaw, and we retreated backstage to the sound of fists and boots behind the stage door.

I remember standing there with Jackie and other members of the band, listening to the mayhem going on just a few feet away. We just shrugged our shoulders and got changed: business as usual. About half an hour later, when the crowd had gone home, or had gone off to beat somebody else up, we emerged from the dressing room. The stage had been trashed. Beat and Specials road crews had protected most of the equipment, but there were bent mike stands everywhere and a lot of microphones had been stolen. The following day, the PA company we were travelling with presented us with a bill which bit a sizeable chunk out of our profits for worthwhile causes.

While we were making our way out to the bus, Jerry was being harangued by this drunken girl: 'Give us yer hat! Give us yer hat!' Jerry declined and said he liked it and didn't want to give it away. Not to be deterred, the girl persisted. 'Go on . . . give us yer hat, you can always buy a new one. Go on. Give us yer hat. Give us yer hat.' I wanted to slap her. To make matters worse, we couldn't get out of the club, the exits had been locked and chained, so we had to traipse back through the building, across the stage, across the bloodstained and glass-littered floor and out the front entrance, this awful girl whining away about Jerry's hat. Jerry didn't give her the hat!

Apparently, violence at Dublin shows was common at that time, and a lot of bands had removed the city from their touring schedules. The Stardust Ballroom burnt down a couple of months later, killing forty-eight people. They couldn't get out of the smoke-infested building because the fire exits had been allegedly locked or obstructed!

Undoubtedly the best date on the trip was in Galway, at the Leisureland, a big modern hall. We decided to reverse the bill and went on first. It was great. The nerves I always got during an opening band's set weren't there. The audience were fantastic and The Specials played great. The Beat rose to the challenge and were superb. I stood with Neville at the sound desk as 'Jah Peters', their brummy sound engineer, mixed. We all piled on the stage for 'Stand Down Margaret', Dick and Rico joining Saxa to make a glorious horn section. Wonderful. After the show, it was my turn to be harangued by a local inebriated female. I took my trousers off and gave her my sweat-soaked underpants!

The last show in Cork had a strange vibe, but we'd played so great the previous night it didn't seem to matter. The sound was horrible – whether it was the dodgy acoustics in the hall or Dave Jordan going cold turkey I don't know – and after the show, when Brad asked him, DJ punched him in the stomach, cracking one of Brad's ribs. Luckily we weren't playing the next night.

We were to fly home from Cork the next evening. We were all on the plane, waiting to take off, when we realized tour manager Pete Hadfield wasn't there. Rick got off to look for him. Pete had been detained by customs with the £8,000 we had raised during the trip. We had contravened some Irish currency laws, apparently, and it looked like Mr Hadfield was guilty of taking a load of money out of the country.

Pete and Rick stayed over in Cork while the rest of us flew back to Birmingham. The eight grand was confiscated by airport officials and passed on to the Irish Government, who seemed unable to pay it to the appropriate charities. The money languished in Ireland for almost fifteen years until it was released to our accountant. It got split up between us. No Protestant and Catholic children went on holiday. I might have bought a new settee, I can't remember.

The '2-Tone live' movie *Dance Craze* was released at the end of January, and there was a big bash at the Sundown Disco (is this the in place to be?) in Tottenham Court Road, London. It was an embarrassing media-fest, but my parents came down and they thought it was all very exciting. There was a very negative vibe towards the movie, especially from the London 2-Tone posse, but I thought it was a brilliant document – still do. Here were the bands doing what they did best. Admittedly The Specials and The Beat were the only bands who didn't doctor their soundtracks like the others appeared to. (Where *do* all those backing vocals come from on The Bodysnatchers' tunes?) The camerawork was sound. The-live-album-of-the-movie was released on 7 February and did a lot better than the film. *Dance Craze* is currently owned by Stiff Records, and I'm sure I've seen a copy of it on DVD somewhere. (My copy is a bootleg video.)

13

Power Plays, Mosquitoes
and Ghost Towns

We were in a real quandary. Playing a Specials concert was like being in a western movie. Would our wagon train reach its destination before it got ambushed by injuns? How long could we defend our Alamo? (Up until 'Gangsters' was preferable!) We wanted to play, sure, but not as part of the rock 'n' roll circus that was the norm. Jerry and I had this wacky idea of having seven separate small stages strategically situated round the hall. (Hey, try saying that after a night out!) Each member of the band would have his stage, the idea being that there would be no actual focal point for the band. Luckily it never got passed the ideas stage, but it reminds me of how frustrating Special-world was becoming. We considered just playing at weekends, like semi-pro bands do. It was not met with a particularly positive response. Our management reminded us that it was a lot cheaper to hire the enormous amount of PA, lights and staging and the appropriate vehicles to transport them in at a monthly rate than to just pick them up for the weekend. Also some of the band members actually wanted to be rock stars with all the hedonistic accoutrements included, despite the fact that these excesses were one of the factors responsible for our gradual disintegration.

While I was in America last year, the rest of the band (except Jerry, who, I think, was also on holiday at the time) went into a studio that Brad had found in London. Six songs had been recorded, Dave Jordan producing, Dick Cuthell playing bass, and I think Dick or Lynval playing the keyboards. The highlight of the session, for me, was a very sparse, spooky version of '96 Tears', which Terry sang. There was a version of The Paragon's 'Wear You to the Ball', two rather cool reggae instrumentals which Brad and Dick wrote, one of them becoming the song 'Racist Friend', which appeared on the *In the Studio* album. The other two tunes were an original version of 'Why?', Lynval's song, written about his beating at the hands of three racist thugs the previous July, and a tune that Roddy had written called 'Sweet Revenge'.

The whole thing was ostensibly demos for the next Specials album, but the vibe around the project seemed to me to be 'we can do this without Jerry'. The fact that the majority of the work was uninspiring did not seem to enter into it. It had all the markings of a power play.

While the fractures were widening within The Specials, in the real world the Two-Tone bubble was bursting. Madness were going on to be a mainstream pop band; Charly Anderson and Desmond Brown, both lynchpins of The Selecter's sound, had quit the band during the recording of the band's second album, which was eventually released six months late to positive critical acclaim, but no sales; The Beat were in the process of 'doing a Clash' and carving out a sizeable niche in America; vocalist Rhoda

Dakar and bass player Nicky Summers had been sacked from The Bodysnatchers, who would reinvent themselves at the atrocious Belle Stars; The Swinging Cats all fell out with one another and split; Bad Manners, a 2-Tone band that wasn't on 2-Tone, continued to play skinhead-troubled gigs around Britain and the Continent and released a version of 'The Can-Can'. Pork pie hats, Harrington jackets and Crombie coats were being replaced by zoot suits, frilly shirts and tall hair. Style magazine the *Face* said so. We had to move with the times and leave Buster Bloodvessel and the boys to it. At the Chrysalis offices, they took down the poster of The Selecter's *Too Much Pressure* album and replaced it with 'We Don't Need This Pressure On', Spandau Ballet's 'Chant No. 1' that followed 'Ghost Town' up the charts in July. When you're hot, you're hot, when you're not . . . they take your posters down.

For The Specials, the early part of 1981 was 'keep your head down' time. There were various interviews to keep the pot boiling, and the *Dance Craze* LP stayed in the album charts until June. It was 'solo project' time.

Both Neville and Brad started their own record labels. Nev's label was called Shack, and 21 Guns, the band formed by our old road crew Rex and Trevor, were his first release. Brad's venture into the indie label market was called Race Records. He signed London reggae band Night Doctor and Coventry soul band Team 23, who had toured with us on the More Specials tour. As we still had bags of credibility with the music press, both labels were given their fair share of column inches in the music weeklies, but the product issued didn't appear to find favour with the record-buying public. Roddy started up his own band,

The Tearjerkers, and started doing shows in and around Coventry.

Me, I decided I needed a laugh. I had bought early rap records by Grandmaster Flash and The Furious Five during our first trip to America, and these 12-inch singles were rarely off my turntable. I thought it would be good to have an English rap record, but in an 'oop North' style. I and some old college friends I had been reacquainted with invented the mythical Yorkshire King of Rap, 'Barnsley Bill'. Various writing sessions, which usually ended in side-splitting, rolling-across-the-floor-in-laughter disarray, resulted in 'The Barnsley Rap'. I'd recently met a Coventry drummer, Rick Medlock, who played with local jazz/funk band Pizzazz. He and I became firm friends for several years and, together with various other local musicians, we cut our first comedy record over at Woodbine Studios, in the basement of John Rivers's tiny terraced house in Leamington Spa. I sent a copy of the tape down to Stella Clifford, who at that time worked at Arista Records. Her boss thought it was pretty funny and wanted to release it. I said it was essential that my name was not included on any of the credits, it was not exactly what you'd expect from one of The Specials, for goodness' sake. The single (released on Mother-In-Law Records) got a reasonable amount of airplay on the radio but never sold. The whole thing cost me about £300 all told and put a smile back on my face for quite some time. It seemed worth it.

Romance-wise, things were changing, too. Jackie and I had outstayed one another's welcome, and she was going back to work in America anyway. This and the fact that I'd started seeing Clare, the girl who caught my eye at Mix gigs. Pretty soon Clare and I were very much in lust, if not love. She went off to work in Haarlem, near Amsterdam, for a couple of months and moved into my London Road flat on her return.

There was no plan, I suppose. My recollections of the beginning of '81 don't amount to a great deal, Specials-wise. Apparently, we were supposed to be doing a concert in St Lucia in the West Indies with Bob Marley and The Wailers headlining, but it came to naught. Bob Marley died in May. Rico's first album on 2-Tone, *That Man Is Forward*, came out in March. It was recorded with Dick at the end of 1980 in Jamaica, half of it with legendary reggae rhythm section Sly Dunbar and Robbie Shake-speare, the other half with guys from the Skatalites era. The old guys won, hands down as far as I was concerned. It is still a lovely record. I got mine signed by the man himself: 'To Horace, peace and love, from Rico'. Thank you.

We continued to do sporadic one-off shows. We played in Amsterdam at an ice-skating rink with Madness. Our stage collapsed towards the end of our performance – no stage invasion, just lots of jumping around. We flew to Oslo to do a festival. Us, Ian Dury and The Blockheads and Toots and The Maytals. Rented equipment, no sound check and I remember we played a blinder. It was as plain as the nose on your face that we were not a happy bunch, but it was on stage where we became ascloseasthis. Every now and again we'd pull off a fantastic performance and come off stage like the buddies we all were in 1979. Then we'd all just retreat back into our shells, or go off, and the malaise would creep back in. The performances made up for the discontent and seething. Almost. In Oslo

I remember being so knocked out with our show I drank far too many bottles of very strong lager; I staggered onto the coach to our hotel, my bonhomie turning to loathing as I berated everyone in the band. A pathetic sight. I was dreadfully ill the next day.

Back in Coventry, rehearsals started for a new single. We congregated upstairs at the General Wolfe pub in Foleshill Road. Brad had taken delivery of one of the new Simmonds electric drum kits. It didn't seem to work very well, and an inordinate amount of time was spent sifting through bass drum sounds. Boring, to say the least.

The atmosphere was bordering on the unbearable. We all stood as far away from one another as was humanly possible. The room did not have seven corners, but, if it had, each would have been occupied by a member of The Specials. To get us to all play together was a triumph of the will. A fourth chord was put into the verse structure of Lynval's tune 'Why?' to make it a bit more interesting than the three-chord trick and 'Message to You' vibe that it had. It worked, of course, but no one seemed enthusiastic about it. I remember Jerry getting so frustrated he stormed out of the room, close to tears. I managed to get him back, and we continued playing, but the atmosphere was dreadful.

We worked on a song that Terry had written, a wonderfully dry story of weekend Coventry folk, 'Friday Night and Saturday Morning'. Jerry added the hook line 'I go out on Friday night, I come home on Saturday morning' over this simple keyboard motif that Terry had composed on his recently acquired keyboard. It had a very cool reggae vibe to it. The other song was one that Jerry had just written: 'Ghost Town'. When we finally got to playing it, it sent shivers down the back of my neck. Not since 'International Jet Set' had I played anything as good. The changing key of the middle-eight, from a minor to a major, then back to the minor key for the next verse, was inspired. Fantastic, and played in a very deadpan style that mirrored our distance from one another. Neville began scat singing over the descending chords of the chorus, and soon Lyn and Terry were joining in, wailing like banshees. It made the song moodier and very spooky indeed. This might actually have been done during the recording, I'm not sure.

We recorded it at John Rivers's Woodbine Studio over in Leamington Spa on an 8-track machine. I was thrilled. It was true to our punk-rock roots, and our reggae roots for that matter. Expensive studios didn't guarantee you a good record, you needed a good tune, and we had three of them. London reggae buff John Collins (who had apparently sent a tape to 2-Tone) was chosen to produce. He had lo-fi roots credentials and was severely into early reggae, especially dub stuff. His own project, a band called The Detonators, harked back to Lee Perry's Black Ark material, and he had just had a UK reggae hit with 'At the Club' by Victor Romero Evans.

Like the rehearsals, the recording sessions were tense, Roddy kicked a hole in the studio door, much to the fury of the generally placid John Rivers, who engineered. We played an extended version of 'Ghost Town' to facilitate a trombone solo/dub section for a 12-inch release. John Collins very wisely took the tapes away with him and mixed them down, on 2-track, in his front room in Tottenham. The whole thing was not a pleasant memory, but the finished result made up for it. It is undoubtedly my favourite Specials song. Rico's solo on the extended version is sublime, and the dub effects are wonderful. The rest of the band didn't think so, and I recall Brad saying that 'Why?' should be the A-side because of its anti-racist stance, but he may have said that just to wind Jerry up.

The Specials had ultimately become a job. Turn up, tune up, play and go away. Jerry seemed more and more despondent, Brad blustered away, Roddy snarled and Lyn, Terry and Nev sat together looking miserable, which is why Dave Jordan named them The Fun Boy Three.

To have my fun, I was playing blues and R&B with my drummer friend Rick Medlock. He had been playing with some characters from Leamington, and I was roped into the collective of musicians called The Mosquitoes. We played alcohol-inspired R&B: Chuck Berry, Sonny Boy Williamson, Dr Feelgood-style riffy stuff with biting harp and bar-room humour. It was great. We played in small, sweaty Midlands pubs. You could see the whites of the audience's eyes and, on occasion, smell their beery breath. It was exciting, it was the fun I wasn't having in my 'day job'.

One time during a break between sets I'd made mention of my first forays into pop music in the sixties and how I'd been a member of The Searchers' fan club. 'Oh!' said Nick, The Mosquitoes' vocalist. 'Tony Jackson, their bass player, lives in Leamington. He works at the Granada shop in Regent Street, sells TV's.' What! The man I saw on *Thank Your Lucky Stars*, the man who first put the idea of being a bass player into my eleven-year-old head?

The next day I headed over to Leamington, my heart pounding. What should I say to the man – not exactly my hero, but one of my 'founding fathers', so to speak? I found the shop and went in. There, at the back, was this little old guy, cheap dark suit, grey hair, bored expression.

'Er... Hi I'm Horace Panter from the Specials and it's great to meet you you were the guy who first made me want to put on a bass guitar I can't believe it this is fantastic!' I stopped for breath. The old guy looked at me quizzically. It *was* Tony Jackson – somewhere. He seemed very nervous and took a step back, nearer the banks of television sets on the back wall of the shop. 'Er . . . do you want to buy a television?' he asked in a not-very-Liverpool voice. He had this hollow look about him, a thousand-yard stare. This was the shell of a man. The bottom did not exactly drop out of my world – I could almost be excused for making a complete twat of myself – but in some sort of karmic, spiritual kind of way, something happened. A circle had been completed – or broken. I left the shop and walked back to my car, somehow a little wiser.

At the end of April, The Specials did a short European tour, culminating in a UK gig at London's cavernous Rainbow Theatre. Jerry wanted Rhoda Dakar, recently ejected from The Bodysnatchers, to come with us to sing 'I Can't Stand It' with Terry. (They duetted together on the album). There was some mix-up with the flight tickets, and Rhoda didn't have one. On the way down to London on the coach, I realized that I'd forgotten my passport. Was I trying to say something? What a prat. So, Rhoda and I got a train up to Coventry from London. I retrieved my passport, then lugged over to Birmingham airport, where I could pay for Rhoda and me to get a flight to Amsterdam, from where we got a train to where the band's first gig was, Zwolle, in Holland. Rhoda did get to sing 'I Can't Stand It' with Terry after all.

Jerry came on tour with his big ghetto-blaster tape machine and a cassette of Public Image Limited's *Flowers of Romance* LP. The album was practically unlistenable, but Jerry insisted on playing it very loudly most times when the band was together. He may have been trying to educate us musically, or he might have just wanted to wind us up. If it was the former, he failed.

The tour was memorable only in the fact I don't remember too much about it. I know we went back to the Metropole in Berlin. After the show we were travelling in convoy with the equipment truck down to Munich. We waited while the gear was being loaded, passing the small hours in a bar which was inhabited by large, moustachioed, leather-clad gays all listening to Wagner. Hmm. Glad I had my mates with me. We got searched by dour-looking East German bodyguards, and Jerry stormed off when we reached Munich because we were booked into a Holiday Inn. (It was probably his usual objection to expensive hotels, but the whole thing about Holiday Inns is that they're cheap, isn't it? Never mind.)

During the crazy 'free-form' solo in the middle of the Terry/Rhoda tune 'I Can't Stand It', Jerry shouted over to us, off mike, 'Go completely mad!' No need, mate – we already were.

The final gig, at the Rainbow, was held on 1 May, May Day (or Labour Day), to raise money for a Liverpool-to-London March for Jobs. (Unemployment was a staggering 3 million back in 1980!) The show was heralded by the music press as a triumph, and I do remember the house definitely was rocking. A big 12-feet-deep chasm at the front of the stage ensured that the audience stayed where they were, but everyone seemed to be having too much fun dancing. The concert raised just over £3,000. I felt righteous again.

Coventry was always known as a multi-cultural city. People of all nationalities had lived and worked together since the late forties, when the call went out to the 'Empire' to rebuild Britain after the Second World War. As it was one of the UK's main industrial centres, Coventry had an influx of workers, skilled and unskilled, from all over the world. By 1981, though, the city was starting to come apart at the seams. There had been a rise in the number of racist attacks in the city, with both the National Front and the British Movement openly recruiting on the streets. On 18 April, Satnam Singh Gill, a twenty-year-old Asian student, was murdered in the city centre. A sixteen-year-old white youth was subsequently charged with the crime. The following day, the Coventry Committee Against Racism was formed. In May, CCAR organized a march from the Foleshill area of the city to Coventry Cathedral. It was attended by nearly 10,000 people. There were clashes with skinheads and older racists, and seventy-four arrests were made. The police were criticized for not containing the counter-demonstrators. According to reports the police attributed the trouble to the sixty or so ultra-left Revolutionary Communist Tendency. This was bad. This was very bad. This city had enabled a multi-cultural group like The Specials to be created. The problem had to be confronted, the sooner the better.

The Specials organized a 'Peaceful Protest Against Racism' concert at the Butts athletic stadium on 20 June for people to come and show their support for the city's stance against race hate and raise money for CCAR, other anti-racist groups and Satnam Singh Gill's family. Coventry singer/actress Hazel O'Connor was on the bill, as were The Reluctant Stereotypes, Brad's Race Records new signing The People and The Bureau (Dexy's Midnight Runners without Kevin Rowland). It was pop music putting its money where its mouth was, so to speak. Local residents were up in arms about the show, with fears of violence from the racists, but they needn't have bothered. I would have preferred it if they hadn't bothered at all, as the turnout was pretty poor, considering the 5,000 that we needed for the show to break even. An overcast sky and rumours of crowd trouble meant that less than 3,000 people turned up, but it was more than enough to make a 'noisy and colourful blow for racial harmony' as the *Coventry Evening Telegraph* said the following Monday. The Specials were £8,000 out of pocket on the show. There was a huge, specially built festival-type stage, a massive PA system and a lighting rig. While I was playing, I could see the people in the Spon End flats opposite dancing on their balconies. We played real good, which made up for the somewhat indifferent reaction we got when we played our home town the previous year. The local councillors and civil dignitaries were all full of praise for our 'actions speak louder than words' enterprise. Unlike other cities in Britain during the summer of 1981, Coventry had no major civil disturbances.

'Ghost Town' was released in early June. *Sounds* didn't know what to make of it, *New Musical Express* were less than impressed, but *Melody Maker* said it was 'magnificent'. It entered the charts at number twenty-one, going up the next week to six, or nine, or seven, depending on which chart you looked at. *Top of the Pops* again, then, and, as all of us were in the same place at the same time, a chance to talk. Even having played some 'good-cause' concerts and having a single going up the charts again was not enough to bring us back from the brink. We continued to bicker and seethe, and our demented stage presence miming 'Ghost Town' seemed to say it all. Sad.

The following weekend we played a free outdoor concert in Rotherham, oop North again, as part of some city celebration or something. The line-up for the afternoon was The Specials, a local covers band and a local heavy-metal outfit, the stunningly named Panzer Division. The highlight of the day for me was the fly-past, during the Panzers' metal onslaught, of a Royal Air Force jet bomber. It was, to be perfectly honest, the ultimate heavy-metal experience: the combination of Rolls Royce turbo-jet engines and distorting Marshall amplifiers in a slow stereo pan from stage left across to stage right and off towards Sheffield. Awesome. The guys from Panzer Division were not as impressed as I was when I breathlessly told them about it backstage after their performance, but they probably thought I was some nutter anyway. Skinheads appeared during the cover band's set and made their lives hell. The cute girl singer left the stage in tears, poor thing. Someone mentioned that there was traditional rivalry between youth from Rotherham and those from Sheffield, and this was apparent from the marauding gangs of skinheads who now converged near the stage. By the time we went on, there was a double line of police right down the middle of the audience. Rotherham on one side, Sheffield on the other. So much for unity. Stage time was around 5 p.m., and it was still daylight when we ejected a dozen or so local girls from our coach and headed down to London to film a video for 'Ghost Town'.

Now that was cool. I got to drive the black 1962 Vauxhall Cresta. Three-speed column-shift gear stick. Yeah, man. Filming started at around midnight and carried on until about 7 the next morning. We drove the car back and forth through the Blackwall Tunnel, through some deserted East End derelict slums and finally through the City, the financial district, deserted at five in the morning. During one of the runs through the tunnel, the camera, which was fixed to the bonnet by means of a gigantic rubber sucker, came loose and fell onto the bonnet of the car. They kept it in the video, but the guy who owned the Vauxhall was less than happy with the scratch on his paintwork. He'd been plied with cans of lager since shooting started and was somehow placated. It might have been money, that usually worked.

The completed video was tremendous, complementing the song brilliantly. The video is still played today on the music video channels. We played a special 900th edition of *Top of the Pops*. We still wouldn't talk to one another.

On 4 July we played the 'Carnival Against Racism' in Leeds. We drove into the city during a National Front march. Heavy. I was used to having a guitar and a stage to protect me, but not now. Come show time, Dave Jordan hadn't showed, so we had to do the gig without him. We went on stage and were absolutely crap. In front of 12,000 people, our biggest-ever concert in the UK. It was a really important anti-racist show, too, and we were awful. Too fast. No groove, just bludgeon away. There was even a fight down the front. A music lover probably. Rico sussed it. He wouldn't play his solo in 'Ghost Town'. I remember coming off stage furious. Dave Jordan finally turned up and said that no one had informed him that show time was 4 p.m. Don't worry, Dave, you didn't miss anything. I rode home to Coventry in the equipment truck, seething with frustration. The next week, 'Ghost Town' was at number one, and that Saturday I played the Green Dragon in Stratford-upon-Avon with The Mosquitoes. A brilliant gig.

Starting on 8 July and lasting for the next two weeks, riots broke out in Britain. There were civil disturbances in the Woolwich, Walthamstow, Brixton, Battersea, Dalston, Southall and Streatham districts of London. The Toxteth area of Liverpool and the Moss Side area of Manchester endured two days of rioting. Handsworth in Birmingham, Chapeltown in Leeds and the Highfields area of Leicester all suffered looting. Other normally placid centres of population kicked off too: Aldershot, High Wycombe, Huddersfield, Luton, Stockport. British youth had had enough. Whites, Asians, Blacks just erupted out of sheer frustration at a government that had 'left its youth on the shelf'. Unemployment, police 'SUS' (stop and search) laws, racist attacks, and over the top of it was this eerie tune, recorded on 8-track in Leamington, and mixed in a front room in Tottenham. Chilling. Never had pop music captured the time and the place so well. Never. It was incredible.

It was during this time that The Bodysnatchers' tune 'The Boiler' was included in The Specials' set. A sixties R&B twelve-bar vibe, over which Rhoda had constructed the spine-chilling tale about a girl who is picked up by a man who subsequently rapes her. It was not exactly easy listening, but nevertheless relevant to the bands' 1981 political stance. It would be released as a single on 2-Tone the following year.

A couple of weeks later, with 'Ghost Town' still at number one, if I remember right, The Specials played Liverpool Royal Court Theatre. During Neville's talk-over part in 'Why?' ('with a Nazi salute and a steel-cap boot') some kid started Sieg-Heiling. What a jerk. We'd showed him the peace sign, or something resembling it.

24 July 1981. It was to be our last UK show.

14

Going West. The Specials
Finally Fizzle Out in America

Why we went to America in August is a mystery. We had a meeting round at Pete Hadfield's flat, just a couple of doors down from Jerry – neutral ground you understand. It was just plain obvious that any attempts to 'reunite' the band were impossible, and, unbeknown to us, Terry, Lynval and Neville had plans well advanced to form their own band. It was hardly surprising that nobody sussed, given the lack of communication prevalent at that time. Although we were going nowhere fast, we ended up going to America.

I suppose we still had a good reputation over there, although I have no idea how *More Specials* fared in the American album charts. The shows we were set to do were in reasonably big theatres, not in small clubs as before. The schedule seemed reasonably relaxed, in fact. The whole thing was billed as a 'works outing', a holiday with gigs attached. The band very kindly paid for Clare to come over as well. No one else brought their partner with them . . . except Rico, who arrived at Heathrow with a girl who looked young enough to be his daughter! I can't for the life of me remember her name. They bickered constantly throughout the whole tour.

Our first show on this American trip was in New York, Pier 51, overlooking the Hudson River, one of a series of concerts sponsored by the Doctor Pepper soft drinks firm. The crew were setting the equipment up when Paul Heskett's dodgy string machine keyboard blew up. He'd changed the voltage to 110, as this is what the Americans use, but hadn't told Jim or Cedric. We took our own equipment with us on this trip and used a step-up transformer, which converted 110 to 240 volts. Hence the strange smell and blue-grey smoke coming from Paul's keyboard. He used it to play the Ice Rink Strings bits on 'Do Nothing', but not any more. Support act for this show were The Go-Gos – well, who else? They all looked very posh and polished and may even have played 'Our Lips Are Sealed'.

I suppose we played all right. The only thing I can remember is during 'Nite Klub', when Terry sang 'I won't dance on a pier like this, all the girls are slags and Doctor Peppers tastes like piss'. It always reminds me of the taste of toothpaste to be honest. Bernie Rhodes showed up backstage and could see from the way we interacted with one another that things weren't right. He apparently sidled up to Rick Rogers and said, 'That's another band you've ruined, then.' Hmm. Good old Bernie. I never got to hear Rick's undoubtedly robust riposte.

From New York, we flew to California. We were scheduled to play at Perkins Palace in Pasadena, just outside Los Angeles. The gig was uninspiring, and I remember being slagged off in the press for berating stage divers.

Shut up and play yer guitar, Horace. I also remember getting very drunk afterwards, possibly due to the appearance of ex-girlfriend, Jackie. Ah, guilt! Waking up the next afternoon, I realized I'd lost my camera.

There were a few days off before our next show, and Jerry, Pete Hadfield, Paul Heskett, Clare and I decided to 'get out of town' and head for the border. We hired two cars and ended up in Ensenada in Baja California, that straggly peninsula bit below Tijuana.

Crossing the border from San Diego to Tijuana was like going from West Germany to East Germany, but with heat. It was the nearest I'd got to seeing poverty, and this was a prosperous part of Mexico. On the drive down our hire car was overtaken by a beat-up old pick-up truck driven by locals who pelted us with beer bottles. Ensenada was tacky and touristy, and we managed to get rooms in a motel. The food was awful. Clare and I spent two days on the beach watching pelicans dive into the sea. We got sunburnt quite badly and were pestered by small children, some of whom threatened to drown the cute puppy they had if we didn't buy their sister. The sister went unsold, and I can only guess what happened to the dog. Clare was looking as red as a lobster and not feeling well at all. On our return to the US, she looked really ill and had to go and be sick when we got to the customs point at San Diego. It made us look a very motley crew in the eyes of the US officials. Tijuana was a regular drug paradise for Californians with too much money and little brain. Still is, come to think of it. Mr Hadfield was not impressed. We had schedules to meet – no time to get slung into a San Diego jail. Sunstroke or not, you can't stop rock 'n' roll!

From Los Angeles we flew to Canada to play a big

outdoor show near Toronto, with The Police headlining. It was a far cry from the 'secondary markets' venues of the previous year. The 'Police Picnic' at the Grove Racetrack, Oakville, attracted 70,000 people. To this day it remains the largest audience I've played to.

Also on the bill were The Go-Gos (of course!), Killing Joke and Iggy Pop. We rocked. We were really, really good. It always baffled me how one night we could be dull and going through the motions and the next night (or afternoon in this case) we could be fantastic. I couldn't explain it, perhaps it was the sense of occasion. People as far as you could see – unbelievable. I have a picture in my mind of Jerry, trousers round his ankles, standing on his keyboard with this ludicrously large sombrero and equally ludicrous large grin. Someone introduced the band with the 'are y'all ready to rock?' cliché. Hilarious. We encored with 'Ghost Town'. I remember it as a truly sublime Specials moment. Yee-haw, rock 'n' roll, fan-bloody-tastic.

Brad had befriended Iggy Pop, who referred to him as Dirk (Bogarde, I suppose – perhaps Brad was wearing white socks, who knows?). Even the appearance of famously tough UK promoter John Curd and our favourite man-mountain Steve English didn't dampen our spirits. Looking back, it made our inevitable split even more tragic. Apparently, back at the hotel in Toronto Jerry had a big row with Rick and sacked him. No one told me.

The next day at the airport we met the guys from Killing Joke. They seemed even more miserable than us. They were on their way back to England, and one of them had a rather large bag of grass that he didn't want to be found with. Clare relieved him of it, but now the problem was, what could she do with it? We gave it to Rico, who placed the leaves between the pages of his bible and thanked us gratefully. Rasta always find a way, y'no see' it.

Back in New York, and we checked into the Royalton Hotel, a pretty nondescript mid-town hotel, apart from the 3-inch cockroaches in the bathroom. The hotel's advantages were, one, it was in Manhattan, and two, it was over the road from the Algonquin, where Groucho Marx used to stay. The bar at the Algonquin was fantastic – old-style, like in the twenties. Clare and I spent a lot of time there drinking rather a lot. We had a few days to kill before our last few shows and we 'slummed it' big time.

One night various Specials found themselves at the Peppermint Lounge. Clare was talking to the presumably reinstated Rick Rogers, and I was looking into space somewhere, feeling the effect of several drinks. All of a sudden, someone comes up to Clare and, with a whiny London accent, tells her to shut the fuck up. It was Johnny Rotten. There was a sound of hand slapping cheek, and before I knew it, there was my girlfriend, rolling over the floor, slapping, clawing and grappling with the lead singer of The Sex Pistols. This was not good. I unsteadily got off my bar stool and walked over to the pugilistic couple at the same time as Mr Lydon's telephone-box-sized black American bodyguard. This was it, then. Might as well die in New York as anywhere. Luckily, at that moment, Clare and her famous assailant disengaged. Mr Telephone Box escorted his charge off stage left, I helped Clare to her feet, and we exited stage right. She always maintains she gave the last slap!

The next night, we were all scheduled to go and see Chaka Khan at somewhere or other. During the afternoon the phone rang in our room. It was Pete Hadfield. 'Listen, Horace, John Lydon's going to be at the Chaka Khan show tonight. Better keep Clare away.' 'Pete,' I replied, 'Clare's going to be at the show tonight, better keep Johnny Lydon away,' and put the phone down. Rock stars. Who do they think they are? And who pays my tour manager's wages anyway? As it happened, both Clare and Johnny were at the Chaka Khan show. They greeted one another like old friends: 'Har har har,' crowed JL. 'We showed those facking Americans, didn't we.' Clare nodded, grinned and put her hand over the carpet burns on her elbows!

Three more shows: Staten Island, Long Island and Boston, then home. We played the cavernous Paramount Theater on Staten Island, a show fraught with crowd trouble. I remember Terry looking back at Roddy and me, furious at us that we weren't down at the lip of the stage with him to repel the next load of boarders. The Long Island show was at a club – a fairly smallish affair, well attended if I remember. Towards the end of the show Neville just walked off the stage. The ill-feeling, the seething, the years of personality clashes, arguments, sarcasm, cynicism, egos and conflicts had finally made it to the stage. The only place where the band made any sense at all. It was over, and Nev, of all people, was the first to throw in the towel. I find this odd in hindsight, as plans for The Fun Boy Three were well advanced. Terry and Lynval were keeping their lips sealed and their heads down, and that was all Neville needed to do. Perhaps it all became too much for him, I don't know. Even our two weeks of sun-drenched high life in America was not enough to keep The Specials together.

No one spoke in the dressing room afterwards. I got

changed and went out to find Clare. Luckily, I had someone to distract me from all this. Everyone just seemed to close down, or put up an aggressive front to protect themselves.

The last gig was at the Bradford Ballroom in Boston. A bootleg exists of the concert. We hired a bus to take us there. In New York, Neville would not get on the coach and stayed up in his room at the Royalton. I went up to talk to him, and he went on about how nobody wanted him to be in the band. He knew it was finished, too, but I managed to persuade him to come and play this one last show. The gig was in the ballroom of an old hotel (the Bradford, presumably). We checked in and nipped downstairs to do the sound check. Luckily we didn't have to spend too much time hanging around.

At show time, there was no Dave Jordan. He'd been out all night with Keith Richards and was finally found unconscious in his hotel room. Monitor engineer Nick Baker said he'd do our out-front sound, and we finally got on stage about an hour late. The bootleg is pretty good. We played well, Neville rising to the occasion and returning to his stage-hurtling form. Some of us knew it was the end, some of us wished it was the end; some of us just didn't seem to care.

After the show, I was collared by a journalist and asked what the future plans for The Specials were. I didn't know. I can't remember our return journey. I know that Jerry stayed over in New York. Not long after his return, he was visited by Terry, who said he, Lynval and Neville were leaving. In a matter of weeks, The Fun Boy Three were in the papers, being managed by Rick Rogers, and their records being produced by Dave Jordan.

I don't remember having any ill-feeling towards them; the whole thing had an air of inevitability about it anyway. Roddy went full tilt into his Tearjerkers band, with Rick Rogers at the managerial helm. That left Brad, Jerry and myself. Despite all my Exegesis positivism, I was stunned into a stupor. Something that I had helped create and take to such emotional heights had crumbled.

By October it was official. The Specials had split, and would you please welcome Chrysalis recording artists The Fun Boy Three. Their single 'The Lunatics Have Taken Over the Asylum' was released later that month.

Brad, Jerry and I agreed to stay working together, and Pete Hadfield would look after the business side of things. It was decided that we would 'wait and see'. We still retained the name The Specials and still had a recording contract. I don't know whether Chrysalis were sympathetic to us, but they adopted a 'wait and see' policy, too. To keep a 'business as usual' face, we recorded Rhoda's tune 'The Boiler'. Well, I didn't; Nicky Summers, the Body-snatchers' bass player, did the bass duties. I have an idea there was a significant amount of sour grapes between Nicky and the rest of The Bodysnatchers. Ms Summers had to suffer the ignominy of being slung out of the band that she herself had formed, and this session had some-thing of a retaliatory statement about it. John Shipley, from The Swinging Cats, played guitar, along with Brad with his god-awful electric Simmonds drum kit. Jerry played organ and produced. The session seemed to be mostly taken up with finding the right drum sounds – well, that's what Rhoda said when she and Nicky knocked on my door at 3 a.m. to stay over for the night after the recording finally finished.

The song was released the following January, with Nicky Summers's name in big flowery letters on the cover for some reason. The record got some airplay but was quickly removed from playlists as it was considered 'unsuitable'. It came out at the same time as judge Bertrand Richards gave what was considered a ludicrously lenient £2,000 fine to the perpetrator of the crime that Rhoda's song was all about.

Rico came to our rescue. He had been asked to do a small European tour – mainly universities and jazz clubs. He asked Jerry, Brad and me to be his rhythm section, and we jumped at the chance. The band consisted of the three of us, Dick and Rico, Dick's friend Tony Wymshurst on guitar and old-time Rico compatriot and south London taxi driver Satch Dixon on percussion. Pete Hadfield tour-managed, along with a German chap called Florian (whom Jerry named Two Bob). Jim and Cedric came, too. The gear was transported in a big Mercedes truck, driven by a German husband-and-wife team whose names escape me. I do remember that vehicle security was carried out by an enormous German Shepherd dog. Brad, the crew and I went in the truck, and everyone else in Florian's estate car.

The tour was brilliant. I think it was in the autumn, October even. Whatever, it couldn't have come at a better time. I didn't have to worry about stage invasions, whether I wore the right shoes, or getting tangled up in anyone else's guitar cable. I just had to play music. Not just music, but Rico's music. I'd bought a copy of 'Man from Warieka' soon after Rico had joined the band, and it was a joy to be able to play those tunes with the man himself. We'd played some of his songs in The Specials, and I always looked forward to them. We learnt a version of The Dave Brubeck

Quartet's 'Take Five', but in 4/4 time (!), and a song Rico had heard Stevie Wonder play at a Sunsplash concert called 'What You Talkin' 'bout (You Say You Don't Like the Reggae Beat)', and a terrific African-type tune called 'Jungle Music'. At some of the shows, we just played and played and played. Two hours plus, some of them; it was wonderful.

The tour was joined by Jamaican dub poet Oku Onura, who ranted his poetry over a taped rhythm track. We also did some shows with Linton Kwesi Johnson. The tour is still one of the best musical memories of my life. We played in Holland, but I cannot remember where. I know we played with LKJ in Berlin at the legendary SO36 club (it's pronounced 'Esso, sex and dry sick', which is pretty appropriate) and stayed in an empty flat in the centre of the city. I did a tourist trip over to East Berlin, Checkpoint Charlie, war memorials and stuff. We played in Zurich, at the anarchist 'Rotte Factorie', and Berne, where we continued to play on despite a power cut, percussion and brass, until the power was restored – it brought the house down. We played in Bonn to a meagre audience. Most of the city's young folk were demonstrating out at the airport for some reason.

The trip seemed to grind to a halt, rather than end. There were problems getting paid, and I think the last few shows were cancelled. I remember a rather stroppy Onura becoming somewhat belligerent towards poor old Two Bob. We set off back to London in high spirits, but by the time we got back to the capital, Jerry seemed morose again.

Back in Coventry, we cobbled together two of the tunes from the Rico tour and came up with 'Jungle Music' – the rhythm tracks, aided by John Shipley's guitar, were recorded over at the new Woodbine Studios in Leamington. Brass and percussion were added in London. The B-side, 'Rasta Call You', was another tune from the recent tour. I feel the recorded version did not do the tune justice. 'Jungle Music' received a fair amount of airplay but did not 'transmit to sales', as they say. It did keep the 2-Tone flag flying, as did a second Rico album, *Jama Rico*, which was issued in 1982. I got to play on some of the tracks, a fact that I am very proud of.

Clare became Mrs Clare Panter on 15 January 1982. A register office job, followed by a cheap and cheerful reception upstairs at the Bull's Head on Binley Road. There was a foot of snow, and Clare's younger brother appeared in the photographs wearing Wellington boots. I was very happy. Still am.

It has been quite astounding to look back and see how much work the three of us actually did during the time from Terry, Lynval, Neville and Roddy's quitting to my eventual departure in April. Jerry wouldn't stop. He started to look progressively worse and became more difficult to be around. It seemed to me that he showed all the signs of meltdown but he was fine and battled through it. My continued involvement in Exegesis was not helping matters either. According to Jerry, I was on a mission to brainwash as many people as possible. I saw it was a way of helping people to help themselves. Relations between Jerry and me continued to deteriorate.

John Shipley was added to our line-up, and we booked time over in Leamington to rehearse and record. The sessions were fraught, to say the least, but out of it came some of the most challenging music I have played in my life. A painfully slow New Orleans-type tune that became the song 'Alcohol', the lazy funk that became 'Girlfriend' and an incredibly hard 'reggae in 5/4 time' piece of music that became 'War Crimes'. 'Free Nelson Mandela' notwithstanding, the three tunes I played on the *In the Studio* album are the best three cuts on it. That's not being big-headed, that's listening to the record almost twenty years later. ('Break down the Door' is a good tune too!)

I would arrive in time for the session, which started at midday. Brad, who would commute from London each day, would generally be there by half-twelve, accompanied as often as not by a bottle of vodka – his way of coping, I suppose. Jerry would appear at around three and want to go for breakfast. We'd start work around five.

The atmosphere was unbearable, and I just couldn't cope with it. It was like attending a funeral every day of the week. Eventually it was worth losing the £100 I got every week not to be there. I was not happy creating music in such circumstances (despite the fact I did). I visited Jerry and Pete Hadfield to try to get the sessions stopped so that we could somehow change the atmosphere in the studio. It was to no avail. Jerry's determination to continue had turned into tunnel vision.

The next day I quit. Horrible, horrible, horrible. I felt like I had stabbed my best friend in the back. It was a decision I hated making, but for my own sanity, knew I had to make. It was the worst day of my life. It still saddens me to think about it, over twenty-five years later.

Epilogue

And that, as they say, was that.

I left the phone off the hook for a couple of days, and Clare and I took off for a change of scene somewhere. It was like a mental amputation. I had been involved in that band from its inception, had done my best to make it work and had felt totally powerless to prevent it falling to pieces. For years I felt guilty that I didn't say this, or do that, or stopped somebody doing something or other. Hindsight can be a very cruel companion. The main reason for writing this book was to be able to look at it from an objective viewpoint and make some sort of sense of it all. It has definitely helped.

I go around telling everybody that I ceremonially burnt my green sweat-encrusted Two-Tone suit, but I didn't. I just threw it away, but the symbolism remained.

I continued playing R&B with my Leamington buddies, and we even attempted some 'real' music, but my heart wasn't in it. I was 'played out'.

I joined forces with Clare in running the punk clothing shop she had recently opened. Pretty soon I had relearnt the silk-screening skills I'd acquired at college, and we began making clothes. We soon got ourselves a small factory unit together and started selling stuff around the Midlands. It was what I needed. It bonded Clare and me together. We worked a fourteen-hour day, seven days a week, and it helped restore my self-esteem and get the 2-Tone blues out of my system.

By mid-1983 The Fun Boy Three were regular fixtures in the UK charts, and I was itching to get back playing again. (FB3 split up in '84.) The (English) Beat had just called it a day, and Dave Wakeling and Ranking Roger had just started a new band, General Public. I called Dave and announced that I was their new bass player. He agreed, and there I was. The music was a kind of reggae-tinged AOR pop. We toured America pretty much constantly through '84 and '85. The first album, *All the Rage*, did really well, and we were 'MTV darlings' for a while. Our live shows were very exciting and well received, but our rather sterile second album stiffed dreadfully. Christmas 1987, Dave Wakeling announced he was leaving the band, effectively splitting it up.

I was OK about this, to be honest. My son, Laurence, had arrived the previous April, and life priorities had instantly changed with parenthood. I continued to work with Ranking Roger, but despite gigs in the UK and America, not to mention a cracking good band, it became pretty obvious that nothing was happening. I made ends meet during 1989/90 working for a transport firm, until a phone call to join Specialbeat (Ranking Roger, Neville Staple, Brad and myself). We made a good living playing our old repertoire to (mainly) Americans, who had finally got wise to the music we had played ten years previously. It was really a glorified tribute band, but we had a lot of fun and played some very exciting concerts. We toured America for three months solid in 1991, and I missed Laurence's first day at school. This made me think hard about stuff, so I quit the band and enrolled on a teacher-training course, qualifying in 1993, which is when Specialbeat threw in its towel. Lynval, who had joined the band after I left, went on to produce other people's records, and Brad, after a brief stint in Pauline Black's reformed Selecter, stopped playing altogether and got a 'real job' with computers. After The Specials got signed in 1979, Brad moved down to live in London. He still lives there, and I have recently heard rumours that he's started playing drums again.

You'd think I'd had enough of playing 'Too Much Too Young' and 'Concrete Jungle', but no. Neville, Lynval, Roddy and I reconvened in 1993 to record an album of ska and reggae covers with Desmond Dekker. Trojan Records released it as *Desmond Dekker and The Specials*, which I was not very happy about, but it gave me some money, which, after almost two years living on a student's allowance with a family to support, was something akin to a godsend. The project soon snowballed into a regular band, from one-off gigs in Europe at the weekends to a full-blown five-week American tour. People flocked to the shows, and the new American ska scene took to us like returning heroes, but there was no Jerry Dammers to give us new ideas. There was no Terry Hall to make the live shows just that little bit sharper. I was married, had a family and all its accompanying responsibilities. I was a different person to the young, wide-eyed adventurer of 1979.

The reconstituted Specials fizzled out in Japan in the

autumn of 1998. I had jumped ship earlier in the year, claiming health reasons for my departure. The doctor said hypertension, I diagnosed exasperation. Subject closed.

These days I play music for fun. I'm a schoolteacher by day but can generally be found most weekends playing my bass in various pubs around Coventry and Warwickshire. I like it like that, thank you.

Roddy Radiation still lives in Coventry and still fronts his own band. It's called The Skabilly Rebels these days. They play out from time to time.

Neville Staple, after an eight-year sojourn in California, is back in town too, complete with burgeoning solo career.

Lynval fell in love during the 'reconstituted' era and now lives in Seattle. He's the one who takes the trouble to keep us all in touch, bless him.

Jerry has built up an impressive collection of dodgy keyboards and long-playing records. These days he makes a living playing the latter rather than the former. *His* book should prove very interesting reading . . . when he writes it.

Terry has carved himself an impressive niche in British pop music since he quit The Specials. He has managed to keep his integrity intact and hasn't had to resort to the 'tribute route' that the rest of us (apart from Jerry) have at some time or other done. He, like Brad and Jerry, lives in London at the time of writing. These days I get phone calls from Lynval and Christmas cards from Jerry and Rod.

Looking back, it seems that I've been in The Specials forever. I've played those songs for the past quarter of a century in some form or another. Those twenty-odd tunes relate to the defining moments of my life and still form an integral part of who I am. Occasionally I'm stopped in town by someone I vaguely recognize. 'All right, Horace!' Yep, that's me – the guy from The Specials.

Index

INDEX

extracts reading groups
competitions books new
books discounts extracts extracts
competitions discounts
books new reading groups events reading groups
events books extracts
extracts books new titles reading groups discounts
interviews events
events extracts discounts
discounts extracts new books events events books
events new new events interviews books extracts

www.panmacmillan.com

discounts extracts discounts books
extracts events reading groups
competitions books extracts new